410
FI

LANGUAGE AND COMMUNICATION

A CROSS-CULTURAL ENCYCLOPEDIA

ENCYCLOPEDIAS OF THE HUMAN EXPERIENCE

David Levinson, Series Editor

LANGUAGE AND COMMUNICATION
A CROSS-CULTURAL ENCYCLOPEDIA

Michael Shaw Findlay

ABC-CLIO

Santa Barbara, California
Denver, Colorado
Oxford, England

Library of Congress Cataloging-in-Publication Data

Findlay, Michael Shaw.
    Language and communication : a cross-cultural encyclopedia /
Michael Shaw Findlay.
        p.   cm. — (Encyclopedias of the human experience)
    Includes bibliographical references and index.
    1. Language and languages—Encyclopedias.   2. Communication—
Encyclopedias.   I. Series.
    P29.F47   1998   410'.3—dc21   98-12300

ISBN 0-87436-946-0 (alk. paper)

04 03 02 01 00 99   10 9 8 7 6 5 4 3 2   (cloth)

ABC-CLIO, Inc.
130 Cremona Drive, P.O. Box 1911
Santa Barbara, California 93116-1911

This book is printed on acid-free paper ⊗ .
Manufactured in the United States of America

To my wife, Denise,
with love and appreciation
for her patience and support

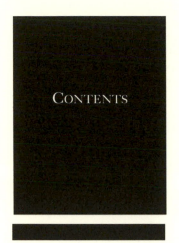

CONTENTS

Contents

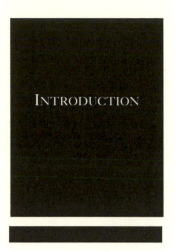

Introduction

When a person speaks to others a complex series of events unfolds. The person doing the talking must organize his or her thoughts into an ordered, coherent, logical pattern. After the central themes of what will be said are conceptualized, the same person must convert those thoughts into verbal-audible speech. For the speech to be understood, the audience of listeners must share basic knowledge regarding the meanings of the sounds being uttered by the speaker. Otherwise what is being said will be nothing more than gibberish. In other words, the speaker "encodes" language into coherent spoken language by constructing sound combinations based on shared linguistic knowledge. The audience must "decode" what is being said to make sense of the utterance. This description, however, makes up only a small part of a typical communicative exchange. Each individual participating in the speech-based communication must rely on shared cultural knowledge before actual interpretations of what is being said can be made. The speaker's body language must be read; the speaker must know something about the audience: What is their primary spoken language—English? Swahili? Bantu? Do the listeners perceive themselves as having higher or lower status than the speaker? What happens when the speaker is a male and the listeners are females? What might happen if the speaker uses certain hand gestures to emphasize what is being said? What if the hand gestures used by the speaker are considered offensive to the listeners? These are the kinds of questions that linguists, anthropologists, and intercultural communication specialists raise in their attempts to describe and understand language and communication from a cross-cultural perspective. Moreover, many of the central questions raised here with this simple example of a communicative exchange are addressed throughout this volume in broader cross-cultural terms.

Humans have been fascinated with language and communication for thousands of years. Both written and oral traditions tell us that ancient peoples were concerned with fundamental questions of language, communication, and cultural difference. In fact, many of the fundamental questions raised by ancient peoples regarding language and communication are still relevant today. How did human language originate? Why are there so many different human languages? Are there aspects of language and communication that go beyond the structure or grammar of a particular language? Why, for instance, does nodding the head up and down mean *no* in some parts of the world and *yes* in others? Are features of language and communication arbitrary, or do underlying universal patterns prevail? Although many early attempts to resolve these questions were clumsy and uninformed, some of their assessments were remarkably insightful. The Greek philosopher Democritus, for example, described how human language must have derived from the basic human tendencies for social behavior and prehensility (grasping and articulation of fingers and hands). Contemporary theorists point out that much of human communication is essentially an extension of social behavior. Moreover, articulated language relies on the evolved ability to place the tongue precisely at various locations along the human vocal tract, which allows human beings to make a significant number of contrasting sounds necessary for producing speech. This ability might be linked to the early human capacity for the articulation of finger and hand gestures, as these might have facilitated nonverbal communication.

Addressing these kinds of issues requires a comprehensive approach. In this volume a cross-cultural perspective is taken, which helps to prevent what social scientists call an ethnocentric bias (a biased focus on one group, society, or tradition). In the past—and too often in the present—Western European scholars have tended to study their own people exclusively. From their studies false generalizations regarding human behavior were often generated. In psychology many of Freud's theories of human behavior were based on descriptions of Austrian-German aristocrats who had a

wide variety of mental disorders. Extending his explanations for human behavior to non-European peoples constituted the assumption that the underlying causes of behavior in Austrian-German aristocrats were universal. Taking a cross-cultural perspective provides us with a wide and diverse range of human linguistic and communicative behavior, thus freeing us from the limitations of a narrow view based solely on European subjects. In reading this volume the reader will be reminded that Europeans are not exclusive or isolated from the rest of the world but are part of it. English, for example, is rapidly becoming a dominant international language. Yet the forms of English emerging in various parts of the world are being shaped and reshaped by many indigenous languages and forms of communication. Also, through the cross-cultural analysis of language and communicative systems, a more complete and detailed picture of how Western and non-Western traditions are influencing one another emerges. Creole or composite languages, for example, arise in culture contact situations where several fundamentally different cultural and linguistic groups are forced to live together. In many cases these creole languages are made up of European and non-European languages.

Finally, this volume addresses a central integrating concept in communication studies having to do with the cultural rules for organizing and carrying out communication. This central idea is what the linguist Dell Hymes calls "communicative competence." This refers to the sociocultural rules that an individual must learn in order to use language. Knowing what is appropriate or inappropriate in a given social or cultural context is, to a large extent, a function of learning and acting on shared cultural rules for "proper" behavior. The concept of communicative competence, perhaps more than any other, explains why so many miscommunications arise as members of differing cultures attempt to communicate. Of course, language differences represent a formidable barrier to communication. In some cases, however, language is not so much a problem as is knowing how to use it to say the right thing or to organize social interaction in a culturally appropriate manner. By exploring how people from differing cultural backgrounds rely on traditional and emergent (newly acquired) cultural rules for social interaction when they attempt to communicate and by learning more about differences in language structures, we can help to ease many of the communication barriers that exist in the world today.

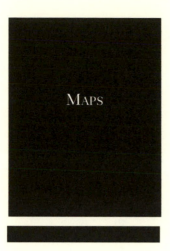

MAPS

The following maps show approximate locations of the cultures mentioned in the text.

Africa and the Middle East

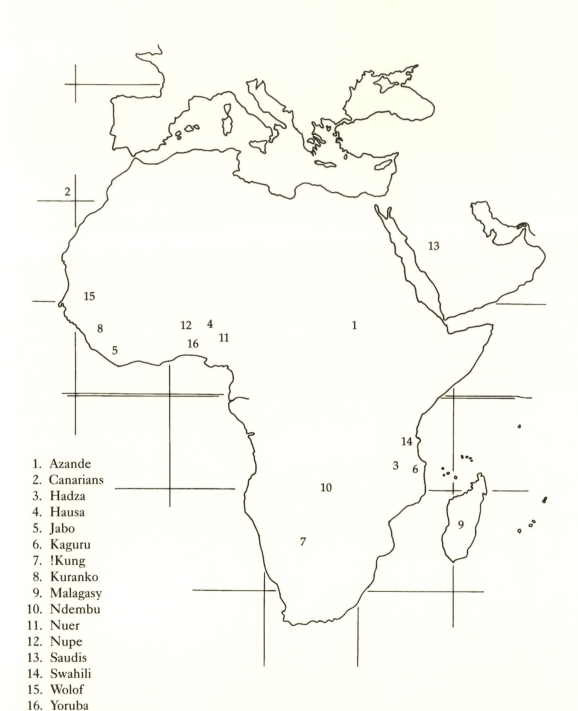

1. Azande
2. Canarians
3. Hadza
4. Hausa
5. Jabo
6. Kaguru
7. !Kung
8. Kuranko
9. Malagasy
10. Ndembu
11. Nuer
12. Nupe
13. Saudis
14. Swahili
15. Wolof
16. Yoruba

Central and South America

1. Antiguans
2. Canela
3. Cuna
4. Huastec
5. Huichol
6. Kickapoo
7. Maya
8. Mazateco
9. Mehinacu
10. Tchikrin
11. Yanomamo

Europe and Asia

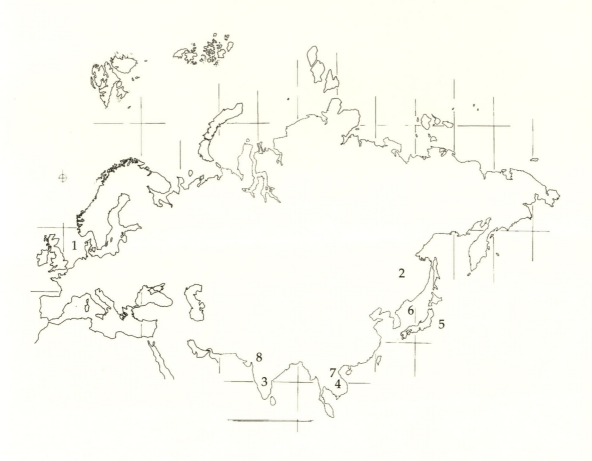

1. British (Cockney-speakers)
2. Chinese
3. Hindus
4. Hmong
5. Japanese
6. Koreans
7. Mien
8. Panjabi

North America

1. Chehalis
2. Cherokee
3. Cheyenne
4. Cree
5. Creek
6. Haida
7. Hopi
8. Inuit
9. Iroquois
10. Kiowa
11. Kwakiutl
12. Lakota
13. Naskapi
14. Navajo
15. Salish
16. Sea Islanders (Gullah)
17. Serrano
18. Tlingit
19. Tolowa
20. Western Apache
21. Yurok
22. Zuni

Oceania

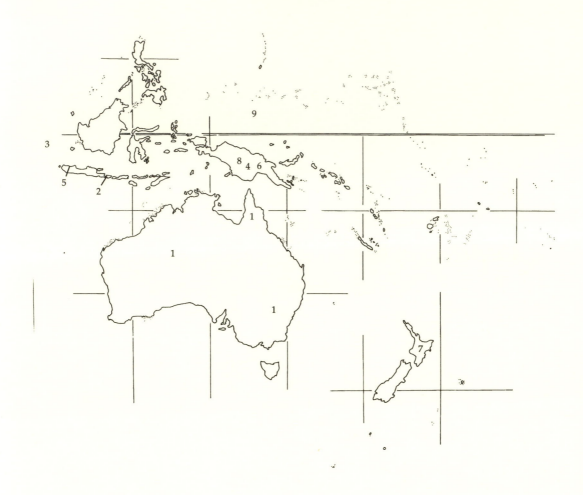

1. Australian Aborigines
2. Balinese
3. Benkula
4. Enga
5. Javanese
6. Kaluli
7. Maori
8. Samo
9. Trukese

LANGUAGE AND COMMUNICATION
A CROSS-CULTURAL ENCYCLOPEDIA

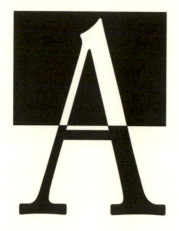

fit of new members who speak a different language from that of the larger group. Accommodation of this kind typically occurs in contact situations where language-minority speakers are present. Often members of the larger speech community use more nonverbal cues (exaggerated hand, arm, and facial gestures) as a way of organizing communication with the newer members.

See also BILINGUALISM.; LANGUAGE ACQUISITION.

ACCOMMODATION In conversation people often unconsciously modify their own speech to conform to the speech of others. This type of adjustment linguists call accommodation. Ethnographers (cultural anthropologists) concerned with language socialization (acquiring the rules for using language) describe the important role of accommodation in cross-cultural studies of language use. Infants, children, and young adults in all societies model their speech after that of adults and their peers. Thus, the differences in the way language is used to reinforce various cultural ideas (especially when emphasizing differences in status by age, gender, and experience) are, at least in part, learned through modeling language and speech behavior.

Accommodation also refers to the adjustments or adaptations made by an entire speech community for the bene-

ACQUISITION The process by which a person acquires knowledge of a language is, as linguists use the term, acquisition. The term generally refers to language acquisition (the acquisition of some aspect of language, a whole language, or a second language). Acquisition has also been used to describe how people learn the rules for using language in the real world. The anthropologist and linguist Dell Hymes calls this type of knowledge "communicative competence" (knowing the appropriateness or inappropriateness of an utterance). Hymes points out that children acquiring knowledge of a language must also acquire the sociocultural rules for using language across a variety of social and cultural contexts.

Acquisition is the central concept associated with theories of language acquisition. These theories range from explanations that assume that people learn language because they are genetically programmed to do so, to theories emphasizing the roles that environment and social interaction play in the overall process.

See also COMMUNICATIVE COMPETENCE; LANGUAGE ACQUISITION.

Hymes, Dell. (1971) "Competence and Performance in Linguistic Theory." In *Language Acquisition: Models and Methods*, edited by R. Huxley and E. Ingram, 3–28.

———. (1971) "On Communicative Competence." In *Sociolinguistics*, edited by J. B. Pride and Janet Holmes, 269–293.

ACROLECT

An acrolect is a type of creole language (a language made up from elements of several languages) that is a standard or prestige language of a region or country. Acrolects contrast with basilects or creole languages that are stigmatized (viewed negatively).

See also CREOLE.

ADDRESS, FORMS OF

Forms of address are specific terms or phrases used to express social and personal orientations among people who are communicating. Forms of address include formal (polite) and informal personal pronouns, personal names, kin terms (including family and clan names), formal titles, nicknames, and special terms for specific situations (greetings and addressing people of differing statuses and roles).

Rules for what forms of address to use vary significantly across cultures and by situation. Ethnolinguists (anthropologists who study language) recognize that some forms and uses of address seem to appear in all human societies. For example, most cultures make use of specific speech codes that emphasize either formal or informal relationships among members. Address forms that are formal reinforce social distance between speakers. Informal address forms imply social solidarity (social closeness). In cases of informal address the terms used are reciprocal (all speakers involved in verbal exchanges use the same term). Alternations (switches) in forms of address signal differences in relationships as situational contexts change.

An ethnolinguistic study of Navajo women who were living in Los Angeles, California, indicates that some Navajo speakers use last names (family/clan names) when addressing elders and personal first names when addressing peers. Also, when younger speakers address elders, generational kin terms (mother, father, grandmother, grandfather) are added to the clan names to acknowledge generational differences between the speakers (even to unrelated elders). Shirley Fiske, the linguist who carried out this study, suggests that differences in the selection of address signal or mark social relationships that are indicated primarily by differences in age. In addition, respect for elders is indicated through the use of formal forms of address. These Navajo women also use formal terms of address when they talk to non-Navajo speakers.

Pronouns as address forms can vary in type and use across cultures and languages. French speakers employ the second-person plural pronoun *vous* when addressing a group of people. *Vous* is also used as the formal second person singular form in some circumstances. This type of plural pronoun exists in some languages, but does not exist in standard English. Some pronoun types indicate gender while others carry no gender marking at all. Southeast Asian Hmong speakers use gender-neutral pronouns only. The linguistic equivalents of the English pronouns *he, she, her,* and *his* do not exist in Hmong. Instead, gender-neutral pronouns such as *kuv* (I), *koj* (you, your, and you've), and *lawv* (they) are used. Knowing these differences may be important if a translation from one language to another is being made. Often exact equivalents for specific pronouns between languages do not exist; therefore approximate pronouns or words that classify like pronouns must be found for a translation to work.

Unusual terms of address may also arise as a result of changes in the political order. In China, after the 1949 Communist revolution, the term *tongzhi* (comrade) came into use. *Tongzhi* is used as a form of greeting, but it also implies affiliation with the Communist Party and to a general sense of national patriotism. Moreover, not using *tongzhi* as a form of greeting could signal informality (as greetings might be carried out in private households) but might also be interpreted as conveying a negative attitude toward the Communist Chinese government.

Criteria for deciding who is or is not a member of a person's kin group is typically defined by culture (although biological relationships are recognized in all societies). In all cultures many of the terms used to address kin (real and fictive kin) mark particular kinship categories. In most non-Western societies kin terms are used for address more frequently than in the West. Among the Yanomamo of Venezuela and Brazil a strict taboo against using personal names of close relatives exists. From the Yanomamo perspective, using a person's personal name brings unwanted attention to that individual. The belief is that using a person's personal name might attract violent spirits that could enter the person's body and cause illness or even death. To avoid this problem the Yanomamo use descriptive kin terms to address people as well as to refer to relatives not present. Descriptive kin terms merely state in a concise manner the particular relationship between the speaker and the person being addressed ("mother's brother," "husband," "husband's uncle"). This allows the Yanomamo to avoid the use of personal names (only people not related can use personal names). Similarly, in Turkey descriptive kin terms such as "mother's brother" are used instead of abstract specific terms like the English term uncle.

Among the Cheyenne of the American plains, when addressing relatives, kin terms are often used in conjunction with age indicators. *Naʔniha* means elder brother. A relative degree of respect is conferred upon an elder. Conversely, *naːsima* means younger brother and implies a lesser degree of status.

Sometimes special terms of address have been developed to maintain military alliances. Among the Samo of

Papua New Guinea a specific set of terms is sometimes used when addressing members of a neighboring group when an alliance relationship has been formed. For example, *oosoo buoman*, "those who sit together," marks an alliance relationship and is a form of address used at intervillage festivals. For the Samo some alliances were created through marriage. In such cases kin terms would be incorporated in an address. The term *koiman* refers to individuals who are allies by marriage. If the ally is a female of one's mother's age the term *uyo* is added to show respect for an elder. If elder male allies are being addressed, *koiman* (ally) also implies father, so the kin term is not added. Since British colonists outlawed warfare among the native populations of New Guinea, alliance terms of address have declined in use. Other forms of address, particularly kin terms, have persisted.

In most societies special terms exist to denote occupations, sociopolitical position, and other forms of official function. The Laotian Hmong use *nom tswv* when addressing a chief (patriarch) and *xib fwb* for master or teacher. These terms are always used to show respect and are often used during special public events (settling disputes, opening marriage ceremonies, and generally while initiating and carrying out public events).

Terms of address are important features of language and communication across cultures. They function to reinforce cultural norms for social organization. Depending on the form of address used, a person can indicate social distance and respect, social closeness, or differences in occupational roles. Terms of address thus reflect the particular social norms of a given society.

See also KINSHIP TERMS.

Bliatout, Bruce, Bruce T. Downing, Judy Lewis, and Dao Yang. (1988) *Handbook for Teaching Hmong-Speaking Students.*

Bonvillain, Nancy. (1993) *Language, Culture, and Communication: The Meaning of Messages.*

Chagnon, Napoleon A. (1992) *The Yanomamo*, 4th ed.

Fang, Hanquan, and J. H. Heng. (1983) "Social Changes and Changing Address Norms in China." *Language in Society* 12: 495–507.

Fiske, Shirley. (1978) "Rules of Address: Navajo Women in Los Angeles." *Journal of Anthropological Research* 34(1): 72–91.

Hoebel, E. Adamson. (1960) *The Cheyennes: Indians of the Great Plains.*

Hong, Beverly. (1985) "Politeness in Chinese: Impersonal Pronouns and Personal Greeting." *Anthropological Linguistics* 27: 204–213.

Shaw, Daniel R. (1996) *From Longhouse to Village: Samo Social Change.*

ADORNMENT

Adornment is the practice of the placing, wearing, or engraving culturally significant decorations or symbols on the human body. All societies provide for the artistic expression of culture through the use of body decoration or adornment. The use of body paints, jewelry, scarification, tattooing, and many other ways to communicate cultural ideas by modifying the human body are found throughout the world. Although the cultural functions for adornment vary significantly on a global, cross-cultural basis, the most common function seems to be to communicate role and status differences among members of a society. For example, members of the Iroquoian False Face Society were required to wear special masks during important ceremonies. These masks, adorned with horse hair, copper eyes, elaborate paint designs, and images of contorted faces, marked the wearer as a member of that important society of Iroquoian shamans (traditional religious healers).

Body adornments often serve multiple cultural functions. Among the Laotian Hmong, shamans, while conducting healing ceremonies, wear a veil. The veil serves the dual purpose of supporting Hmong religious belief—Hmong shamans say that the veil shuts them off from this world so that they may travel in the spirit world—and of serving as the public expression of Hmong shamanhood. A similar use of body adornment can be seen in the Huichol shamans of the western central highlands of Mexico. Huichol shamans use various natural pigments—typically yellow body paints—to draw religious designs on their legs and faces. The forms are often abstract designs such as swirls, zigzags, stars, and circles. Some of the forms represent the Sun, the Moon, deer, rabbits, and other images derived from nature. The Huichol say that these body paintings are to assist shamans in their endeavors to cure people and to assist in the regulation of ritual activities.

Across cultures, body adornment is used most often to communicate changes or differences in social status

All societies provide for the artistic expression of culture through the use of body decoration or adornment. This young woman of Nunivak Island off Alaska's southwest coast wears chin and nose ornaments.

among members of a particular society. In many cases individuals who go through rites of passage are, upon receiving their new status, given a new set of clothes to wear, a tattoo, scars, or some other overt sign of their new position in society. Among the Nuer of Africa's Sudan, young boys, upon becoming men, have their heads shaved and their foreheads cut with sharp knives. The six horizontal cuts indicate that these boys should now be considered full adults in Nuer society. The scars, as cultural markers, represent a permanent statement of the social position of the young men and, by extension, are viewed by the Nuer as symbols of male authority.

Similarly, among the Tolowa (a Native American group from northwestern California), girls, upon going through their rite to adulthood, acquire tattoos on their chins. These tattoos, as in the other cultures mentioned above, indicate a change in status. In addition, the linear pattern of the tattoos also mark tribal membership in that the patterns differentiate Tolowa women from neighboring groups such as the Hupa, the Yurok, and the Karok.

Adornment is often used in ritual contexts. Among South American groups, particularly in the Amazon Basin, sharp sticks are sometimes driven through the nasal septum of women before the celebration of a feast. Men often use lip plugs—made of wood and sometimes tobacco—before and during highly charged ceremonies. Among the Yanomamo of Venezuela and Brazil men adorn themselves with lip plugs and body paint before entering a neighbor's village. The adornments, in this particular context, communicate village affiliation, the intentions of the visitor (peaceful or nonpeaceful), and the overall status of the individual in relation to members of his group. The Tchikrin of Brazil use ear plugs, lip plugs, marked clothing, and variable hair length to indicate a complex array of cultural meanings. For example, hair length connotes degrees of sexual power, with long hair representing full sexual potency.

Various ideas have been suggested by social scientists to explain the widespread use of body adornments. The sociologist Erving Goffman, for example, suggests that adornments act as "display" in much the same way as a male peacock shows off his feathers as a means of attracting a mate. Goffman has pointed out that human beings (men and women) spend considerable time making themselves up in various ways to attract potential mates. The anthropologist Edward T. Hall has observed that body adornments serve a number of complex functions through a general capacity for nonverbal communication. Hall suggests that clothing, jewelry, perfumes, and body paints can delineate a person's occupation, sex, subcultural affiliation, and age. In general, linguistic anthropologists view adornment as a feature of extralinguistics or nonverbal communication. The cultural messages that are communicated through the use of adornment are often subtle or implied; but, as many anthropologists have pointed out, the content of the messages is typically culturally important to the people who use them.

See also NONVERBAL COMMUNICATION.

Eastman, Carol M. (1975) *Aspects of Language and Culture.*

Evans-Pritchard, E. E. (1968) *The Nuer.*

Goffman, Erving. (1967) *Interaction Ritual.*

Good, Kenneth. (1991) *Into the Heart: One Man's Pursuit of Love and Knowledge among the Yanomami.*

Hall, Edward T. (1959) *The Silent Language.*

Myerhoff, Barbara G. (1974) *The Peyote Hunt: The Sacred Journey of the Huichol Indians.*

Turner, Terence S. (1969) "Tchikrin: A Central Brazilian Tribe and Its Language of Bodily Adornment." *Natural History* 78: 8.

AGGLUTINATING LANGUAGES

Some languages contain a high number of complex words that are constructed by placing together ("gluing") several words into lengthy cohesive sequences. The Cree (an Algonkian-speaking Native American group) have the word *athapaska*, which, literally translated into English, is "reeds-that-grow-here-and-there." Cree speakers utter this word phrase as a single word.

Many of the world's languages are agglutinative. Inuit (Eskimo), Algonkian, Wakashan, Turkish, Japanese, and Swahili are a few examples of this language type.

ANIMAL COMMUNICATION

All animals obtain information from their environment. Obtaining such information constitutes a rudimentary form of communication. Even primitive multicellular organisms receive stimuli from light sources, movement of other organisms, and chemical changes occurring in the environment. Understanding these rudimentary patterns of communication helps scientists to understand the basis for communication as it is carried out in complex higher-order organisms—including human beings.

Anthropologists are interested in animal communication, especially for higher-order primates, because it may tell them something about the evolution of human language and communication. Higher-order primates such as the anthropoids (the great apes) are im-portant to this type of research because of their closeness to human beings in evolutionary terms. Most researchers working in this area (anthropologists and primatologists alike) describe non-human primate communication as "closed." This means that communicative "calls" made by these primates carry only one meaning at a time (one call, one meaning). Howler monkeys, for instance, are unable to combine and recombine calls to generate more complex and detailed communication. In contrast, human beings are capable of using a narrow range of sounds (consonants and vowels) to make an infinite variety of communicative utter-ances. Human communication is therefore "open."

There may be cases that represent exceptions to the sharply defined separation of nonhuman primate and human communication. Dorothy Cheney and Robert Seyfarth have conducted extensive research on East African vervet monkeys *(Cercopithecus aethiops)* and have concluded that vervets use a variety of contrasting calls to differentiate among types of danger. For instance, these monkeys use separate calls for signaling the presence of eagles, snakes, and large predator mammals. There is clear evidence that vervet monkeys use separate calls for each of these types of danger because predictable responses consistently follow each call. If the threat is from hawks or eagles the call given causes the vervets to look up. If the threat is from a snake a call is produced that causes vervets to look down. If a large predator cat is nearby a call is produced that causes vervets to climb trees. Apparently the calls not only differentiate among types of danger but

In the 1980s renewed interest in chimpanzee language stimulated new research projects. Here, Dr. Roger Fouts and seven-year-old Tatu converse in American Sign Language at Central Washington University's home for gifted chimpanzees (1983).

also communicate what appropriate responses should be taken. It is interesting to note that vervets responding to an alarm react accordingly before they actually see the danger.

Research on chimpanzees has also raised certain questions pertaining to the assumed sharp delineation between human and nonhuman communication. In the late 1960s Alan and Beatrix Gardner conducted studies of chimpanzee communication through teaching chimpanzees sign language. A young common chimpanzee *(Pan troglodytes)* named Washoe was taught American Sign Language (ASL). According to the Gardners, Washoe, through the use of signing, demonstrated the ability to construct simple sentences to carry out basic conversations with human beings. Herbert Terrace, working with a chimpanzee named Nim Chimsky, stated that chimpanzees are not capable of producing a sentence. Instead, these chimpanzees seem to be mimicking or patterning their signing behavior after their human teachers and apparently do not comprehend the meaning of the signs they are making. After the announcement of Terrace's results, most research on chimpanzee communication was shut down.

In the 1980s renewed interest in chimpanzee language stimulated new research undertakings. Sue Savage-Rumbaugh began working with pygmy chimpanzees *(Pan paniscus)*. Her work was largely based on descriptions of the communicative behavior of a small group of pygmy chimpanzees (bonobos, as they are sometimes called). Although her work involved several chimpanzees, much of the research was concentrated on the behavior of a chimp named Kanzi. Savage-Rumbaugh's research indicates that although chimpanzees cannot vocalize human speech (they cannot produce consonants), chimpanzees are capable of comprehending human language and, through the use of a special electronic board, can produce simple sentences. This research also suggests that for Kanzi communication is open; he can comprehend statements that he has never heard before, statements constructed by new combinations of words that Kanzi already knows. Moreover, Kanzi appears to be capable of displacement, which is the ability to comprehend references to things not in his immediate visual field.

Studies of animal communication, especially those of higher-order primates, have far-reaching implications for understanding human language and communication. Theories that attempt to place human language and communication into a comprehensive evolutionary framework indicate that at this broad level human beings share many behavior traits with nonhuman animals. As more research is conducted on the communicative behavior of other animals, answers to central questions regarding our relationship to other organisms may to some degree be answered.

Cheney, Dorothy, and Robert Seyfarth. (1991) *How Monkeys See the World*.

Gardner, Beatrix, and Alan Gardner. (1969) *Teaching Sign Language to a Chimpanzee*.
Parker, Sue T., and Kathleen R. Gibson. (1990) *Language and Intelligence in Monkeys and Apes: Comparative Developmental Perspectives*.
Pinker, Steven. (1994) *The Language Instinct: How the Mind Creates Language*.
Savage-Rumbaugh, Sue. (1991) "Language Learning in the Bonobo: How and Why They Learn." In *Biological and Behavioral Determinants of Language Development*, edited by N. A. Krasnegor, D. M. Rumbaugh, R. L. Schiefelbusch, and M. Studdert-Kennedy.
Terrace, Herbert. (1979) *Nim*.

APPLIED LINGUISTICS

Applied linguistics is the application of linguistic methods, analyses, and theories to the solution of language and communication problems. This wide-ranging field includes forensic linguistics (using analysis of language to solve crimes), language translation/interpretation, intercultural communication, and applied sociolinguistics (reconstructing the use of language and speech in situational contexts).

Perhaps the most generally used approach to applied linguistics is intercultural communication. This approach involves descriptions of communicative exchanges among people of fundamentally different cultural backgrounds. With intercultural communication the emphasis is not so much on direct translation (finding word-for-word correspondences) as it is on interpretation (finding comprehensible terms and phrases that correspond) and isolating cultural differences in social interaction.

Businesses that operate outside their home countries have made the most extensive use of intercultural communication resources. For example, U.S. firms doing business in Japan during the 1950s found that collaboration efforts and decision-making protocols were often hindered by profound but subtle cultural differences. During the 1960s and 1970s intercultural communication specialists formed consulting firms that assisted various businesses who were operating in other cultural settings. During the 1980s and 1990s intercultural communication expanded into such areas as education, health care, the legal domain, and everyday work settings.

Other forms of applied linguistics have been used for translating verbal and written texts from one language to another (or others). This is sometimes called *interpretation* because direct word-for-word translation often renders texts incomprehensible. Interpretation requires finding appropriate terms and phrases for the target language that approximate the central ideas contained in the original version. For instance, the linguist Peter Farb points out that the English word *home* as used by British English speakers carries a significant degree of connotative meaning (suggested meaning). To a British English speaker *home* refers to the place of a person's origin, the quality of a person's background associated with that homeland, and the subjective sense that *home* resides in one's soul. *Home*, therefore, does not merely refer to the physical space where a person lives. Thus, translating a British novel into Mandarin (a Chinese lan-

guage) might require finding an appropriate term or phrase that closely represents the British meaning for *home*. Translations that are made by the effective use of interpretation are generally considered to be more reliable. Moreover, this type of translation is typically based on an understanding of the specific cultural patterns underlying the verbal and written texts of a language.

Since the 1980s applied linguistics has been used to resolve problems of communication across a wide variety of social and cultural situations. Interpreters are often called into courtrooms when language barriers become problematic. Many hospitals now employ language specialists who act as cultural-linguistic brokers. These brokers facilitate verbal communication and, through interpreting a variety of cultural beliefs and behaviors that may impede communication, are generally able to resolve problems of social protocol (knowing the correct rules for social interaction). For example, cultural-linguistic brokers can often regulate how people should be introduced to one another. To illustrate, among the Japanese it is important to address elders first when introductions are made. Using a formal speech form is also required. Someone who has been trained to recognize this cultural pattern would be able to do the introductions and explain the cultural pattern to non-Japanese.

Some applied linguists analyze the vocabularies of different languages in order to make use of specific semantic constructs (for example, the way words are related to one another: "fish, trout, types of trout"). Semantic information of this type is important because some languages contain detailed semantic categories for certain phenomena. Other languages may lack useful categories in specific areas of knowledge. A classic example of borrowing a semantic field (words organized from general to specific levels by meaning) is demonstrated by English-speaking geologists, who have incorporated as part of their working vocabulary Hawaiian-Polynesian terms for various types of lava. Because Hawaiians have a long history of living in close proximity to volcanic eruptions, their knowledge of—and therefore terms for—lava is quite detailed. Instead of inventing new terms, English-speaking geologists (volcanologists in this case) use the native Hawaiian terms. *Aa,* for example, refers to thick, slow-moving lava with protruding jagged rubble, while *pahoehoe* is fast-moving, extremely hot, fluid lava.

See also INTERCULTURAL COMMUNICATION.

———

Burrus, Thomas L., and Herbert J. Spriegel. (1976) *Earth in Crisis: An Introduction to the Earth Sciences.*
Farb, Peter. (1978) *Word Play: What Happens When People Talk.*
Hickerson, Nancy Parrott. (1980) *Linguistic Anthropology.*
Samovar, Larry A., and Richard E. Porter, eds. (1991) *Intercultural Communication: A Reader,* 6th ed.
Trudgill, Peter. (1984) *Applied Sociolinguistics.*

What is said and how something is said can be viewed by members of a society as either appropriate or inappropriate according to prevailing cultural norms. The selection and use of an utterance that is deemed correct by the general population of speakers of a language is called appropriateness. Knowing whether a statement is appropriate or not depends on the individual speaker's ability to judge the impact the statement will have on others across a variety of social and cultural situations. Appropriateness is therefore more a function of being able to interpret and understand the subtleties of a wide variety of sociocultural contexts. The concept of appropriateness, as it has been applied to sociolinguistics, is typically associated with communicative competence (having the ability to use language to communicate culturally appropriate messages).

See also COMMUNICATIVE COMPETENCE.

———

Hymes, Dell. (1971) "Competence and Performance in Linguistic Theory." In *Language Acquisition: Models and Methods,* edited by R. Huxley and E. Ingram, 3–28.
———. (1971) "On Communicative Competence." In *Sociolinguistics,* edited by J. B. Pride and Janet Holmes, 269–293.

APPROPRIATENESS In any given society certain ways of communicating are considered normal.

ARCHAISM In all language systems some words, through time, fall out of general use. Sometimes these words are maintained for use in special circumstances (such as poetry, proverbs, and children's stories). Old or archaic words that lose their use in the general spoken language are called archaisms. For example, in Newfoundland Canada the archaic term *drite* is sometimes used to state that the air is dry. This term is not generally used outside of Newfoundland.

ARCHING

Arching is a strategy in conversation whereby a person responds to a question with another question. Arching, as a strategy, serves several functions. First, by answering a question with a question, a speaker may be making a negative comment on the initial question. Second, the use of arching may be a way of avoiding the substance or content of the initial question (especially if the question is embarrassing to the person responding). Finally, arching sometimes functions to signal a change of topic.

AREAL LINGUISTICS

Some linguists are concerned with describing the shared properties of languages that are associated with a particular geographic region. The description and analysis of language properties shared by languages in a given region is called areal linguistics. Areal linguists are not merely concerned with languages that are genetically related (that is, related languages that diverged from an earlier language); often these linguists want to know how unrelated languages of a particular region have influenced one another.

To illustrate the kind of problem areal linguists might engage, consider the case of Tlingit (a Native American language of the Pacific Northwest coastal region). In 1915 the linguist Edward Sapir stated that Tlingit was related to the Athapaskan languages of the interior of British Columbia (such as Carrier, Sarcee, and Chippewyan). Sapir believed that although the Tlingit language did not share a significant number of words with the Athapaskan languages, there were sufficient similarities in grammar and phonology (the sounds used in a language) to warrant the connection. If Sapir was correct, a larger grouping of the Athapaskan languages was necessary. This larger grouping Sapir called Na-Dene.

Subsequent linguistic analysis by areal linguists indicated that the similarities between Tlingit and the Athapaskan languages may have resulted from convergence (coincidental similarities) and borrowing (exchanging linguistic items). Many areal linguists felt that Tlingit was not an Athapaskan language. However, knowing the geographical as well as the linguistic relationship between the two language groups was still useful. The question of whether Tlingit is or is not Athapaskan is still being debated.

See also LANGUAGE FAMILIES.

Sapir, Edward. (1915) *The Na-Dene Languages: A Preliminary Report.*
Thompson, Lawrence C., and Dale M. Kinkade. (1990) "Languages." In

Handbook of North American Indians, Vol. 7, *Northwest Coast,* edited by Wayne Suttles, 30–51.

ARGOT An argot is an exclusive vocabulary used secretly by groups of people who wish to separate themselves (sometimes only periodically) from the general society. The terms *cant* and *jargon* are synonymous with argot. The primary function of argots seems to be to deny outside members—that is, members of the general society—access to communication being carried out within the exclusive group.

Argots occur across cultures, appearing in a variety of contexts and serving numerous functions. Secret vocabularies are often used by religious specialists to contact the spirit world and to reinforce their role as mystics; they may be used by members of warrior societies to reinforce their special status as brave fighters; they may also be used by political figures who wish to hide aspects of their activities from others. Criminals in various parts of the world have used argots to avoid communicating important information to their jailers. Argots have also been used by children to distance themselves socially from adults and for practicing their oratory skills.

Among the Haida of the northwest coast of North America (British Columbia, Canada), shamans (traditional religious healers), during moments of religious ecstasy, switch from the Haida language to a broken version of Tlingit (spoken by a neighboring group). Switching from one language to another in religious contexts like this

is called *xenoglossia*. Haida shamans who do this are essentially using an argot. Most Haida speakers are not competent in Tlingit, and thus the shamans' use of Tlingit hides what is being said and creates a sense of awe in their audiences.

In Panama, Cuna children use a form of argot by adding linguistic material to the front of words (prefixing). This is similar to the use of "Pig Latin" among English speakers. Peter Farb has observed that Cuna children add *ci* "before every syllable and then stress the syllables in the normal form." Thus, the Cuna word for friend, *ai*, is changed into *ciAcil*. The medial *ah* sound after the initial *ci* is stressed (said louder and at a higher pitch). Farb suggests that this form of linguistic manipulation has two functions: first, it is a form of linguistic play (merely having fun with word play), and second, it allows Cuna children to prepare for public oration (similar to tongue twisters), which is culturally emphasized in Cuna culture.

Toward the end of the eighteenth century and continuing throughout much of the nineteenth century, many British convicts were shipped to Australia, where they were subsequently incarcerated. Many of these prisoners were from London's East End and spoke a dialect called Cockney. On their voyages to Australia the prisoners made extensive use of Cockney as a secret code language. Most of the guards and prison officials who were traveling on board the prison ships could not understand Cockney, especially when it was exaggerated or embellished. This, like the Haida example, constitutes the use of a complete language (not merely a vocabulary) as an argot. Through the use of Cockney dialect many of the prisoners were able to organize and carry out activities with a certain degree of secrecy.

The linguist Susan Philips has observed Western lawyers using "legalese" (legal jargon) as a secret language. Philips recorded how law students acquire this special vocabulary and described how, after receiving their law degrees, lawyers use the highly technical jargon of their profession to confuse, intimidate, and frustrate the lay public. This jargon has been extended to written documents as well. Some social scientists have suggested that this form of argot has been maintained by legal professionals to prevent the public from settling disputes without the assistance of lawyers. Many lawyers argue that the legal field, like other professions, makes use of specific terms and concepts that cannot be conveyed through common everyday language.

See also XENOGLOSSIA.

Chambers, J. K., and Peter Trudgill. (1980) *Dialectology.*

Farb, Peter. (1978) *Word Play: What Happens When People Talk.*

Philips, Susan Urmston. (1988) "The Language Socialization of Lawyers: Acquiring the 'Cant.'" In *Doing the Ethnography of Schooling: Educational Anthropology in Action*, edited by George Spindler, 133–175.

Swanton, John R. (1905) *The Haida.*

AVOIDANCE

Avoidance refers to culturally sanctioned rules for regulating abstinence or refrainment from particular behaviors, most often avoidance of interaction between specific members of extended kin groups (members of a family unit beyond the immediate family, such as cousins, aunts and uncles, and distant relatives). Avoidance rules may also direct food taboos, choice of linguistic codes (polite versus impolite, formal versus informal, direct or indirect conversation, and greeting forms), and ritual observances.

In many small-scale traditional societies people commonly observe avoidance rules for certain members of extended kin groups. The Ju/'hoansi (!Kung) of the Kalahari Desert of Namibia and Botswana divide kin groups by an "avoidance-joking" relationship dichotomy. Hence, all members of Ju/'hoansi society would be designated as either "kin-to-be-avoided" or "kin-with-whom-to-be-familiar," depending on the relationship from the individual making the judgment. Avoidance among the Ju/'hoansi is not absolute, but it is expected that interactions between people for whom an avoidance relationship exists be kept brief, formal, and without levity. Avoidance relationships among the Ju/'hoansi are designated for same-sex siblings, members of one's parent's generation, and members of one's children's generation. The underlying reason for these avoidance rules seems to be to maintain social distance between generations and, to some extent, rival siblings of the same sex. Maintaining social distances from elders is desirable because important decisions are typically made by older members of society, and a certain degree of respect is given to these elders to maintain the social order.

These recurring cultural patterns assist in the regulation of numerous and complex social/communicative interactions. Knowing the cultural rules for how people should and should not interact can tell outsiders a great deal about the internal dynamics of a cultural system. For example, the Iu-Mien of Laos have a strong (albeit implicit) rule prohibiting married women from talking to adult males in private settings (that is, without the husband present). This rule is so strongly adhered to that women caught in this situation are sometimes shunned by the community. In these situations men are expected to approach a house, stand outside, and shout to the woman (in full public view) if the husband is not home. Ethnographers describing such events have to look beyond the overt behavior as isolated occurrences in order to comprehend how the Iu-Mien view social relationships and social interactions in general. For example, maintaining a household with strong family ties is desirable because the family is the basis of the Iu-Mien economy. When an adult male visits a household when the head of the household is away, the potential for adultery increases. Hence the visitation represents a threat to the marriage and to the economic viability of the family and, by extension, to the village.

Among the Canela of Brazil sons-in-law must avoid most contact with the mother of their bride in all social and private settings, and a more moderate application of the rule is extended to all female members of the mother-in-law's generation. Like the Ju/'hoansi, the Canela seem to be using avoidance rules to reinforce relationships where social distance should be maintained and, by contrast, those relationships that should remain close (especially for members who are potential courting partners).

Subtle avoidance rules are often applied to informal discourse. In conversation, for example, sociolinguists have observed that most people tend to avoid harsh, direct, or incisive language. In Western societies even people who claim to be straightforward and direct will make use of euphemistic, indirect language when engaged in conversation. In most societies, for example, speakers typically open a conversation with small talk (e.g., "Hello, what a nice shirt," or "Kind of a big crowd here tonight—Oh, by the way . . ."). Keith Basso, an anthropologist who has studied the Western Apache, has pointed out that the degree to which people will tolerate indirect language (avoiding directness) varies significantly from society to society. Among the Western Apache, as Basso has observed, greeting rituals are kept minimal. Sometimes nothing is said at all. Knowing that someone has arrived is enough protocol for subsequent discourse to take place. In contrast, in some cultural traditions members are subtly required to provide a significant degree of indirect talk before settling on a central issue. In most parts of western central Africa strangers who are being introduced each provide a lengthy narrative of their family, their personal holdings, and other background information before raising central issues related to their meeting (e.g., business, school, and so forth). In the Appalachians of the United States most people consider direct talk rude. One is expected to use pleasantries before broaching the main purpose of a visit.

Imperatives for avoiding certain terminology—also referred to as lexical choice—are quite common across cultures. The Yanomamo have a taboo against using a person's personal name unless the individual is not related, is an enemy, or lives in a distant village. From the Yanomamo perspective, the use of a person's personal name could bring harm to that person by summoning violent spirits. The U.S. military has also developed a highly specific list of terms to use to refer to war-associated phenomena. The linguist Peter Moss has described how these terms have been used to replace more direct, demonstrative language. For example, "collateral damage" is used instead of "civilian dead"; "rapid disassembly" (originally taken from the physicists' term for a nuclear explosion) is used instead of "large explosion." The ordinary terms evoke emotional responses, whereas the newer terms, in the military's view, are neutral. Some linguists have suggested that the military's use of euphemistic terms to describe war events represents a form of avoidance or denial designed to allow for performance unencumbered by emotion (the same way that medical doctors talk about the condition of terminally ill patients). Other linguists have suggested that the military uses such language merely as a way of avoiding negative publicity.

Avoidance rules can in some societies be expressed in the form of food taboos. Among the Inuit of the North American Arctic, it is emphatically forbidden to mix caribou and seal meat. The anthropologist Marvin Harris has suggested that these food taboos reflect more practical aspects of life. Seals were traditionally hunted through the ice during the winter months; caribou was hunted on land during the summer and the fall. Hunting seal through the ice during the summer would have been extremely dangerous because of ice breakup. Hunting caribou during the winter would have meant that the hunting group would not have been located out on the ice, where traditional seal hunting occurred. In precise terms, then, at any given time of year it was impractical either to hunt seal or to hunt caribou. The taboos against combining caribou and seal meat in a meal thus represents the institutional, ritualistic reflection of highly regulated and predictable subsistence activities. Harris has noted that the same observation can be applied to the generalized taboo against eating pork in the Middle East. Orthodox Jews and Muslims have strict taboos against eating pork. From an outsider's perspective this rule may seem unusual, but, as Harris has noted, it makes sense in terms of the subsistence/ecology of the Middle East. In the past the Semitic cultures of the Middle East were primarily pastoralists (herders). Harris has pointed out that herding pigs across a desert environment would have been nearly impossible; pigs require large amounts of water and they cannot travel long distances in a hot climate, and therefore using pigs as herding animals would not have been practical. Thus, highly specific rules of avoidance may reflect cultural ecological concerns.

Avoidance rules in all sociocultural contexts reveal cultural preferences by positing negatives (behaviors to be avoided). Those behaviors that are to be avoided tend also to illuminate correct or preferred norms.

———————

Basso, Keith H. (1979) *Portraits of "The Whiteman": Linguistic Play and Cultural Symbols among the Western Apache.*

Brown, Lillian, and George Yule. (1983) *Discourse Analysis.*

Chagnon, Napoleon A. (1992) *The Yanomamo,* 4th ed.

Chance, Norman A. (1966) *The Eskimo of North Alaska.*

Croker, William, and Jean Croker. (1994) *The Canela: Bonding through Kinship, Ritual, and Sex.*

Harris, Marvin. (1985) *Good to Eat: Riddles of Food and Culture.*

Lee, Richard B. (1993) *The Dobe Ju/'hoansi.*

Moss, Peter. (1985) "Rhetoric of Defense in the United States: Language, Myth, and Ideology." In *Language and the Nuclear Debate: Nukespeak Today,* edited by P. Chilton, 45–63.

See CREOLE.

BILINGUALISM

Bilingualism refers to a situation where an individual or a community of speakers is competent or fluent in two or more languages. Bilingualism also refers to bilingual education—the practice and philosophy of teaching in two or more languages.

Linguists often refer to bilingualism as *polyglottism*—literally, the ability to speak more than one language. Thus, a person who is able to do this is a polyglot. Linguists also distinguish between simultaneous bilingualism, in which the languages are acquired at the same time, and sequential bilingualism, which occurs when competency in a new language(s) is added to that of a first. Recently the term *multilingualism* has been applied to situations in which individuals are able to speak more than two languages.

Bilingualism is generally viewed by linguists as advantageous. Knowing more than one language allows for greater depth in comprehension, flexibility in communicative situations, and, as some research has suggested, a greater ability to understand language process in general. In 1984 Kenji Hakuta conducted a study of Spanish-speaking students in a New Haven, Connecticut, elementary school. Hakuta concluded that the bilingual speakers had a better working knowledge of language than did those who

BACKCHANNEL CUE

A backchannel cue is a verbal or nonverbal cue used by a listener to maintain a conversation when the comprehension of the listener is low or nonexistent. Among English speakers, periodically using backchannel cues such as "oh," "is that right," or "hmmm" makes it possible to continue a conversation while avoiding in-depth comprehension of what is being said. Nonverbal backchannel cues have also been observed. Head nodding and eye and hand gestures are often used to facilitate the continuation of a one-sided conversation. Backchannel cues allow listeners to avoid the embarrassing admission that what someone is saying is boring. These cues thus function to ease social interactions, especially interactions in which the potential for conflict exists.

See also COCKTAIL PARTY EFFECT.

If it weren't for the English subtitles on the signs and the American cars in the parking lot, this photo could pass for that of a shopping area in Asia instead of Monterey Park, California. However, in most parts of the world, bilingualism is the norm.

could speak only one language (either English or Spanish). Hakuta's research also suggests that the students who were bilingual had greater cognitive flexibility (the ability to think through) with regard to comprehension and use of language grammar. He went on to point out that this flexibility most likely results from bilinguals' being able to contrast grammatical rules specific to each of the languages spoken; these students, in other words, had a richer array of grammatical examples to choose from as part of their linguistic repertoires. Moreover, bilingual students demonstrated a greater ability and flexibility than monolingual students with regard to social skills. This suggests that lan-

guage competence influences the range of social interactive skills a person will have.

Linguistic anthropologists have long recognized the importance of being bilingual. A cultural anthropologist who goes into the field to study a society must take the time to learn the native language of the group being studied. Anthropologists assume that if an ethnographer (field cultural anthropologist) learns a native language, then that language can be used as a kind of perceptual window into the lifeways of the culture being studied. For example, learning native terms for plants and animals might provide insight into the many ways that people organize information into semantic groupings (relationships of meaning).

Knowing how a language is structured grammatically may also provide some sense of how a group of people view time, or spatial relationships among subjects, objects, and action words (verbs). For example, Harry Hoijer has studied the internal structure of Dine (Navajo) and has concluded that the Dine language is verb oriented. In fact, the Dine do not seem to use nouns in the same way that English speakers do. The subjects and objects of sentences (in English always nouns) function more like verbs. For example, the English word "bridge" would be most accurately translated from Dine into English as "bridging." Thus, most nouns are used as verbs of being, such as "tree" to "treeing," "house" to "housing," and "rock" to "rocking." Viewed from this perspective, an English speaker acquiring fluency in Dine would not only have to learn the grammatical conventions of Dine, he or she might also have to acquire a slightly different view of reality.

Bilingual education emerged in the 1970s and has become one of the dominant forms of educating language-minority pupils in the United States and Canada. Ironically, bilingual education did not begin as a recognizable approach for teaching English as a second language. In 1974 in *Lau v. Nichols*, the U.S. Supreme Court ruled that students who were not being taught the curriculum in a manner that they could understand—such as through their native language—were being denied their right to a public education as guaranteed by the equal protection provisions of the Civil Rights Act of 1964. Bilin-

gual education thus began as a civil rights issue and only subsequently developed as an instructional approach to assist in teaching language-minority students.

Since 1974 a significant amount of research has been conducted on bilingual education. Increasingly, research on bilingual education has moved away from psychologically based testing to studies based on direct observation of language acquisition in naturally occurring everyday situations. Stephen Krashen and Tracy Terrell suggested in 1983, in a now-famous publication, that second language acquisition can be carried out as quickly and efficiently as primary language acquisition if the natural conditions under which the first language is learned are simulated for the second. Children learn language in a stress-free environment where language is modified by adult speakers so that children will constantly comprehend what is being said (this is referred to as "comprehensible input").

Some of this "context-oriented" research has been anthropological or cross-cultural in method and theory. Most anthropological studies view bilingual education as a function of two-way cultural adaptation. For example, while language-minority students (in any education setting) are adapting to their new situation, schools have also had to adapt by developing programs to accommodate language-minority students. What makes anthropological studies different from psychological studies of bilingual education is that anthropologists view schools as communities that are embedded in larger cultural contexts. The emphasis is therefore not on individual performance but on the entire range of naturally occurring behaviors that, taken as a whole, assist researchers in understanding how language-minority students negotiate various communicative situations in school and other social settings.

The author, for example, spent an entire school year (1991–1992) observing a small group of American Hmong high school students. (The Hmong are refugees from Southeast Asia.) The students were observed interacting in classrooms, hallways, the cafeteria, and after school at home. The rates at which these students acquired an understanding of English varied considerably, as English acquisition was influenced by numerous factors. For these students the acquisition of English was part of the larger process of cultural adaptation. They found it necessary not only to learn English, but also, in order to function well in their new societal setting, to acquire an understanding of how language could be used across a wide variety of social and cultural circumstances. Bilingualism resulted from the complex linguistic and cultural adjustments that primary Hmong speakers made on a day-to-day basis in a predominantly North American English-speaking community. Hence, bilingualism and biculturalism appear to be closely associated.

Some anthropological studies of bilingual education have focused on the various ways entire native communities have used multiple languages to communicate a comprehensive curriculum to their students. Gloria Gilmore has described how the Dine (Navajo) have developed bilingual approaches to teaching and learning in their reservation Contract Schools. In these schools most of the curriculum is taught in the Navajo language, and English is taught as a second language, though significant portions of the lessons used (especially writing lessons) are conducted in English. This type of bilingualism reflects the community's use of Navajo in domestic settings and the use of English in official public settings, where communication outside of the immediate community is necessary.

In most parts of the world bilingualism is the norm. In New Guinea most natives are multilingual, speaking the languages of their neighbors and, quite often, pidgins and creoles that are used as trade languages (lingua francas). The same situation exists in Indonesia, where several hundred languages are present. Even in Jakarta, the capital of Indonesia, it is difficult to find locals who speak only one language. Since before the colonial period, Javanese has been an important trade language throughout much of the central region of the Indonesian archipelago. Most Indonesians who live in this region (even beyond Java) speak a variety of local languages as well as a generic form of Javanese. In central Europe having the ability to speak more than one language (three or four languages is not uncommon) is typical. In Switzerland and Austria many citizens speak German, French, and Italian, and many speak English as well.

See also ACQUISITION; COMMUNICATIVE COMPETENCE; LINGUA FRANCA.

Crawford, James. (1993) *Bilingual Education: History, Politics, Theory, and Practice.*

Emerson, Gloria. (1983) "Navajo Education." In *Handbook of North American Indians*, vol. 10, edited by Alfonso Ortiz, 659–671.

Findlay, Michael Shaw. (1992) "American Hmong High School Students: An Ethnographic Study of Communication and Cultural Adaptation." Ph.D. dissertation, University of Oregon.

Hakuta, Kenji. (1990) "Language and Cognition in Bilingual Children." In *Bilingual Education: Issues and Strategies*, edited by A. M. Padilla, H. H. Fairchild, and C. M. Valadez, 47–59.

Hoijer, Harry. (1951) "Cultural Implications of Some Navajo Linguistic Categories." *Language* 27: 111–120.

Krashen, Stephen D., and Tracy D. Terrell. (1983) *The Natural Approach: Language Acquisition in the Classroom.*

Saville-Troike, Muriel. (1989) *The Ethnography of Communication: An Introduction*, 2d ed.

BLACK ENGLISH

As a result of the slave trade that brought West Africans to the Caribbean and to the southeastern region of North America, a significant degree of linguistic mixing occurred. Slaves from Africa spoke a variety of different West African languages, such as Ewe, Fante, Hausa, Ibo, and Yoruba. The plantation owners (who governed slaves) spoke English in the southeastern region of North America, French in Haiti and Martinique, and Spanish in Cuba and Hispaniola. In the English-speaking portions of the New World, especially in what would later become the southern region of the United States, emergent populations of African Americans developed languages that are known collectively as Black English. Black English has been variously labeled Black Vernacular English (BVE) and sometimes Black English Vernacular (BEV).

Black English has been described by some linguists as a creole. Most linguists describe Black English variations as whole languages that contain extensive English vocabularies, with retained elements (primarily of grammar and narrative style) of the West African languages. The degree of reliance that a New World Black language has on a European language (English, French, Spanish) depends largely on the geographical and historical associations that arose in New World contexts. For example, many of the Caribbean creole languages (languages composed of several languages) and North American Black English varieties contain a high number of West African elements (words, grammar, narrative styles, and so forth). Black English speakers of the United States, for example, retain grammatical elements specific to the West African languages: double negatives are often used by Black English speakers ("Don't never say that"), third person singular is dropped (such as *he* instead of *his*), as are the possessive forms (*'s*) and plurals used in standard English ("Her four apple" instead of "Those four apples are hers").

Along the coasts of Georgia and the Carolinas of the southern United States, a form of Black English called Gullah is spoken. Gullah has numerous West African elements in it; in Gullah reliance on African linguistic elements exists to such a degree that Gullah is unintelligible to many speakers of southern American English. Other, more common forms of Black English (both rural and urban), although distinctive in many ways, are essentially variable forms of English.

The use of Black English is controversial. Black English is viewed by many as an inferior language; however, linguists who have studied Black English have pointed out that all forms of Black English contain a full range of grammatical rules, rich use of figurative expression (metaphors, analogies, and expressive adjectives), and extensive and complex vocabulary inventories. These linguists have noted, however, that Black English is stigmatized by a large portion of the American public. It is this stigma that causes some members of the general population to perceive Black English as an inferior language. These perceptions are not based on a systematic analysis of the languages themselves. For example, some English grammarians make the assumption that English is a highly efficient, economical (streamlined) language system because the rules for grammar and spelling were standardized during the eighteenth century. If we contrast English and Black English using the efficiency model, an interesting comparison emerges. In some cases Black English may be more efficient than the more standard versions of English. The sociolinguist Dorothy Seymore, for example, compared an archaic Black English sentence: "There be four book on the table" with the standard English version "There are four books on the table." With the standard version three linguistic markers for pluralization are used *(are, four,* and *s).* From the standpoint of efficiency and economy, two of the

plural markers are not necessary (they are redundant). With the archaic Black English example, only one plural marker is used *(four).* By the criteria of striving for efficiency and economy of language, the archaic Black vernacular sentence is more concise and efficient than its standard English counterpart.

The stigma on Black English has even affected the ways in which some educators view African American students. In the late 1940s and early 1950s some educators subscribed to a theory of language called *language deprivation theory* (LDT). In this theory it was assumed that inner-city African Americans grew up in economically and socially deprived environments and as a result were deprived of the potential for acquiring competency in a full or complete language. Linguists working in the 1960s (William Labov in particular) demonstrated that there is no empirical evidence to support LDT's central claim. Labov found that there are significant differences between Black English and standard forms of English, but these are only of kind and not of quality.

See also CREOLE; SOCIOLECTS.

Burling, Robbins. (1973) *English in Black and White.*

Labov, William. (1970) *The Logic of Nonstandard English.*

———. (1982) "Objectivity and Commitment in Linguistic Sciences: The Case of the Black English Trial in Ann Arbor." *Language in Society* 11: 165–201.

Seymore, Dorothy Z. (1975) "Black English." In *Introductory Readings on*

Language, edited by Wallace L. Anderson and Norman C. Stageberg, 239–245.

Stewart, William A. (1975) "A History of American Negro Dialects." In *Introductory Readings on Language*, edited by Wallace L. Anderson and Norman C. Stageberg, 246–255.

BLENDING

Blending is the mixing of two separate communicative calls to form a new call. Calls are distinctive sounds (screams, screeches, cooing) made by animals to communicate simple messages such as warnings, threats, and indicating social bonding.

In 1960 the linguist Charles Hockett proposed that the blending of calls in early hominids (early human beings) represented a significant step toward the development of full human language. Hockett described the sounds (calls) made by gibbons, observing that for some circumstances dilemmas arose when two instantaneous calls were needed. For example, gibbons sometimes had to use a call that indicated the presence of food at a moment when a threat was imminent (which required a separate warning call). This created the need for an entirely new call that resulted from the blending of the two original calls. For gibbons, the addition of a new call represents a communicative innovation and contributes to the increased complexity of their call system.

Linguists refer to the exclusive use of calls to communicate as "closed communication." Closed communication is the use of one sound to correspond to one basic meaning (a scream might be a warning, cooing might signal social closeness). In contrast, human communication is open. A limited number of sounds can be combined and recombined to produce an infinite number and variety of statements. Hockett speculated that early hominids who made use of an extensive complex call system (closed system) faced an increasing need to blend calls in order to create more detail and precision in their communication. Hockett suggested that blending, in part, may have stimulated the emergence of an early open system of human communication.

See also ANIMAL COMMUNICATION; ORIGINS OF LANGUAGE.

Hockett, Charles F. (1960) "The Origins of Speech." *Scientific American* 203(3): 88–96.

BOASTING

Boasting is a form of performance speech designed to impress listeners by drawing attention and praise to the person doing the speaking. Emphasis is typically placed on the deeds or actions of the speaker. Sociolinguists view boasting as a form of word play that sometimes leads to verbal dueling.

Boasting is found in many societies. It is somewhat rare in small-scale traditional societies where emphasis is placed on group cohesion rather than the individual, but it occurs frequently in larger-scale societies. In New Guinea and throughout much of Melanesia as well as other parts of the world there is a type of tribal leader called a Big Man. Big Men often make use of boasting when organizing certain rituals. Marshall Sahlins has noted that Big Men in New Guinea are obligated to procure resources for ritual giveaways (Mokas), bride payments, festivals, and for paying for rank in secret societies. To generate such capital a Big Man must convince members of his society that he is worthy of such gifts; this is done through persuasive speech making. In these speeches Big Men often make reference to successful Mokas and festivals that they organized in the past. They often draw attention to their work ethic, their skills at obtaining alliances with other groups, and generally to their abilities in bringing wealth into the community (typically through long-lasting relationships with neighboring groups). Boasting among New Guineans is thus a communicative form specific to males of high rank. Their skill at maintaining high rank often depends on their ability to draw attention to themselves (through boasting) without jeopardizing the social fabric of the community.

Roger Abrahams has observed boasting behavior among African Americans. In his article "Black Talking on the Streets," Abrahams describes various speaking styles used by African Americans, including "running a game." Running a game involves the use of speech in which the content of the discourse establishes the "credentials" of the speaker. Credentials are the known skills or abilities associated with an individual. Abrahams's analysis points to the complex relationship between variable uses of speaking styles and social rank. For instance, running a game might involve an individual boasting about past verbal duels with members of the immediate group or describing interactions with outsiders where the individual doing the boasting generated a "put-down" (a clever insult). Running a game is only one form of using speech style as a means of establishing a *rep* (reputation).

Abrahams, Roger D. (1977) "Black Talking on the Streets." In *Explorations in the Ethnography of Speaking,* edited by Richard Bauman and Joel Sherzer, 240–262.

Sahlins, Marshall. (1963) "Poor Man, Rich Man, Big Man, Chief: Political Types in Melanesia and Polynesia." *Comparative Studies in Society and History* 5: 285–303.

BYNAME

A byname is an additional name given to a person to assist in differentiating among people in a community who have similar personal names. Eric the Red was a Norse explorer who sailed off the coast of North America. At that time (circa A.D. 894) many Norse/Viking men had the first name Eric. The byname "the Red" was added to indicate reference to the specific individual associated with the Norse exploration of North America.

Through time bynames can become surnames (family names). Among English speakers, surnames such as Carpenter, Smith, and Driver were, in the past, most likely bynames. For instance, John the blacksmith became John Blacksmith, which eventually became John Smith.

Among the Ju/'hoansi (the !Kung) no surnames exist. Moreover, only a small number of personal names are used. This situation created a built-in need for more differentiation in naming people. To compensate for having so few personal names, the Ju/'hoansi use bynames, which are added to personal names. The bynames typically refer to observable physical or behavior traits associated with specific individuals: *Toma* (short one), *Debe* (big belly), and *N!ai* (short face) are a few examples.

See also NAMING.

_____

Alford, Richard D. (1988) *Naming and Identity: A Cross-Cultural Study of Personal Naming Practices*.
Lee, Richard Borshay. (1993) *The Dobe Ju/'hoansi*.

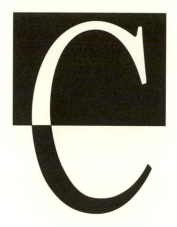

circumlocution is not only tolerated but also is more desirable because indirect conversation allows for social relationships to develop before concise topics are broached.

See also CONVERSATION.

Ochs, Elinor. (1996) "Norm-Makers, Norm-Breakers: Uses of Speech by Men and Women in a Malagasy Community." In *The Matrix of Language: Contemporary Linguistic Anthropology*, edited by Donald Brenneis and Ronald K. S. Macaulay, 99–115.

CALL SYSTEM

See ANIMAL COMMUNICATION.

CANT

See ARGOT.

CIRCUMLOCUTION

Circumlocution refers to the use of excessive words either to avoid or to delay settling on a concise meaning or topic. For most urban American English speakers, circumlocution—talking around a subject—is not considered a desirable form of social discourse. In rural areas of North America and generally across most non-Western cultures,

CLOSED SYSTEM

See ANIMAL COMMUNICATION.

COCKNEY

Cockney is a distinctive dialect of British English spoken in communities situated in the East End of London, England. Cockney contrasts with standard forms of British English by way of its dropping of the *h* sound *(house* becomes *ouse),* through the constant glottalization of the *t* sound *(bottle becomes boʔhl),* and by representing the *th* sound with *v (mother becomes muhver).*

Cockney is viewed negatively by most speakers of standard British English. It is typically associated with lower-socioeconomic communities that are concentrated primarily in the working-class

Michael Caine overcame the working-class status associated with his Cockney origins when he became a celebrated film star during the 1960s.

neighborhoods of London's East End. In the past Cockney was more widespread in London. In fact, historical linguists have determined through the analysis of written documents that Cockney, or rather an archaic form of the dialect, was the predominant way of speaking for Londoners during the eleventh century. When "countryside" aristocrats began to establish businesses and residences in London (during and after the twelfth century), Cockney became stigmatized. The term *Cockney* is most likely a contraction of "cock's egg," an idiom for odd or unusual, no doubt leveled at Cockney speakers by their aristocratic neighbors.

***

Chambers, J. K., and Peter Trudgill. (1991) *Dialects of English: Studies in Grammatical Variation.*
Trudgill, Peter. (1990) *The Dialects of England.*

COCKTAIL PARTY EFFECT Listeners who rely on a variety of communicative cues (backchannel cues) to create the illusion of comprehension in communicative exchanges are producing what psychological linguists call the "cocktail party effect." This effect allows listeners to maintain conversations despite their minimal participation in and comprehension of the conversation. To generate the cocktail party effect, listeners rely on frequent head nods (indicating comprehension) and the use of brief verbal responses such as "oh," "uh-huh," "I see," and "really?"

The cocktail party effect often emerges in situations of cross-cultural communication. When, for example, comprehension of a second language's content is low or nonexistent, listeners often rely on nonverbal backchannel cues to avoid the embarrassment of revealing their lack of comprehension. This situation often arises when speakers of two languages (each with little or no understanding of the other's language) attempt to carry out a conversation.

The author of this volume has observed Hmong students (Laotian immigrants to the United States) generating the cocktail party effect in situations in which linguistic comprehension is low. In one instance, a Hmong student who had been in a fight was brought before the school principal for a disciplinary lecture. The lecture session took approximately ten minutes. The principal, speaking English, explained how fighting would not be tolerated at school. As the lecture unfolded, the principal occasionally asked for a response from the Hmong student, using such statements as "Is this clear?" or "Do you understand?" At each of these junctures the principal used a rising tone at the end of the question, followed immediately by an extended pause. The Hmong student did not understand the content of what was being said, but he did respond to the principal's cues (the rising tone and the pause) with a positive head nod. In a later interview with the Hmong student the author noted that although the Hmong student did not know specifically what the principal was saying, reading the gravity of the situation (context reading) allowed the student to make sense of the event in terms of its general significance. The principal, also in a follow-up interview with the author, stated that he was "pleased with the student's responsiveness."

See also BACKCHANNEL CUE.

Bonvillain, Nancy. (1993) *Language, Culture, and Communication: The Meaning of Messages.*

Findlay, Michael Shaw. (1992) "American Hmong High School Students: An Ethnographic Study of Communication and Cultural Adaptation." Ph.D. dissertation, University of Oregon.

CODE MIXING

See CODES (SPEECH).

CODE SWITCHING

See CODES (SPEECH).

CODES (SPEECH)

Speech codes are differing forms of speech used by members of speech communities (aggregates of people who share cultural knowledge for the use of speech) across a variety of cultural, linguistic, and social-situational contexts. Speech codes can be different languages or variations of a single language. Speech codes have been organized using a wide variety of criteria and terminology: *registers* signal differences in formal and informal codes (for example, the difference between addressing one's grandmother or one's peers); *marked codes* signal membership in social and ethnic groups (such as using computer jargon to indicate affiliation with computer specialists or using an ethnic dialect to signal membership in that group); and *emphatic codes* (using precise and clear directives) indicates communication in special circumstances (a job interview, for example).

Although speech codes are often classified according to type and function, they are sometimes described in terms of how they become altered as situational contexts change. Changing a speech code to fit a change in situation is called *code switching*. Sociolinguist John Gumperz has organized speech codes and code switching by way of the code type and the function and pattern of switching. For example, *code alternation* refers to switches that are necessary to overcome major obstacles to communication, such as switching from one language to another. *Style switching* involves altering code markers (codes that indicate age, ethnicity, socioeconomic class) either to emphasize membership in a group or to distance oneself momentarily from a particular group. Gumperz points out that code switching reveals important information about the cultural, social, and emotional relationships that exist among members of a given speech community. As an illustration, imagine a schoolteacher who in the course of disciplining a student uses a firm, commanding voice (a formal code). Later the same teacher might be heard speaking to the same student under more friendly circumstances. Here the teacher might use a more informal manner of speech, emphasizing familiarity with the student (an informal code). This use of differing speech codes suggests that relationships among individuals do not remain constant. However, the teacher was able to adjust the nature of the teacher/student relationship as different circumstances arose. In this case variable use of speech codes indicated either social distance (through reprimand) or social closeness (through informal speech).

Sociolinguists have also observed code mixing. Code mixing involves bilingual situations that result in more than one language being used to construct a sentence; typically a second language is mixed with a base language. For example, throughout California and most of the southwestern portion of the United States, Spanish and English are often combined in single-sentence constructions. A typical sentence using code mixing might be: "Hola [hello], so where are we going tonight" or "Mi amigos [my friends], it's good to see you again."

Recognizing speech codes and developing an understanding of their cultural functions is important because it allows linguists and anthropologists to explore more subtle aspects of communication and social interaction. The mere shift from a formal speech code to an informal one in a given cultural context not only can tell the researcher what has transpired linguistically, but it can also provide important clues as to the social relationships that exist among speakers.

_____

Gumperz, John. (1982) *Discourse Strategies*.

McClure, Erica. (1977) "Aspects of Code-Switching in the Discourse of Mexican-American Children." In *Linguistics and Anthropology*, edited by Muriel Saville-Troike, 93–116.

Valdes-Fallis, Guadalupe. (1978) "Code-Switching among Bilingual Mexican-American Women: Toward an Understanding of Sex-Related Language Alternation." *International Journal of the Sociology of Language* 17: 65–72.

COGNATE A cognate is a word that derives from a single common linguistic source. For example, English kin terms such as *mother* and *father* can be traced back to their original source language, Indo-European, by way of their shared genetic relationship to related contemporary languages. In Hindi—also an Indo-European language—*mother* is *matar,* and *father* is *patar.* English and Hindi kin terms are thus cognates. After comparing Hindi and English, historical linguists discovered that the two languages share a significant number of cognates. Therefore it is assumed that the two languages emerged from a single linguistic source that existed in the past.

Cognates are typically words found in the common or basic inventory of terms (lexicon) for a language. Words for kin, numbers, body parts, and colors tend to be maintained over time and thus are useful in determining historical relationships among languages assumed to be related.

See also GLOTTOCHRONOLOGY; LANGUAGE FAMILIES.

COMMUNICATION

Communication refers generally to the process by which information—sometimes simple stimuli—is received by an organism or organisms. At its most basic level, communication involves the sending and receiving of information. In communication theory this process is stated in the form of a simple model: A (message source) to N (noise or interference) to B (receiver). This simple model (sometimes called the *conduit model*) plots the course of a message (from A to B) and assumes that at times there will be obstacles (noise or interference) that impede the transmission of the message. Communication theorists typically describe interference in a variety of ways. When discussing communication for human beings, for example, interference may be caused by actual noise (a jackhammer pounding while two people are talking) or by ideological/psychological noise (when a person distorts a message by passing it through his or her own ideological filter).

Communication theory, as it has been applied to higher-order organisms (including primates and human beings), can be characterized as departing from the simplistic sender-receiver model. For human communicators the process of communication is viewed as a complex set of interactions, transacted (negotiated) across a wide spectrum of cultural and situational contexts. For instance, imagine two people sitting at a table. Person A says, "Fishing is out of the question." Person B responds, "What about next week?" On the surface this seems like a simple exchange, yet on closer inspection some of what is being communicated is implied and not explicit. The statement "Fishing is out of the question" implies that there were plans to go fishing in the immediate future (sometime before the following week). The statement made by person B ("What about next week?") is not merely a straightforward question designed to create the potential for fishing the following week; it may also function to keep options open in ongoing discourse. In this exchange there are explicit (stated) messages being sent through the statements; however, flexibility in communication is maintained through negotiating statements or questions ("What about next week?"). This exchange, therefore, is not a closed two-way exchange. It represents an ongoing

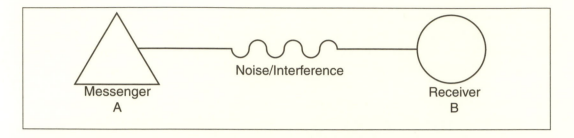

At its most basic level, the communication process is stated in the form of a simple model: A (message source) to N (noise or interference) to B (receiver).

communicative exchange between the two communicators and will most likely be negotiated through continuing discourse.

The anthropologist Anthony Wallace calls this more recent approach to communication the analysis of equivalence structures. Equivalence refers to a communicative "fit" or "agreement." In conversation, ambiguity or confusion often arises. When ambiguity occurs speakers must engage communicative exchanges that seek to clarify issues. Meaning or equivalence is therefore negotiated. Wallace and Fred Gearing, also an anthropologist, have applied the idea of equivalence to explain the culture transmission process (*enculturation*, or how a person acquires cultural knowledge). If culture is merely information or knowledge, then its acquisition must be regulated through communicative exchanges that are negotiated between adult speakers and younger individuals in a given society. Because cultural information is apparently transacted through these "give-and-take" interactions, the content of what is said, together with the way something is said, must be regulated by culture-specific rules. Therefore equivalence can be extended to an understanding of intercul-

tural communication (in which a person from one culture attempts to communicate with a person from another).

Communication, as a unifying concept, has also been used to provide an understanding of social symbolic systems. This approach is called *social semiotics* (the study of signs or symbols that have socially significant meanings). The application of a social semiotic perspective to communication represents an attempt to discover and describe underlying (implied) cultural messages found in recurring social patterns of behavior (including the construction of material culture, such as buildings, parks, house interiors, and so forth). For example, consider a school classroom in which all the desks have been neatly arranged in straight rows. The teacher's desk is at the head of the classroom and faces the desks where the students sit. This particular configuration, according to social semiotics researchers, subtly communicates several culturally loaded messages (formality, rigor, discipline, and the authority of the teacher). Rearranging the desks into a semicircle and placing the teacher's desk at the side of the classroom might communicate informality, exploration, creativity, and social closeness between the teacher and the students. In other cultural contexts these same configurations might communicate entirely different messages. The swastika, for example, because of its association in European/Western history with the Nazi movement, generally carries a negative meaning. Among the Chinese, the Hopi, and many Australian aboriginal groups, the same or a similar symbol has other meanings (unity, the interplay of opposites, and so forth).

Communication is often carried out through nonverbal means. The anthropologist Edward T. Hall has explored the rich variety of nonverbal communicative forms that are expressed cross-culturally. Communication at this level might be carried out through eye movement, facial gesturing, hand and body movement (kinesics), and the use of spatial distancing (proxemics). Physical signs, for example, vary significantly in form and function across cultures. In the Middle East among most Arab populations direct eye contact is desirable in most communicative exchanges. For northern Europeans and North Americans, direct eye contact is avoided in most close conversational exchanges but may be required in some formal situations (formal speech making, reprimanding children, and so forth). In most Southeast Asian societies it is considered impolite to point fingers and toes directly at people. In Thailand pointing gestures are considered to be insulting; westerners who are quite used to pointing often unknowingly insult their hosts. In the Middle East, especially among Arab peoples, the cultural use of space allows for closer distances between speakers in commu-

nication than is normally tolerated by Western speakers. Hall has observed what happens when Arab and Western (European and American) communicators attempt to interact. A kind of dance emerges in which the Western communicators continually back away from Arabic speakers, who are, in keeping with their culture, trying to get closer.

See also ANIMAL COMMUNICATION; INTERCULTURAL COMMUNICATION; KINESICS; NONVERBAL COMMUNICATION; PROXEMICS.

Cathcart, Robert S., and Larry Samovar, eds. (1984) *Small Group Communication: A Reader.*

Gearing, Fred O. (1973) "Where We Are and Where We Might Go: Steps toward a General Theory of Cultural-Transmission." *Council on Anthropology and Education Quarterly* 4(1): 1–10.

Griffin, Em. (1991) *Communication: A First Look at Communication Theory.*

Hall, Edward T., and Mildred Reed Hall. (1994) "The Sounds of Silence." In *Conformity and Conflict: Readings in Cultural Anthropology,* edited by James Spradley and David McCurdy, 61–72.

Hodge, Robert, and Gunther Kress. (1988) *Social Semiotics.*

Malandro, Loretta A., and Larry Barker. (1983) *Nonverbal Communication.*

Samovar, Larry A., and Richard E. Porter, eds. (1991) *Intercultural Communication: A Reader,* 6th ed.

Wallace, Anthony F. C. (1970) *Culture and Personality.*

COMMUNICATIVE COMPETENCE

Knowing the appropriateness or the inappropriateness of an utterance in a given social context is what the linguist Dell Hymes calls communicative competence. Having communicative competence requires an individual to be able to interpret social and cultural contexts (circumstances) and judge the impact a statement or question will have on a given audience. Communicative competence contrasts with the concept that the linguist Noam Chomsky calls "linguistic competence" (knowing the grammar of a language). Hymes points out that merely knowing the grammar of a language is not sufficient for true communication to occur; a person must also know how linguistic utterances are going to be interpreted. For example, if a young person uses an informal greeting with a Japanese male elder (without knowing the elder), this would represent a significant social mistake. If the person who initiated the greeting is unaware of the mistake, Hymes might say that the person lacks communicative competence.

Chomsky, Noam. (1965) *Aspects of the Theory of Syntax.*

Hymes, Dell. (1971) "Competence and Performance in Linguistic Theory." In *Language Acquisition: Models and Methods*, edited by R. Huxley and E. Ingram, 3–28.

———. (1971) "On Communicative Competence." In *Sociolinguistics*, edited by J. B. Pride and Janet Holmes, 269–293.

COMPARATIVE LINGUISTICS

Describing and analyzing elements of two or more languages together in a study is comparative linguistics. Comparative linguists examine languages at all levels through descriptions of sound (phonology), basic units of meaning (morphology and semantics), and grammar (comparative syntax). Comparisons are typically made to determine whether or not two or more languages are related (derive from an earlier parent language).

See also LANGUAGE FAMILIES.

CONNECTED SPEECH

When people speak, the various elements of language unfold in a continuous natural pattern of connected utterances. This natural quality of continuous speaking is called connected speech. In language learning, isolated elements of language (affixes, words, phrases, and pauses) are often practiced as separate from ongoing spoken language. When these isolated elements are placed in continuous speech with its natural rhythms, these elements take on qualities that are not present in isolation. For example, the isolated juncture "sea kelp" might be confused with "seek help." When either of these utterances is embedded in a sentence its meaning becomes apparent: "The anchor was entangled in *sea kelp*. Another vessel was nearby so we decided to *seek help*." The linguistic material surrounding *sea kelp* and *seek help* in the sentences assists listeners in interpreting the meaning. The placement of the sounds as they unfold in the sentence also contrast so that the distinction between the two phrases can be made.

Because language, as it is expressed in overt speech, is regulated by complex shifts in intonation, stress (intensity), pauses, and pacing, knowing how to assemble various elements of language within ongoing speech is crucial for the development of linguistic competence.

See also PARALANGUAGE.

when people get older they tend to lose interest in worldly affairs.

See also CONVERSATIONAL IMPLICATURE; DENOTATION.

Heimbach, Ernest E. (1979) *White Hmong-English Dictionary.*
Johnson, Charles, and Se Yang. (1992) *Myths, Legends, and Folk Tales from the Hmong of Laos,* 2d ed.

CONNOTATION

Connotation is the implied meaning of words and more lengthy utterances. Connotation thus contrasts with denotation, which refers to direct or explicit meaning. For example, to an environmental activist the phrase "conservation is always wise" might connote the idea that it is generally wise to protect the natural environment, but to a social conservative it may connote support for the maintenance of traditional values.

Taking into account connotative meaning when cross-cultural communication is occurring is important because the central meaning of a message is often implied. This is true for all human language-communication systems. For example, consider the following translation of a Laotian Hmong proverb: "Old dogs don't keep watch; old men don't like to discuss court cases." For a non-Hmong this proverb may not make much sense. However, for most Hmong the connotation is clear. The statement "old men don't like to discuss court cases" connotes the general idea that

CONTEXT

Context, as sociolinguists use the term, refers to the circumstances or conditions in which an utterance (a statement or question) is situated. Describing and understanding the role of context in constructing the meaning of an utterance is important for sociolinguists because quite often it is the context that determines meaning. The linguist Steven Pinker uses the statement "stud tires out" to illustrate the importance of context. To interpret this statement the person doing the interpreting has to know whether the statement was made in the context of snowy winter conditions where an automotive supply store just ran out of studded tires, in which case the word *tires* is a noun, or, if the statement was made by someone visiting a horse breeding ranch, *tires* most likely is a verb. In this case an identical utterance carries two completely different meanings because of differences in context.

Knowing the cultural context for language is extremely important for interpreting meaning in speech discourse.

The linguists George Lakoff and Mark Johnson have noted that West African Hausa speakers do not include themselves as primary points of reference when indicating the spatial relationships of visible objects. Hausa speakers will say, "The ball is on the other side of the rock," although from the perspective of English speakers the ball may be between the person making the statement and the rock. The Hausa speaker says that "the ball is on the other side of the rock" instead of "the ball is between me (the person doing the seeing) and the rock" because he or she is not being included as a spatial marker in the overall frame of reference for objects in the immediate field of vision. Therefore, in order to interpret the statement, some knowledge of the cultural context—in this case knowing determiners for marking spatial relationships—is required.

See also DISCOURSE ANALYSIS.

Lakoff, George, and Mark Johnson. (1980) *Metaphors We Live By.*
Pinker, Steven. (1994) *The Language Instinct: How the Mind Creates Language.*

CONVERSATION Conversation is a form of social discourse composed of informal verbal interactions among two or more speakers. Typically in conversation, topics change quickly, much of the content is implied (not directly stated), and a significant degree of nonverbal action accompanies verbal interaction.

Some linguists have described conversation more as a form of social interaction than as a means of direct communication. Viewed in this light, the function of conversation might be to maintain or alter dimensions of the various social positions of those engaged in conversation. Still other linguists, particularly sociolinguists, point out that using conversation to manipulate social relationships is really a form of implied communication (subtle, not directly stated). The many ways that people use conversation either to reinforce or to alter social hierarchies constitute, as Deborah Tannen has termed them, metamessages. Metamessages are the subtle cultural norms that people bring to situations of social interaction. For example, males and females bring fundamentally different cultural agendas to conversation. Men may be more prone to structuring conversational strategies that emphasize their social position. Women, in contrast, tend to organize conversations in ways that foster inclusiveness or "connection and intimacy." These differences in speech behavior are a result of the different ways that males and females of the same society are socialized to the use of language.

Cross-cultural descriptions of conversational interaction have revealed that there is considerable variation in how conversations are structured and used. This variation is particularly evident in the degrees to which societies will or will not tolerate indirectness in conversation. Elinor Ochs described the conversational patterns of a group of Malagasy speakers. On the island of Madagascar, where the Malagasy live, news from the outside world is scarce because of isolation and governmental

These two women from Provence, France, illustrate the tendency women have to organize conversations in ways that foster inclusiveness or "connection and intimacy." These differences in speech behavior are due to the different ways that males and females of the same society are socialized to the use of language.

restrictions on the media, and so it is considered valuable. In conversing among themselves and with outsiders the Malagasy were often evasive or unwilling to part with valuable information. This evasiveness or indirectness extended even to direct questions that require direct responses. From the Malagasy point of view, a converser must be willing to work for and gain the trust of the other conversers if information is to be exchanged.

In Japan, as the linguist Yoshiko Matsumoto has suggested, there is no sharp distinction between conversation as "informative" and conversation as "interactive." In English, structuring neutral statements conveying mundane information about the world (for example, "The post office is on 15th Street") occur frequently. Japanese conversers, however, tend to avoid statements that are direct and neutral. Instead the Japanese include references to the relationships among the immediate speakers involved in a conversation. Thus, in Japan "The post office is on 15th Street" would most likely be similar to "From where we are standing, as my father has indicated, the post office is two blocks away on 15th Street." In addition, polite and informal forms of speech are selected by Japanese speakers depending on status differences among the speakers. In Japan deferring to elders as high-status individuals is done through the use of a formal or polite speech code. For example, in referring to the building on 15th Street, a speaker of low status (a younger person), if talking to an elder, would be obliged to use a highly formal or polite speaking form to reinforce the formal distance of their social relationship—even when conveying simple directions.

Sociolinguists have also discussed the apparent existence of important cultural differences for the organization of turn taking in conversation. These linguists have suggested that cultural rules for determining who talks at a given time, how much talk is tolerated from conversers, and how changes from one speaker to another are carried out vary significantly across cultures. These same linguists point out that these rules are implied (subtle and not overtly stated), but are nevertheless important when considering cultural differences in discourse style.

Susan Philips, in her study of Native Americans on the Warm Springs Reservation in Oregon, contrasts her subjects' conversational style with that of Anglo-English speakers who lived on or near the reservation. Philips observed that her Native American subjects tended not to talk over one another (talking at the same time as someone else). They also tended to avoid monopolizing talk time; no one person could dominate a conversation. While conversing, they tolerated longer periods of silence between utterances than did the Anglo subjects. Cultural emphasis in conversations among the Native American speakers was focused on group interaction; drawing attention to individuals through competing for "talk time" was subtly avoided. In contrast, Anglo subjects were "speech monopolizers" who constantly competed for "the floor."

See also CONVERSATIONAL IMPLICATURE.

Matsumoto, Yoshiko. (1989) *Politeness and Conversational Universals: Observations from Japanese.*

Ochs, Elinor. (1976) "The Universality of Conversational Postulates." *Language in Society* 5: 67–80.

Philips, Susan Urmston. (1993) *The Invisible Culture: Communication in Classroom and Community on the Warm Springs Indian Reservation.*

Tannen, Deborah. (1990) *You Just Don't Understand: Women and Men in Conversation.*

CONVERSATIONAL IMPLICATURE

In conversation the meanings of messages being exchanged are often implied (not directly or overtly stated). The carrying out of communication through conversation at the implicit level (through implied meaning) is conversational implicature. Implicature refers to the reliance in conversation on subtle or implied content. The philosophical linguist H. P. Grice introduced the concept of conversational implicature to demonstrate the existence of differences in logic and agreement in conversational structure and strategies across cultures and situations.

Conversational implicature may serve a number of functions. One function of implicature, according to sociolinguists, is to assist speakers in avoiding harsh or blunt language; euphemistic language (softer, less harsh speech) is used instead. For example, if a waiter says to a group of diners who are lingering at a table, "I have to go now; someone else is taking my shift," the implicit message of the utterance might be: "Pay the bill so I can get my tip." For the waiter to state explicitly, "Pay the bill so I can get my tip and leave" would go against the prevailing cultural norms for politeness. Thus, the polite-euphemistic statement is used to cover the more basic practical motivations behind the waiter's statement.

See also CONVERSATION; DISCOURSE ANALYSIS; IMPLICATURE.

Brown, Gillian, and George Yule. (1983) *Discourse Analysis.*

Grice, H. P. (1975) "Logic and Conversation." In *Syntax and Semantics*, edited by P. Cole and J. L. Morgan, 41–58.

CREOLE

A creole is a complete language (that is, it contains a full grammar) that has emerged in a relatively short period from a simple composite language (a pidgin). Creole languages, like the pidgins that produce them, arise in contact situations where it is necessary for speakers of fundamentally different languages to communicate on a continuous basis. *Creolization* is the process of producing a creole from a pidgin. For example, various Caribbean creole languages developed as a result of the mixing of West African languages with English, French, Spanish, and in some cases Chinese, Carib, and Arawak. Today creole languages are spoken in many parts of the world. Examples of creoles include Gullah (still spoken in parts of the Carolinas of the United States), Afro-Caribbean-English, Caribbean

Patois (French-influenced Creoles), New Guinea English, and Hawaiian Creole.

The anthropologist Marvin Harris has pointed out that the formation of creole languages is an example of short-term language evolution. Harris asks: "How was it possible for pidgin-speaking children to change Hawaiian pidgin into Hawaiian Creole in such a short time?" Harris wants to know what evolutionary factors contributed to a human capacity for language that allows for the development of a full language (as in the Hawaiian case) in only one generation.

The linguist Derek Bickerton suggests that creoles are formed quickly from pidgins because all human beings have an innate capacity (internal biological blueprint) for grammar. Pidgins, according to Bickerton, do not remain pidgins for long because children from the next generation of speakers, who interact verbally with pidgin-speaking adults, bring complex grammar to the pidgin through their inherited capacity for grammar use.

Bickerton's stance on this question is controversial. Some linguists assume that pidgin languages change into creoles because of the need to communicate continuously at higher levels of complexity. From this perspective creoles are formed because more subtle and specific aspects of language are added (unconsciously) to pidgins to facilitate more refined and detailed communication. Forming creoles therefore represents a way of overcoming functional constraints (limitations) that are characteristic of pidgins.

Linguists classify creoles according to the degree to which they are (or are not) accepted by a general population.

Creoles that are fundamentally different from the dominant language of a country or region and are generally viewed as inferior (stigmatized) by the dominant population are called *basilect* creoles. African American creoles, such as Gullah, are considered basilects because they are generally stigmatized by the dominant Anglo population. In contrast, Jamaican Creole, because it is the dominant language of Jamaica, is an *acrolect* creole (a standard or prestige language). Jamaican Creole contains elements of various West African languages, Spanish, and French, but its grammar and much of its vocabulary derive from English. *Mesolect* creoles are composite languages that fall somewhere between acrolects and basilects; they are sometimes stigmatized, but not to the extent that basilect creoles are. In some cases creole languages may become influenced by noncreole languages. If a noncreole language dominates a creole language through time (replacing creolized elements), the creole may lose its composite nature. This process is called *decreolization*.

See also LINGUA FRANCA.

Bickerton, Derek. (1981) *Roots of Language*.
Harris, Marvin. (1989) *Our Kind*.
Sebba, Mark. (1986) "London Jamaican and Black London English." In *Language and the Black Experience*, edited by D. Sutcliffe and A. Wong, 123–135.
Wong, Ansel. (1989) "Creole as a Language of Power and Solidarity." In *Language and the Black Experience*, edited by D. Sutcliffe and A. Wong, 109–122.

CURSING

The word *curse* derives from the Anglo-Saxon word *curs*, which means to use verbal magic to bring harm to someone. Cursing, as the term was originally used, literally referred to imposing harmful magic on a person through the use of esoteric (hidden) language. Today cursing refers to the use of words and phrases that are prohibited or taboo in most social circumstances. The term *swear* is sometimes used as a synonym for curse.

The extent to which cursing is tolerated varies significantly across cultures and social situations. As a general rule, because cursing represents the use of informal (impolite) language in the extreme, its use can generally be found in informal settings. Moreover, terms selected as curse words (in many societies) often make reference to human genitalia and sexual behavior. In southern Mexico the term *huevos* (literally, eggs) connotes testicles. The expression *"no huevos"* indicates a lack of courage and thus is an insult.

The cultural functions of cursing also vary according to cultural and situational conditions. Typically, cursing is used as a form of insult. In some societies cursing exchanges occur among members of lineage segments (kin membership based on descent) where insulting paradoxically reinforces social solidarity. Among the Canela of Brazil the use of extended cursing phrases between nieces and uncles is acceptable behavior. The anthropologists William and Jean Croker recorded a 13-year-old Canela girl insulting her elder great-uncle: "Your penis is screw-turned like a large yam's root, and its naked head is rotten and so is purple like a sweet potato." To which he replied: "Your vagina is so big from use that it needs the grinding of a penis as large as a manioc pestle with a rutting goat's energy." For the Canela, insulting of this type is carried out to maintain ongoing joking relationships between nieces and uncles. Thus, the use of insults allows for social closeness by way of maintaining informality among close kin. Similarly, among English-speaking American and British men, using coarse language signals male attributes of masculinity. In this case cursing for purposes of maintaining solidarity is specific to men.

In other societies the use of curse (taboo) words may produce more serious consequences. Among the Nupe of west-central Nigeria the use of prohibited language may be cause for accusations of witchcraft and thus may result in an individual's being severely stigmatized or physically harmed. The Nupe are so concerned with avoiding such terms that they readily borrow substitute terms from Arabic. The Arabic terms do not carry the same antisocial potency as do the Nupe terms. The anthropological linguist Peter Farb has observed that the Nupe seldom use their own terms for sexual intercourse, menstruation, and semen. The Nupe curse word *dzuko* for vagina is seldom used; the Arabic term *kafa* (opening) is preferred.

Croker, William, and Jean Croker. (1994) *The Canela: Bonding through Kinship, Ritual, and Sex.*

Farb, Peter. (1978) *Word Play: What Happens When People Talk.*

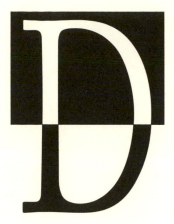

See CREOLE.

The idea of deep structure was developed by the linguist Noam Chomsky. Deep structure refers to the underlying structure of grammar. A sentence can be arranged in a number of ways (surface structure), but, according to Chomsky, each sentence has a concise underlying structure (deep structure) that does not vary to a significant degree.

See also GRAMMAR.

Chomsky, Noam. (1957) *Syntactic Structures*.

Denotation refers to the direct correspondence of a word to its core meaning. For instance, in the statement "The cat just ran away," the term *cat* most likely refers to a real cat. Therefore the term *cat* denotes the animal to which the term directly refers. Denotation contrasts with connotation. Consider the same term (cat) in the following sentence: "Cat get your tongue?" Here the term *cat* does not literally refer to a cat, but is used to refer metaphorically to a person who does not talk much. Therefore the meaning of the sentence is understood by reading the connotation. It is important for linguistic anthropologists to differentiate between denotative and connotative meaning when they are obtaining linguistic information from native speakers. Confusion may arise if the researcher is not sure how a native speaker is actually using a term.

See also CONNOTATION.

Perhaps the first and most important step in conducting research on language and communication is describing, in an objective and systematic fashion, the basic elements of a language and communication system. Descriptive information (collectively called data) is obtained by linguists across all dimensions of language and communication. Describing the sounds of a language (phonology), the minimal units of meaning in a language (morphology), the grammar (syntax), and word meanings (semantics) all represent the descriptive domains of linguistics. Sociolinguists describe how people use language across a wide spectrum of social situations.

Linguistic anthropologists are interested in descriptive methods because the validity of their claims regarding cross-cultural patterns of language and communication emerge out of the descriptive information they collect in the field. If their descriptions are not accurate, then their conclusions will be questionable.

Description contrasts with *prescription*. Prescriptive grammar involves the use of agreed-upon (standardized) policies for language structure and use. Correcting someone's grammar is a function of prescription. Observing grammatical structures as they exist in a given language system (without judgment) is description.

DETERMINISM, LINGUISTIC

Linguistic determinism is the assumption that the language a person learns will, through its particular structure, predispose a person to see the world in a particular way. The central idea of linguistic determinism is that language will determine the nature of recurring behavioral and perceptual patterns for individual speakers of a language. Hence, the language a person learns will structure and organize how that person conceptualizes the external world. The idea that language can predispose a person to see the world in a particular way has sometimes been called the Sapir-Whorf hypothesis.

See also LANGUAGE AND CULTURE.

DIALECTS

In most of the world's languages, differences or variations in the way people speak emerge as a result of geographical or socioeconomic separation. Recurring differences in speaking form and style in which mutual intelligibility (understandability) is maintained are referred to by linguists as dialects. Dialects are produced when speakers of a single language become geographically, socially, or economically isolated. If enough time passes, emerging dialects may become mutually unintelligible. These languages (formerly dialects) could then be classified as separate but related languages.

Dialectical differences can arise as a result of differences in socioeconomic background. These dialectical forms are sometimes called *sociolects*. In many stratified societies in which a single language dominates, numerous variations of that language may be present. In some cases the type of speech used may overtly mark a person as a member of a particular class. This is often the case in India. While Hindi and Panjabi are the two dominant languages of northern India, multiple variations of these two languages are used across a wide and rigidly defined social, religious, and economic class system. Many of the dialects are regional, while others are associated with caste (extremely rigid class distinctions). Linguistic diversity at the level of dialects is so common in northern India that most people must learn to speak several varieties. For instance, the linguist Lachman Khubchandani has observed speakers in Bihar (a state in northeastern India) using formal Hindi when addressing elders, but in more mundane settings using a local vernacular (common dialect) when speaking to peers. Formal Hindi thus is considered a high-prestige dialect, and the local dialect is perceived as a low-prestige form of speech. Khubchandani also observed that formal Hindi was used exclusively when performing rituals, while the common dialect (called "bazaar Hindustani") was used in most informal situations. The linguist John Gumperz observed a similar situation in Khalapur in northern India. In Khalapur there are 31 endogamous castes (that is, castes in which the members must marry within the same caste). Hindi is used as the high-prestige form by members of high-status casts, and the local Khalapur dialect (related to Hindi) is used by members of the lower castes.

Low-prestige dialects are often viewed negatively by members of the same society who speak more prestigious dialects. In the United States, for example, Black Vernacular English (BVE) is described by sociolinguists as a stigmatized dialect. In fact, many "nonstandard" dialects are perceived as inferior by speakers of more standard varieties of English. Sociolinguists and dialectologists (linguists who study dialects) have pointed out that regional and social dialects may be viewed by a majority population as inferior, but in reality these dialects are full or complete languages. William Labov has pointed out that Black Vernacular English, as well as many other stigmatized inner-city dialects (particularly in New York, where much of Labov's research was conducted), make rich use of metaphor, spontaneous word play, and a wide variety of linguistic innovations. For example, many speakers of standard English carry the belief that, when

asked questions, speakers of Black Vernacular English use only monosyllabic responses (such as "yeah, "no," "ugh"). Labov noted that when African American children were being questioned by white authority figures, the responses of the children were often monosyllabic. Labov pointed out, however, that these children tended to respond this way in situations that they perceived as threatening. In other contexts, the same children were observed interacting with their peers using a full range of complex linguistic responses.

Dialects represent forms of language variation that emerge through time as groups of people become separated geographically, socially, or economically. Linguists view the development of dialectical differences as a form of linguistic divergence (splitting off). In some cases, however, dialectical elements can, in language contact situations, appear as a result of linguistic diffusion (the borrowing or spreading of linguistic elements). For example, English speakers in New York have made use of many Jewish/German Yiddish terms, such as *schlemiel* and *schlock*. Along with the adoption of words might come changes in tonal, nasal, and other sound qualities. Added linguistic elements coupled with sociocultural differences among speakers tend to create new dialectical qualities of speech.

See also BLACK ENGLISH; LANGUAGE AND CULTURE; LANGUAGE CHANGE.

Gumperz, John. (1964) "Linguistic and Social Interaction in Two Communities." *American Anthropologist* 66(6, part 2): 137–153.

47

Khubchandani, Lachman. (1983) *Plural Languages, Plural Cultures: Communication, Identity, and Sociopolitical Change in Contemporary India.*

Labov, William. (1970) *The Logic of Nonstandard English.*

Saville-Troike, Muriel. (1989) *The Ethnography of Communication: An Introduction*, 2d ed.

DIFFUSION

See IMMERSION; LANGUAGE CHANGE.

DIGLOSSIA

Diglossia, a term coined in 1959 by the linguist Charles Ferguson, refers to situations in which it is necessary to use more than one language or language variety. Ferguson developed the term to describe how people living in the suburban areas of New York City altered their speech in numerous situations (such as home, work, while on vacation, and so on). The basic concept of diglossia, however, can be used to describe any situation in which code switching (altering speech or language) occurs. Diglossic situations are divided into two categories: "in-diglossia" (altering speech within a community of speakers) and "out-diglossia" (altering speech to communicate outside of a community of speakers).

Examples of in-diglossia can be found in France, where rural dialects known as "patois" (dialects such as Occitan, Breton, and Alsatian) are often abandoned when patois speakers visit major urban centers. People living in or near French urban centers typically speak forms of French that are marked for high status; various forms of patois, in contrast, are considered "bad French." The social stigma attached to patois puts pressure on its speakers to switch to more standard forms of French in settings where standard varieties dominate. Some patois speakers refuse to employ code switching in diglossic situations; this reveals a pattern of dynamic tension between diglossic situations and the use of language as a means of maintaining ethnic or regional identity. Resisting code switching in diglossic situations thus represents a statement of social solidarity (social identity).

Out-diglossic situations typically arise when it is necessary to carry out communicative exchanges in bilingual or multilingual situations. Interpreting (translating) utterances from one language to another for purposes of international diplomacy occur in out-diglossic situations. Employing a broker language (a lingua franca) for the purpose of carrying out trade is an example of diglossic necessity. For instance, Swahili, a native language spoken in many parts of Africa, is often used as a lingua franca to carry out trade and international diplomacy. Because Swahili is utilized as a means of communication beyond the boundaries of specific ethnic and linguistic groups, its use constitutes a form of out-diglossia.

The concept of diglossia has provided linguists and other researchers interested in language variation with a model for describing and understanding variable use of speech and language across a wide continuum of situations and cultures. Moreover, through the use of diglossia as an analytic tool, linguists have come to recognize that at some level most people are multilingual (at least in terms of being able to employ a variety of speaking forms).

See also CODES (SPEECH).

Ferguson, Charles A. (1959) "Diglossia." *Word* 15: 325–340.

Haarmann, Harald. (1986) *Language in Ethnicity: A View of Basic Ecological Relations.*

Zuengler, Jane. (1985) *English, Swahili, or Other Languages? The Relationship of Educational Development Goals to Languages of Instruction in Kenya and Tanzania.*

DING-DONG THEORY

See ORIGINS OF LANGUAGE.

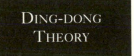

DISCOURSE — Verbal or written texts that extend beyond the level of a single sentence are referred to by linguists as discourse. Discourse is expressed in a wide diversity of forms or genres. For instance, informal conversation, narration, short and lengthy written texts, jokes, riddles, poems, gossip, and formal speeches are all considered to be forms of discourse.

See also DISCOURSE ANALYSIS.

DISCOURSE ANALYSIS

Discourse analysis is the description and analysis of discourse texts or utterances (either verbal or written utterances longer than a sentence) carried out through the examination of how these texts are situated in specific social and cultural contexts. The linguist Malcolm Coulthard defines discourse analysis as "the analysis of situated speech."

Although a specific, uniform (standard) method of conducting discourse analysis has not been developed, a set of shared methodological strategies, with several agreed-upon key concepts, typically emerges when linguists conduct discourse analysis. For most linguists who use discourse analysis, four concepts are often used to assist in the integration and interpretation of discourse data: *reference*, which is what is being referred to—literally, the relationships between words and things or actions; *presupposition*, which is the knowledge that people bring to situations, including shared cultural knowledge; *implicature*, which is the implied meaning; and *inference*, which is the ability to make sense of what is being said.

To demonstrate how a general discourse analysis works, let us consider the following statement: "I am leaving now; someone else will take over." Without some knowledge (presupposition) of the context in which this statement was made, interpreting (inference) will be difficult. Let us assume that we know more about the particular situation associated with the statement.

For instance, if we assume that the statement was made in a restaurant, we now have more presuppositional knowledge to assist us in our interpretation. We might guess that the statement was made by a waiter who wishes to inform patrons that another waiter will soon be taking over. But are there more subtle messages being sent through this utterance? To interpret more subtle messages that may or may not be implied in the statement, we must use the concept of implicature (what messages are being implied?). Again, we might rely on our presuppositional knowledge to assist us. In this case we know that waiters must make sure that their clients pay their bills. Therefore an implied meaning for the statement "I am leaving now; someone else will take over" might actually be "Pay the bill." Again relying on our presuppositional knowledge, we know that waiters make part of their living through obtaining gratuities (tips). The statement may contain an even subtler message: "I want my tip." Of course it would not generally be socially acceptable for a waiter to walk up to a table and demand a tip. Thus, the original statement was used not only to communicate a fact (this person's shift was ending) but also to communicate several implicit messages (pay the bill and give me a tip) that could not be stated overtly. By using our knowledge of restaurants (presupposition) and knowing what the person was referring to (reference) at an implied level (implicature), we might have been able to interpret (inference) what the actual message of the statement was.

Using discourse analysis involves working at two levels. First, the linguist must record what is actually said. This is working at the level of *text*. In our example, the text is: "I am leaving now; someone else will take over." We know that it is possible that other messages may have been implied in the statement. Working to interpret implied messages is analyzing *subtext* or meaning that is conveyed beneath the level of text. "Pay the bill" and "Give me a tip" are subtextual messages. We would not be able to infer what was actually being communicated, though, without knowing the situational context of the original statement.

Sociolinguists and linguistic anthropologists have observed that discourse analysis has significant value when one is attempting to describe and understand gaps in communication. Some linguists, for example, have applied discourse analysis to research conducted with language-minority students. When educators talk to language-minority students there is often not a great deal of shared presuppositional knowledge. Moreover, many language-minority students know enough about using nonverbal cues to create the illusion of comprehension in communicative exchanges. In observing language-minority students (Latinos, Hmong, Lao, and others) the author of this volume has noted that language-minority students often nod their heads in agreement when teachers ask: "Do you understand?" In many instances (though certainly not all) these students did not comprehend the content of the lessons that had preceded the teacher's question. Applying discourse analysis, the author suggested that before the question regarding the student's comprehension was asked, there might have been little or no shared knowledge. However, students responding with head nods were acknowledging that a question had been asked. That much presuppositional knowledge, albeit minimal, was shared between the teacher and the students. The author, when working with these same students, did not merely ask, "Do you understand?" but went on to ask, "Will you tell me what you know?" When the students could not respond to the second query by describing what they had learned in the previous lesson, "comprehensible feedback," as the author calls this condition, did not occur. At this point it became apparent that a significant lack of presuppositional knowledge was blocking communication between the researcher and the students. In this case study, discourse analysis assisted in locating, in specific terms, the nature of an ongoing communication problem.

Discourse analysis has also been used to assist in the translation of verbal and written texts. Translating texts from one language to another involves much more than literally translating (word for word, phrase for phrase) what is said in the text of the language being translated. An effective interpretation involves taking into account the cultural rules that govern the use of language in specific circumstances. For instance, in many Asian societies the liver is considered to be the most important organ for sustaining life. Thus, literal translations such as "Go with your liver!" might not make sense to an English speaker. The term *heart* might be substituted for liver as the best analogous term for preserving the essential meaning of the statement. Using discourse analysis, an interpreter has to know how the statement is typically used in the original cultural context (not just the linguistic context) before selecting workable terms and phrases in the translation. Again, knowing or inferring what a person is saying (reference) is always based on cultural knowledge (presupposition).

Since most cultural rules are implied (not stated), implicature is a valuable tool for translation. To illustrate, consider idiomatic sayings such as: "The cat's out of the bag." For most English speakers, the meaning of the statement is fairly obvious. Important news of some sort has inadvertently been revealed. The meaning of the statement is implied; a cat did not literally get out of a bag. To infer what has been said requires some cultural knowledge of how such a statement is used. There are no formal or explicit rules for using idiomatic language like this; however, knowing the implicit cultural rules for using figurative language as well as knowing a wide range of culture-specific idiomatic phrases allows for fluent interpretation. Because all human language systems make use of figurative, idiomatic language, discourse analysis is useful for conducting culturally meaningful translation and interpretation.

Brown, Gillian, and George Yule. (1983) *Discourse Analysis*.

Clyne, M. (1981) "Cultural Discourse Structure." *Journal of Pragmatics* 5: 61–66.

Coulthard, Malcolm. (1985) *An Introduction to Discourse Analysis*.

Findlay, Michael Shaw. (1994) "Structure and Process in Speech Subcommunities of Hmong Students at a Northern California High School." *Language and Education* (6)3: 245–260.

———. (1995) "Who Has the Right Answer? Differential Cultural Emphasis in Question/Answer Structures and the Case of Hmong Students at a Northern California High School." *Issues in Applied Linguistics* (6)1: 23–38.

Freeman-Larsen, Diane. (1980) *Discourse Analysis in Second Language Research*.

Gumperz, John. (1982) *Discourse Strategies*.

Hatch, Evelyn. (1978) "Discourse Analysis and Second Language Acquisition." In *Second Language Acquisition*, edited by Evelyn Hatch, 401–435.

Kramsch, Claire. (1981) *Discourse Analysis and Second Language Teaching*.

DOUBLESPEAK

Illogical, evasive, confusing, and incoherent language is what linguists and rhetoricians (experts in logic) call doublespeak. In some cases, doublespeak is used persuasively to produce emotional responses in audiences—through creating the illusion of coherence—while the content of what is actually being said makes little sense. Politicians, lawyers, and professional pundits of various sorts often make use of doublespeak to their advantage, particularly when they deem obfuscation (obscuring a message) necessary.

DRAMA

Cultural anthropologists have long recognized the importance of dramatic performance as a means of communicating cultural knowledge. All human societies make use of dramatic performance through a variety of forms, including ritual, dance, narration, character role playing, and improvisation. Drama, as it is expressed in various cultural contexts, functions primarily to communicate both positive and negative cultural values. Anthropologists who have described culturally constructed dramatic behavior have observed that cultural information is generally organized into performance formats that are easily recognized by members of a society. Moreover, cultural norms are communicated through the content of these performances.

Some social scientists have noted that cultural information contained in drama seems to be communicated at two fundamental levels. First, dramatic performances make use of explicit or manifest (obvious) culture, where cultural knowledge is acquired through interpreting what characters in narratives, plays, and songs actually do and say. Second, and perhaps more important, cultural norms are often communicated through what characters and narrative texts suggest or imply. For instance, in Europe and throughout most of North America, Christmas pageants are performed on or just before the celebration of Christmas. On the surface, these performances celebrate the birth of Jesus Christ, the central figure in Christianity. At a more subtle level, a host of other cultural values are being communicated. Gift giving, feasting, and singing are all behaviors that reinforce social solidarity (social togetherness). These performances function officially to celebrate the birth of an important religious figure, but unofficially they may rein-

The importance of dramatic performance as a means of communicating cultural knowledge is evident in the Hopi Snake-Antelope Dance. The dance provides a way for the Hopi to communicate their ideas regarding weather and to incorporate young males into adulthood. It also provides an opportunity to address ongoing social agendas.

force cultural values of social bonding. Some social scientists have suggested that Christmas performances, coupled with other aspects of Christmas, may communicate cultural values of competitiveness and commerciality while maintaining all of the surface trappings of Christian virtue. If this is the case, then these performances may serve to mask cultural values that conflict with the stated positive aspects of Christmas.

The sociologist Robert Merton developed the ideas of manifest (obvious) and latent (hidden) functions to articulate the dual function of dramatic ritual performance. By describing ritual performance at two levels, Merton was able to make sense of the Hopi Snake-Antelope Dance. The Hopi are a Native American society that currently live in north-central Arizona. This particular ceremony, always performed in August, involves dramatic dancing in which men and older boys handle live snakes (some are poisonous). Merton's Hopi consultants told him that the purpose of the Snake-Antelope Dance was to call on kachinas (rain and weather spirits) to bring rain for the crops; it was also performed as a rite of passage to adulthood for young males. Merton also observed that the Snake-Antelope Dance was a ceremony that was anticipated with a great deal of excitement by the entire Hopi community. When the nine-day ceremony was carried out, Merton noted that a significant degree of socializing, courting, and negotiating between families took place.

Thus, the Snake-Antelope Dance provided the Hopi with a way to communicate their ideas regarding weather and the appropriate way to incorporate young males into adulthood, but it also allowed the Hopi an opportunity to address ongoing social agendas.

Throughout the 1890s and extending into the early twentieth century the anthropologist Franz Boas collected a significant amount of information on the Kwakiutl, a Native American group that still lives along the central coastal area of Canada's British Columbia. Among Boas's field records are written descriptions and photographs of the Kwakiutl Hamatsa (cannibal) Dance. This dance was often acted out at potlatches (ritual gift-giving ceremonies set up by high-status individuals, typically important chiefs) and was usually performed by shamans (traditional religious healers). The dance was designed to bring forth a sense of fear and bewilderment in the audience. The Hamatsa dancers, dressed in torn hides and wearing large cedar-bark necklaces, danced in circles, often turning suddenly toward the audience to display grotesque faces. For this reason the dancers did not wear masks, as required in most other Kwakiutl dances. It was important for the audience to see the hideous facial contortions of the dancer to create a sense of awe and fear. Boas suggested that the dramatic effect of the Hamatsa Dance was designed to enhance the mystical role of shamans. Other anthropologists have suggested that the Hamatsa Dance communicates positive Kwakiutl values through dramatic use of the contrast between positive and negative behaviors. The Hamatsa character, described by Kwakiutl storytellers as a cannibal who lives in the forest and likes to devour wayward children, is a figure that stands in sharp contrast to ideal Kwakiutl behavior. References to Hamatsas in Kwakiutl narratives also tend to emphasize major differences between the village environment, where life is safe and predictable, and the forest environment, where life is dangerous and unpredictable. Through this division between village life (culture) and the forest (the unkempt wilderness) the Kwakiutl are able to convey the basic idea that they see their society as essentially ordered and civilized.

In some societies dramatic performance is used to act out mythic stories. A Native American group from north-central California, the River Patwin, used drama in their ritual dances to retell various myths, including their creation myth. These ritual performances were associated with an all-male group called the Kuksu society. The Kuksu society was organized around a seasonal ritual cycle that began with a ceremony called Hesi. In the Hesi ceremony, as was the case in most Kuksu rituals, dancers impersonated mythical spirits, such as Moki and Tuya ("big-headed dancer"). Although the overt function of the rituals was to initiate boys into adulthood, the constant reference to mythology in the dances indicates that a primary function was to retell (reinforce) the mythic traditions of the Patwin. Here the cultural functions of performance parallel narrative traditions and lend a certain degree of credibility to the stories through making mythic characters real (concrete). In addition, using dramatic interpretation through role playing serves an educational function in that mythic ideas—abstract in nature—are made concrete and tangible to the children who are viewing the performances.

The use of dramatic performance is widespread in contemporary large-scale societies (particularly among Western societies). Unfortunately, the sheer amount of messages sent through dramatic formats by the modern media (television and radio) is overwhelming. Moreover, the complexity and mixed nature of cultural messages associated with dramatic performance in modern media have, according to many social scientists, created a chaotic social pattern that stands in sharp contrast to those of small-scale traditional societies (such as the Hopi, the Patwin, and the Kwakiutl), in which cultural norms were consistently passed down through generational lines. The societal messages distributed through modern media formats do not always reflect a consistent set of cultural norms. Programming is organized to service clients (advertisers) and various segments of society that watch or listen to media productions. On a typical evening, one television channel might have shows that emphasize middle-American family values, while another channel might be showing a series of situation comedies that portray the American family as being in a state of constant deterioration. Thus, in contrast to the Hopi and the Kwakiutl, members of contemporary large-scale societies must, through the continued interpretation of multiple themes —often inconsistent—in mass-media performances, cope with cultural content that communicates these mixed cultural messages.

Boas, Franz. (1966) *Kwakiutl Ethnography.*

Degh, Linda. (1994) *American Folklore and the Mass Media.*

Dorson, Richard. (1983) *Handbook of American Folklore.*

Frickeberg, Walter, et al. (1968) *Pre-Columbian American Religions.*

Frigout, Arlette. (1979) "Hopi Ceremonial Organization." In *Handbook of North American Indians*, vol. 9, *Southwest*, edited by Alfonso Ortiz, 564–576.

Georges, Robert A. (1969) "Toward an Understanding of Story Telling Events." *Journal of American Folklore* 82: 313–328.

Heizer, R. F., and M. A. Whipple. (1971) *The California Indians: A Source Book.*

Kroeber, Alfred L. (1932) *The Patwin and Their Neighbors.*

Loeb, Edwin Meyer. (1932) *The Western Kuksu Cult.*

McLuhan, Marshall. (1964) *Impact of Electronic Media.*

Merton, Robert K. (1967) *Manifest and Latent Functions.* In *Theoretical Sociology*, 79–91.

Sherzer, Joel. (1976) "Play Language: Implications for Sociolinguistics." In *Speech Play: Research and Resources for Studying Linguistic Creativity*, edited by Barbara Kirshenblatt-Gimblett, 19–36.

DRUMMING

In some parts of the world, particularly in western Africa, drums are used as a form of long-distance communication. "Talking drums," as they are sometimes called, are used by many West African societies to generate signals for communicating information within groups and across

In some parts of the world, particularly western Africa, drums are used as a form of long-distance communication. Here, the "talking drums" of Burundi's Royal Drum Band proclaim the state's independence in 1962.

tribal boundaries. Drum languages generally track the tonal (pitch and tone) patterns of the parent spoken language.

George Herzog, in 1945, described the drum language of the Jabo of eastern Liberia, Africa. Herzog observed that the Jabo use two types of drums. The first type is constructed from hollowed-out tree trunks. These are called "slit drums" because long slits are cut out along the length of the trunk, which allows Jabo carvers to hollow out the

centers of the logs. Herzog described the sound quality of this type of drum as similar to that of bells. The other type of drum used by the Jabo were single-headed skin drums.

Herzog noted that the slit drums were generally used to call for or dismiss official council meetings and to introduce warriors or important dignitaries to the community. Skin drums, in contrast, were used for a wider variety of communicative purposes. They could be used to relay messages to neighboring villages regarding upcoming important events, for negotiating trade exchanges, or for arranging marriages.

The drum language of the Jabo parallels the tonal features of their spoken language. Shifts in tonal patterns can be constructed by alternating beats on several drums that are tuned at different pitch levels. If a particular rising tone and syllabic pattern for a spoken word is shared with another word, the potential in drum language for confusing the two terms becomes real. The rising tone, produced by closely connecting drum beats sequenced from lower to higher tone levels, accompanied by the same number of syllabic beats, produces the same effect as a homophone (a signal with the same sound but different meaning). A prescribed number of syllables (in the form of level drum beats) always accompany a tone marker, allowing the listener to comprehend what word (from the spoken language) was being represented in the drum language. For Jabo drummers, in cases in which two words contained the same tonal marker and the same number of associated syllables, drummers typically added more drum language to place the homophonic

drum words in a recognizable context. For example, in the spoken language of the Jabo the words for leopard and moon have identical tonal and syllabic patterns, and so a listener might not be able to distinguish between the two when they are represented through drum signaling. The drummer, realizing the potential for misunderstanding, might surround each drum word with phrases that facilitate interpretation. For instance, "leopard" might be embedded in the phrase "he who tears up the roof"; "moon" might be embedded in the phrase "looks down upon the earth."

The drum language of the Jabo, as is true of other African drum languages, is capable of communicating different emotional states through the use of prosodic features such as stress (hitting the drum with exaggerated force), pauses (like musical rests that signal reflection or time for response), and varying the pace and speed of a cadence. By using variations in stress and cadence, Jabo drummers could communicate anger, indifference, or joy.

Herzog, George. (1945) *Drum-Signaling in a West African Tribe.*

"What is the significance of the Sun Dance?" (a ritual practiced by Native Americans on the plains), an interviewer might ask the question in the form of a request: "Tell me a little about the Sun Dance." The second form, the request, allows the native consultant more latitude in answering. The consultant is thus able to generate a broad-based context so that the researcher can periodically intervene and ask informed questions related to more specific issues. In the first question form, the word "significance" acts to reduce the question to an elicitation of important aspects of the Sun Dance. If the consultant is allowed to explain in general terms what the Sun Dance is, the importance of the dance will come out naturally and in context as a consequence of the extended discussion.

Sometimes elicitation is used to obtain lengthy narratives or stories. To check for consistency, a researcher might ask several members of a cultural group to recite the same story. Napoleon Chagnon used this approach when he elicited the Yanomamo (a South American horticultural group) story of the origins of fire. Several members of the tribal group recited the same story without knowing that Chagnon had obtained various versions from each of them.

More precise forms of elicitation are used by linguists to obtain and describe detailed grammatical structures of various languages and to elicit native semantic categories (the meanings of words as they relate to native ways of classifying things, attributes, and actions). When working on grammar a linguist might use a form of negation elicitation. A grammatically correct sentence is spoken in

ELICITATION The process by which linguists and cultural anthropologists obtain (elicit) linguistic and cultural information from native consultants is called elicitation. Elicitation can be indirect, as when it is carried out in informal interviews in which consultants select their own questions and responses or through recording native narratives, and it can be direct, as when it is carried out in formal interviews (in which the agenda and questioning are organized by the researcher).

The anthropologist James Spradley, in his book *The Ethnographic Interview,* outlines basic methods for eliciting cultural data from native consultants. In interviews Spradley recommends using "grand tour" questions or open-ended requests that allow the native consultants to direct the responses in directions of their choosing. For example, instead of asking a native consultant, which agreement from the native speaker that the sentence is indeed correct could be obtained. The linguist then moves words around or adds words to see if certain other grammatical constructions can work. When these substitutional constructs do not work for the native speaker, the linguist can flag those constructs as inconsistent (negative cases) or as contrasting with the native's rules for grammar. Thus, a recurring pattern for correct grammar in the language being studied eventually emerges.

Frame elicitation, in which words denoting (referring directly) things, attributes (qualities), or actions contrast with other words, can be used to develop a map of native semantic categories. For instance, the linguists Brent Berlin and Paul Kay used a form of frame elicitation to obtain color term categories as these were organized across a large sample of the world's languages. In each case the linguists asked a native consultant to elicit the most basic term for a color (for example, red). The linguists could then place colors representing similar—but different—shades of red and ask for the appropriate native term, gradually moving away from the basic color red. When a new term appeared the linguists knew that a semantic boundary had been obtained. By proceeding through the entire color spectrum, Berlin and Kay were able to describe native semantic categories for color. It is interesting to note that with this type of research linguistic anthropologists discovered that, although there appear to be universal patterns associated with the evolution of adopted color terms, not all languages divide up color gradients in the same way. In many parts of Asia terms for blue and green are identical. The difference between blue and green from the perspective of many speakers of Asian languages is one of gradation or shade and not one of using two separate color terms (one for blue and one for green).

A wide range of elicitation methods are used by linguists and cultural anthropologists to obtain information from native sources. These approaches represent the basic methodological tools of field researchers who are interested in collecting cross-cultural data.

Berlin, Brent, and Paul Kay. (1969) *Basic Color Terms: Their Universality and Evolution.*
Chagnon, Napoleon A. (1992) *The Yanomamo,* 4th ed.
Spradley, James. (1979) *The Ethnographic Interview.*

ELOCUTION

See ORATORY.

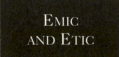

EMIC AND ETIC

The terms *emic* and *etic* are used in ethnography (descriptions of cultures) to differentiate the perspective of the native (emic) from that of the researcher (etic). The terms were introduced by the linguist Kenneth Pike in 1954. Pike coined emic from the word *phonemic.* Phonemics refers to the orientation in phonology (describing the sound system of a language) of a native toward the perception and production of sounds within the native's language. In contrast, *phonetics*, from which the word etic is drawn, refers to the sounds literally described by a linguist. The distinction between the emic perspective (the insider or native's view) and the etic perspective (the outsider's view) is important because readers of ethnographies have to be able to determine what is native knowledge (specific to the group being discussed) and what is knowledge (through method and theory) held by the researcher. Both orders of knowledge are deemed important for interpretation in ethnographic and linguistic research.

Pike, Kenneth. (1954) *Language in Relation to a Unified Theory of the Structure of Human Behavior.*

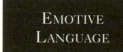

EMOTIVE LANGUAGE

See DOUBLESPEAK.

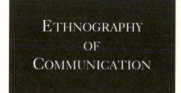

ETHNOGRAPHY OF COMMUNICATION

The general approach that linguistic anthropologists use to collect data on human communication is referred to as the ethnography of communication, and sometimes as the ethnography of speaking. This approach is made up of methods of ethnographic description and analysis, such as direct observation, participant observation (in which the anthropological researcher participates in the daily activities of those being studied), and interviewing, as these methods are applied to communication. The ethnography of communication, as a subdiscipline of linguistic anthropology, was developed by the linguists Dell Hymes and John Gumperz during the 1960s and early 1970s.

As a form of descriptive research, the ethnography of communication involves observing human communication at three levels. First, researchers must produce descriptions of *speech situations*. Speech situations represent the overarching contexts (situations) in which more specific speech behaviors occur. For example, holiday celebrations, school semesters, vacations, important rituals, and so on can all be described as speech situations. Second, *speech events* are described. Speech events are specific contexts (subsumed under speech situations) in which communicative exchanges between two or more people occur. Job interviews, ritual plays (involving actors), song duels (insulting singing), and conversation are salient examples of speech events. Finally, *speech acts* are described. Speech acts are utterances produced by specific individuals. The statement "Don't go into the water" is an example of a speech act. It is an utterance made by one person and thus represents a highly specific action that occurs within broader communicative circumstances (speech events and situations).

To illustrate how this statement might be situated in an ethnographic study of communication, let us assume that the researcher is describing a speech situation that involves the

Speech events are specific contexts in which communicative exchanges between two or more people occur. A job interview, such as the one Oscar de la Renta is giving here, is an example of a speech event.

comprehensive description of a Polynesian coastal village. Polynesians have a long and rich tradition of adapting to the ocean. Understanding the intimate relationship between these Polynesians and their immediate maritime environment would be useful for an understanding of more specific behaviors occurring in this context. Hence, a conversational exchange (speech event) between two Polynesian fishermen could be analyzed according to broader frames of reference that are established at the speech situation level. The various references that Polynesian fishermen make in their conversation—references to fishing conditions, seasonality (espe-

cially with regard to the potential for dangerous storms), the presence of sharks, the condition of their outriggers (boats)—will be composed of utterances relevant to their lives as fishermen in the village being described. The specific utterance "Don't go into the water" (which would of course be said in a Polynesian language) is somewhat vague. However, knowing something about the context in which the statement was made might provide an ethnographic researcher with enough information to make sense of the utterance. The specific utterance, therefore, is not an isolated string of linguistic data. The statement represents a piece of linguistic data that is situated or integrated with larger ongoing social and cultural patterns. The warning contained in the statement might refer to the potential for impending violent storms, the presence of sharks, dangerously low tides, or treacherous riptides. The interpretation of the statement could be made only with some understanding of the speech event itself and through knowing something of the ongoing circumstances (speech situation) surrounding the speakers' lives.

At the level of the speech act, further analysis can be conducted through isolating what is actually said by a speaker (the *locutionary act*), determining the underlying motivation of an utterance made by a speaker (the *illocutionary act*), and observing the reaction that an utterance has on an audience (the *perlocutionary act*). Realizing the nature of these three dimensions of any given speech act depends on knowing how the utterance is related to broader social and cultural contexts. With the example "Don't go into the water," we have the explicit locutionary act (literally what is said). To determine the motivation behind the statement, or why the speaker made the statement (illocution), we have to be able to know what the speaker is referring to (perhaps the reference is to sharks). The Polynesian fisherman listening to the person who made the statement might be able to interpret what is being said by knowing the circumstances surrounding the statement (it might be generally known that sharks have been in the area). His reaction to the initial statement in the form of the response, "There are sharks nearby; I will not go into the water," represents the reaction to the initial statement, and this reaction is the perlocutionary act.

The ethnography of communication contrasts somewhat with discourse analysis. With discourse analysis linguistic researchers analyze specific texts (analogous to speech acts) and attempt to determine meaning through discovering the use of the utterance in a context. Discourse analysis is therefore an inductive process, because analysis proceeds from specifics (speech texts or acts) to more general dimensions of communication (broader sociocultural implications). The ethnography of communication is deductive (general to specific), because ethnographers typically describe broader contexts first and then situate more specific behaviors within those contexts.

Ethnographic studies of communication are important because they provide valuable information on cross-cultural patterns of communication. Researchers using this approach are able to describe language systems in terms of how they are used—not merely how languages are structured—across a wide spectrum of culturally specific circumstances. For example, among the Laotian Iu-Mien (a Southeast Asian highland society) children address elders with formal terms of address—titles such as father, mother, master, and the like. The use of these formalities is highly encouraged; any deviation is considered a breach of cultural etiquette. A researcher using an ethnography of communication approach might describe the cultural rules for regulating social interaction patterns among members of different age, gender, and occupational groups. Knowing what these recurring patterns for social interaction are might assist the researcher in making sense of the variable use of address forms across changing social situations. In the case of the Iu-Mien, address terms communicated across extreme social boundaries, such as large differences in age or other clear status markers, require a high degree of formality. For peers in Iu-Mien society, informal greetings are expected. Again, knowing why individuals select certain linguistic forms (terms of address in this case) depends largely on knowing the situational and cultural circumstances in which the forms (utterances) are embedded.

See also ADDRESS, FORMS OF; DIGLOSSIA; DISCOURSE ANALYSIS.

Gumperz, John, and Dell Hymes, eds. (1972) *Directions in Sociolinguistics: The Ethnography of Communication.*

Hymes, Dell. (1962) *The Ethnography of Speaking.*

Lewis, Elaine, and Paul Lewis. (1984) *People of the Golden Triangle.*

Saville-Troike, Muriel. (1989) *The Ethnography of Communication: An Introduction,* 2d ed.

Searle, John. (1969) *Speech Acts: An Essay in the Philosophy of Language.*

ETHNOGRAPHY OF SPEAKING

See ETHNOGRAPHY OF COMMUNICATION.

ETHNOLINGUISTICS

See LANGUAGE AND CULTURE.

ETHNOPOETICS

See POETRY.

ETHNOSEMANTICS

Ethnosemantics is the cross-linguistic study of language-specific word-meaning categories. Semantic categories are made up of cultural-linguistic groupings of words (nouns, adjectives, and verbs) according to various semantic (meaning) criteria. For example, the English noun *drink* (beverage) can be associated with other words to generate more specific or more general meaning. *Soft drink* is a type of drink. *Orange soft drink* is more specific. Each of the added terms carries a specific a meaning (*soft* means carbonated beverage, *orange* means orange flavor) by way of its association with the word *drink*. The meaning of the word *drink* can undergo semantic change depending on how it is used in a sentence. In the utterance "I could drink an entire bottle," the word *drink* becomes a verb. *Drink* can also be understood by its relationship to more general terms like *liquid* and *fluid*. Deriving meaning from an examination of the relationship among words is *semantics*. Describing how various language systems across cultures organize semantic categories is *ethnosemantics*.

All languages generate semantic criteria (divisions among word types) for organizing and classifying words. The Hmong language (a language spoken in Laos and parts of China) makes use of over 50 noun classifiers. English speakers use only a few (such as *the, this, that*).

In Hmong, to determine which classifier to use, a speaker must know how Hmong nouns are classified (or grouped) by Hmong speakers. The Hmong classifier *daim* can only be used (placed in front of) nouns that denote things that are flat or two-dimensional: *Daim ntawv* (the letter) and *Daim ted* (the field). The Hmong classifier *txoj* is used with nouns that denote linear phenomena (rope, string, and abstract ideas like destiny or fate). For a native speaker of Hmong, knowing the correct classifier depends on knowledge of semantic criteria for organizing nouns. For linguistic anthropologists, being able to describe how native speakers (in this case Hmong speakers) organize words into semantic categories (sometimes called semantic fields) represents an important investigatory tool for obtaining native linguistic and cultural knowledge.

Many anthropologists have described and analyzed native semantic categories for the purpose of obtaining information on social organization. For example, kinship terms are often collected by ethnographers (cultural anthropologists working in the field) and arranged according to semantic criteria obtained from native speakers. These kinship categories provide anthropologists with an insider's (native) view of family and social organization. In many small-scale traditional societies, for example, the same kin terms for father and mother are extended to all male or female members within the same age range as the parental generation. In the Hmong language the term *txiv* (father) is applied to all male members of one's father's generation. Qualifiers are added to denote the social and familial distance from a person's biological father

(*txiv hlob* is father's older brother, and *txiv ntxawm* is father's younger brother). It is sometimes crucial for anthropologists to know these native semantic categories, because language configurations of this sort represent culture as it is encoded in language.

See also KINSHIP TERMS.

Conklin, Harold. (1959) "Linguistic Play in Its Context." *Language* 35: 631–636.

Frake, Charles. (1964) "How to Ask for a Drink in Subanun." *American Anthropologist* 66(6, part 2): 127–132.

Jaisser, Annie. (1995) *Hmong for Beginners.*

Tyler, Stephen. (1978) *The Said and the Unsaid: Mind, Meaning, and Culture.*

ETYMOLOGY

Etymology is what historical linguists call the study of the origins and historical use of particular words and phrases. All words contained in the lexicon (vocabulary inventory) of a language have their own particular histories. For example, the word *poultry* entered the English vocabulary during the eleventh century after the French-Norman invasion of Britain. *Poultry* derives from the French word *poulet* (chicken or domesticated, edible fowl). Some words can be traced back in time to assumed ancient protolanguages (first-form languages). The English word *mother* shows similarities to the Spanish word *madre*. By an examination of numerous kin terms in many European languages (such as English and

Spanish), historical linguists have been able to determine that these languages must be related by way of their relationship to an earlier common language. For most European languages, this original protolanguage is Indo-European.

Through the examination of written texts when they are available for a language, the etymology (word history) of specific terms can be carried out with relative ease. However, with exclusively oral languages the task of establishing etymologies becomes more difficult. Among societies with writing systems, actual written representations exist of specific words as they appeared at different points in time; explicit records of word changes in oral societies do not exist. Therefore linguists who are interested in etymological questions pertaining to oral language systems must rely on comparisons among related languages. For example, the first person pronoun (*I* in English) is *si* in the Apachean/Athapaskan languages of Navajo, Chiricahua, and Mescalero. In the Sarcee language (a related Athapaskan language) *sini* is the first-person pronoun. Linguists can see relationships based on similarities in word form at a given time, but describing the specific changes that have occurred for a word through time is difficult without a written record. In these Apachean/Athapaskan languages, the English word *tongue* is variously represented as *co?zad* (Navajo), *zade* (Chiricahua), and *zude* (Mescalero). These are closely related languages, yet precise etymologies for words like *zade* cannot be fully worked out for lack of a written history of the languages.

Describing the etymologies for words that have been borrowed and used by numerous unrelated languages is also problematic. For example, in Southeast Asia all of the dominant languages (Thai, Lao, Khmer, and Vietnamese) contain high numbers of Chinese (Sinitic or Sino-Tibetan) words. Because of this, historical linguists classified these languages as Sino-Tibetan. However, recent etymological studies of Southeast Asian languages conducted by the linguist James Matisoff suggest that Thai, Lao, Khmer, and Vietnamese are not actually Sino-Tibetan; they are members of other language families associated with southern Asia or Southeast Asia proper. Because of the extensive linguistic borrowing that has occurred in Southeast Asia, etymological research has been difficult, and the results of the work are somewhat tentative.

Folk etymologies are also an important source of linguistic and cultural information. Folk etymologies refer to the historic sources of folk ideas, terms, and expressions typically associated with a particular region or time period. The statement "he was whittled down to size" is a folk metaphor for reducing a person's overblown stature through some unstated means of demotion. This kind of statement was commonly used in the Appalachians of eastern North America. Place names all have their own particular folk etymologies. Canada derives its name from the Iroquoian word *kanata* (literally, "group of dwellings"). Early French explorers of the seventeenth century (Samuel de Champlain among them) are reported to have asked a group of Iroquois—living at that time on the St. Lawrence River—what they called all of the land west of the river. The Iroquois apparently thought the French explorers were referring to their village and responded with the descriptive term *kanata*.

Crystal, David. (1987) *The Cambridge Encyclopedia of Language.*

Cutler, Charles L. (1992) *O Brave New Words: Native American Loanwords in Current English.*

Matisoff, James A. (1990) "On Megalo-comparison." *Language* 66: 106–120.

Young, Robert W. (1983) "Apachean Languages." In *Handbook of North American Indians*, vol. 10, *Southwest*, edited by Alfonso Ortiz, 393–400.

EUPHEMISM

All languages have polite or euphemistic terms and phrases. Polite language is used to avoid harsh or vulgar expressive forms. Vulgarisms are culturally defined as unacceptable forms of expression in most circumstances of public discourse, although they are tolerated in many informal settings. Euphemisms always contrast with these corresponding vulgarisms. For example, in English *rest room* is often preferred over more harsh terms such as *can*, *head*, and *crapper*.

See also AVOIDANCE.

EUPHONY

Some forms of speech, particularly poetry, are perceived to have aesthetically pleasing sound qualities. Although somewhat subjective and constrained by cultural bias, ethnographers, classical linguists, and philosophers have often attempted to define (in objective terms) the "beauty" of language. Most linguists and anthropologists, however, feel that this "quality of language" is not describable in empirical, scientific terms.

EXTRALINGUISTICS

See NONVERBAL COMMUNICATION.

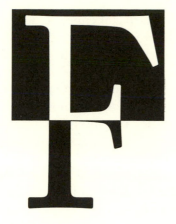

have not developed the refined speaking skills necessary for Big Men run the risk of losing face if their speeches are not well received.

Brown, Penelope, and Stephen Levinson. (1987) *Politeness: Some Universals in Language Usage.*

Goffman, Erving. (1959) *The Presentation of Self in Everyday Life.*

Meggitt, Mervyn. (1977) *Blood Is Their Argument: Warfare among the Mae Enga Tribesmen of the New Guinea Highlands.*

FACIAL GESTURING

See KINESICS; NONVERBAL COMMUNICATION.

FACE

In communicative exchanges among speakers, a person's perceived self-esteem can influence the way in which speaking is carried out. Self-esteem or a person's perceived public image, as it is particularly associated with speech exchanges, is what sociolinguists call *face* (as in "saving face"). Using face as an analytical tool allows linguists to examine power and status relationships (as these are culturally defined) among communicators (interlocutors). When, for example, relations among communicators are highly competitive, speaking strategies are often a function of saving face. In Papua New Guinea, many groups allow for Big Men (men of high status) to organize various rituals, peace ceremonies, and warfare. Status is usually maintained through elaborate speeches given by Big Men at special public events. Individual males of relatively low status who attempt to gain increased status and who

FIGURATIVE LANGUAGE

All human languages incorporate figurative or abstract language. Figurative language involves the use of words, phrases, and more lengthy forms of discourse (sentences, paragraphs, and narratives) to convey nonliteral meaning. The English word *snake,* for example, carries a figurative meaning when it is used to refer to someone who is not trustworthy. If the word *snake* is used to refer to the actual reptile, the meaning is literal. Figurative meaning can be communicated through the use of phrases. For instance, the statement "We were on top of things" is a figurative way of saying "We knew what we were doing" (the second statement is more literal or concrete). Sometimes entire narratives carry figurative meaning. For the ancient Greek philosopher Plato, the allegory of the cave was not merely the story of people literally trapped inside a cave. The true meaning of the allegory is inferred at an abstract level where the people within the cave signify the "unenlightened"; those who eventually leave the cave and see reality in the light of day signify those who have achieved enlightenment.

Figurative language is often expressed through the use of idiomatic phrases (phrases incorporating culture-specific analogies and metaphors). For instance, English speakers who are having a momentary difficulty in speaking sometimes say, "I have a frog in my throat." For most speakers of English (particularly in the United States and Britain) this statement cannot be taken literally. It is an abstraction (that is, abstracted from reality) designed to inform listeners that the person about to speak needs to clear his or her throat.

The meaning of words (semantic attributes) can be plotted along a continuum—depending on the context of use—that ranges from literal (concrete) to figurative (abstract). For example, the English term *stingy* will not translate directly into many other languages—that is, many other languages do not have a specific term that equates with *stingy*. In many Asian languages, the personal behavior characteristic that English speakers call *stingy* might be stated, "He/she does not give away goods easily." *Stingy* is an abstract term, whereas the phrase "He/she does not give away goods easily" is concrete. These two linguistic forms convey the same basic meaning; however, the extent to which they are

either figurative or concrete depends on their placement along a semantic spectrum indicating the degree of semantic abstraction from reality.

The translation of figurative language from one language to another is always problematic. The intended meanings of idiomatic phrases, allegorical narratives, and myths are always derived from culture-specific knowledge. For example, it would be quite difficult to translate the subtle meanings that underlie much of the idiomatic language used in American films without some grasp of American folk culture. The same problem exists when anthropologists and linguists attempt to translate narrative texts for which little or no cultural context exists. This problem has been documented with the case of Ishi. Ishi was a member of a northern California Native American group called the Yahi. In 1911 Ishi was the last of his people; he spoke no English when he first encountered English-speaking whites, and he was the only person alive who spoke Yahi. The anthropologists A. L. Kroeber and T. T. Waterman recorded one of Ishi's long narratives, the "Story of Wood Duck." Although Kroeber, Waterman, and the linguist Edward Sapir spent considerable time attempting to make sense of the story, its central meaning was embedded in the Yahi culture and therefore was lost to them. The story itself must have functioned for Ishi at a highly figurative level, because many of his explanations for the story (mostly communicated through broken English) made use of metaphors, analogies, and other abstractions.

Ishi died in 1915. With his death the true meaning of the Wood Duck story also passed away.

Kroeber, Alfred L. (1925) *Handbook of the Indians of California.*

Kroeber, Theodora. (1961) *Ishi in Two Worlds.*

Lakoff, George, and Mark Johnson. (1980) *Metaphors We Live By.*

FLUENCY

When a person has a complete and competent knowledge of a language and is able to produce coherent grammar using the language, this is called fluency. Being fluent requires a full working knowledge of the grammar of a language and its vocabulary and generally having the ability to construct meaningful utterances. Fluency can be equated with the concept of *linguistic competence* introduced by the linguist Noam Chomsky. The linguist Dell Hymes has added *communicative competence* as a key idea to understanding fluency. For Hymes, communicative competence refers to a person's ability to recognize how language should or should not be used across a variety of social and cultural circumstances.

See also COMMUNICATIVE COMPETENCE.

Chomsky, Noam. (1965) *Aspects of the Theory of Syntax.*

Hymes, Dell. (1971) "Competence and Performance in Linguistic Theory." In *Language Acquisition: Models and Methods*, edited by R. Huxley and E. Ingram, 3–28.

———. (1971) "On Communicative Competence." In *Sociolinguistics*, edited by J. B. Pride and Janet Holmes, 269–293.

FOLK ETYMOLOGY

See ETYMOLOGY.

FOLKLORE

Folklore literally means "the people's (folk) knowledge" (*lore* comes from an Anglo-Saxon word for knowing). For anthropological folklorists, the term is used to denote the subdiscipline (subsumed under anthropology) dedicated to the description and analysis across cultures of folk belief and expression. Folk knowledge is communicated through such genres as oral narratives, riddles, proverbs, poems, word play, and nonverbal display (clothes, body adornment, and so forth).

Ethnographers of communication are also interested in folklore, because a significant degree of cultural knowledge is communicated through "folkloric" forms of expression. For instance, in many parts of the American West, tying a red ribbon around a person's finger is thought to prevent nosebleeds. The folk expression (the ribbon tie) reveals the underlying assumption that red ribbons are causally related—through a vaguely defined supernatural connection between the color red and human blood—to nosebleeds.

Sometimes folk knowledge is communicated through religious activities. Among the Azande of central-eastern Africa, folk beliefs in supernatural power are expressed through the actions of diviners (specialists who interpret oracles for clients). Azande diviners attempt to resolve community disputes by consulting oracles, which take the form of rubbing boards (small wooden boards held down by the diviner's foot), the chicken poison test, and the use of a variety of ordeals (the hot knife test is often used). To illustrate, if a member of an Azande community suspects a neighbor of evil magic (witchcraft) because one of his goats died, he may consult a diviner in an attempt to determine whether or not magic was used to kill the goat. If it is determined that magic was used, the client, working with the diviner, might want to determine the identity of the guilty party. The diviner might use the chicken poison test. For this test diviners give baby chickens poison as questions of the oracle (in this case the chicken) are asked on behalf of the client. The diviner might ask, "Is the death of the goat the result of magic?" The diviner can, through slight-of-hand, control the physical outcome (either the chicken lives or it dies). The diviner can also manipulate the outcome through predetermining how initial questions are framed. If, for example, the chicken dies, the diviner can say "Yes, the death of the goat is due to magic" after carefully omitting which outcome would represent a positive result in the initial question. The diviner could then proceed to the next question, again controlling for a specific outcome. (Through slight-of-hand diviners can regulate the amount of poison given to the chicken; sometimes no poison is given.) This type of folk behavior communicates how the Azande perceive supernatural power, how they resolve or perpetuate community-level disputes, and, in general, how they view ongoing intragroup social dynamics. Azande diviners and their actions thus communicate fundamental cultural presuppositions held by most Azande.

The anthropologist Michael Jackson has observed the Kuranko of Sierra Leone, in western Africa, using folk narratives for the purpose of resolving ethical dilemmas. Jackson describes Kuranko storytellers generating ambiguous situations in their stories. The underlying purpose of these ambiguities seems to be to get listeners actively involved in the stories and to force them to assess critically the ethical dilemmas constructed in the stories. Jackson has suggested that Kuranko folk stories function to communicate and reinforce sociocultural norms by providing narrational vignettes (short dramas) that force listeners to engage their knowledge of correct Kuranko behavior.

Information on material and social culture (food, buildings, tools, and family and kinship structures) have also been gleaned by anthropologists through analyzing traditional oral narratives. The anthropologist Thomas Blackburn has described the oral narratives of the Chumash (a native group of California) and has extracted considerable data on their use of plants, fishing techniques, and elements of their social organization. Blackburn points out that native oral narratives convey more than just ideological themes; stories typically convey a comprehensive range of cultural traits.

Cross-cultural studies of folklore have been used by a variety of social science researchers as a means of understanding culture processes. Folklore represents a pervasive, but subtle, way for people to communicate what they know and think about the world.

Blackburn, Thomas C. (1975) *December's Child: A Book of Chumash Oral Narratives.*

Hand, Wayland D. (1989) "Folk Medical Magic and Symbolism in the West." In *Magic, Witchcraft, and Religion: An Anthropological Study of the Supernatural,* edited by Arthur C. Lehmann and James E. Myers, 192–202.

Jackson, Michael. (1977) *The Kuranko.*

FUSIONAL LANGUAGES

Also called inflecting languages, these language types are characterized by the extensive use of affixes (additions that carry minimal meaning [morphemes]). Word order (grammar) is not as important in fusional languages because affixes modify words by altering their function (marking different parts of speech). In fusional languages the subjects and objects of sentences can often be reversed without loss of meaning. Typically, in fusional languages the subject of a sentence is not indicated by word order; the subject will be marked by the addition of an affix—a prefix, medial affix, or a suffix, depending on the language. Fusional languages contrast with "analytic" or "root" languages, in which reliance on affixes is minimal or nonexistent and word order is crucial.

In the 1960s growing numbers of social scientists became interested in recurring cultural patterns that influence differences in gender behavior. For anthropologists this interest has stimulated some cross-cultural research on gender-specific language use. Recent studies of language structure and use, as these pertain to gender, indicate that the degree of difference between female and male language use varies significantly across cultures. Some linguists have suggested that in some societies women use entirely different linguistic codes (different languages) from the men, while in other societies no gender-specific differences were observed. The linguist Robin Lakoff casts doubt on the suggestion that in some societies the women and the men speak entirely different languages. The Arawak of the Caribbean had been reported to have separate languages for men and women; early explorers reported that Arawak women spoke a language that was not intelligible to their male counterparts. Lakoff points out the obvious flaw in this contention: "But then how could boys communicate with their mothers (who raised them)?" Yet linguists working with different cultures have observed contrasting ways that men and women use language. Moreover, these differences in use often produce miscommunications between women and men.

Gender differences in the use of language range from contrasting forms of pronunciation to word choice, phraseology, and the selection of gender-specific speech codes (styles of speaking). For example, among the Chukchee of Siberia, men use the consonants *c* and *r;* women substitute *s* in words that contain *c* and *r.* The Chukchee word *cumnata* ("by a buck") represents the male pronunciation, while *sumnata* is the female form of the word. Chukchee men say *ramkichin* (people), and Chukchee women say *samkissin.* The *r* and *c* in */r/amki/c/hin* are replaced with *s* in the female pronunciation (*/s/amki/ss/in*).

Since the early 1970s interest in gender and language issues has increased. Questions concerning the relationship between language and power/status differences, and differences in pronunciation and word choice, have stimulated much of the research in this area. In addition, the related roles of social, political, and economic forces as factors contributing to gender differences in language use have become important areas of concern to gender language studies. A basic problem with early studies

GENDER DIFFERENCES

Many sociologists have observed that American men, such as these men sitting around a potbellied stove, in contrast to American women, typically don't face each other directly when conversing—they usually stand at angles. They also tend to use conversation to compete with one another. These differences emerge as a result of the way men and women are socialized in the use of language.

of language is the ways in which linguistic data on gender-related topics were collected. Throughout most of the history of linguistic research, men have been the primary investigators. The results of their studies therefore tend to reflect the male biases of the researchers themselves as well as the attitudes and perceptions of their male native consultants. American English-speaking men, for example, have often characterized "women's speech" as "illogical," "indecisive," and "gossipy." Recent sociolin-

guistic studies have shown that there is no significant difference in the logical coherence of male and female English speech, that women (depending on the context) can be as decisive as men, and that men also gossip.

In some language/societal systems women can, in many contexts, be more direct and decisive than men. The linguist Elinor Ochs has observed Malagasy women using an informal form of speech called *rasaka*, in which confrontational language (arguing and criticizing) in public places is considered to be a normal form of discourse among women. From the male perspective in Malagasy society, arguing in public violates general cultural norms. Men, in contrast to Malagasy women, often use *kabary,* a formal speaking style used primarily during rituals. While using *kabary,* Malagasy men use subtle innuendo and polite forms of criticism in their exchanges with one another. Their arguments, however, must always be masked by polite, hidden forms of argumentation; they cannot be direct or incisive. Men and women use both *rasaka* and *kabary* according to the degree of formality of a situation. However, because the women are more familiar with the use of argumentation in public places, and despite men often saying that women do not argue, men will, if confronted by rivals, frequently ask women to defend them in public. While the women defend the honor of their husbands the men will quietly observe, thus maintaining their perceived public dignity and prestige.

Differences in the way men and women construct and use language often reflect a society's rules for regulating class, gender, and age. In Japan, for example, women tend to use more speech markers (speech that indicates membership in a group or segment of society), showing respect when addressing men, than do men when addressing women. Japanese women are also expected to remain silent in situations in which men are engaged in conversation. Through the extensive use of polite, formal deference to males, Japanese women's use of language reflects the reality that in Japan women generally have lower status than males.

Recent research on gender/language issues suggests that differences in male and female language and speech have been exaggerated. The linguist Sara Trechter has compared her data on Lakota (a Siouan language) with earlier studies conducted on other Native American languages. For instance, the linguist Edward Sapir, working in the early part of the twentieth century, described Yana (a Native American language of northern California) as having two different language subtypes: one for men and the other for women. According to Sapir, these subtypes were exclusive; women could only use one form of Yana and the men the other. The linguist Mary Haas, working with Koasati (a Native American language of the Southeast), suggested that women used modified male words in their speech. Thus, although women used a different form of Koasati from that of their male counterparts, female speech derived from male language forms. Haas, like Sapir, stated that these differences in use fell exclusively along gender lines and could not be compromised by men using female speech or vice versa. In Trechter's examination of Lakota, and through a reexamination of Yana and Koasati (through the descriptions of these languages as obtained by Haas and Sapir), Trechter has reasoned that Lakota women often used "male speech." Furthermore, the most important factor contributing to the use of one speech form over the other was context, not necessarily gender.

In contrast to these non-European languages, English has few explicit differences in female and male language. There are few overtly gender-specific words, special speech codes, or esoteric languages. However, there appear to be some differences (some subtle and others not so subtle) in gender-specific usage and forms, suggesting differences in the general orientation of men and women to the use of language. Sociolinguist Deborah Tannen has described the different ways in which American English-speaking women and men organize conversation. According to Tannen, word choice, body proxemics, and the ways in which conversations are structured reveal status differences between American women and men. Men in conversation typically do not face one another (they stand at angles looking off at the horizon). In contrast, women tend to face one another directly as they talk. Women also tend to use conversational mechanisms designed to include people in talk. Men, in contrast, tend to use conversation to compete with one another. Male conversation, therefore, is a reflection of how men perceive themselves in the overall hierarchical system of American society. Tannen is quick to point out that these patterns do not result from biological differences between males and females; they emerge as a result of differences in the way boys and girls are socialized to the use of language.

Moreover, although men and women in American society use the same words (lexical choice), certain words carry connotative meanings that suggest gender status differences. For example, *doctor* connotes maleness even though many doctors in American society are female. Conversely, *nurse* connotes femaleness, although there are actually many male nurses. Great battles have been fought by academics over the differential use of pronouns. In many publications, es-

pecially those printed before the 1980s, masculine pronouns were used generically (as general references to subjects and objects). For example, consider the following sentence: "If a student experiences difficulty during his first semester, he should consider contacting one of our counselors." The article *a* that appears before the word *student* indicates that the author could be talking about any student (a hypothetical student); yet later in the sentence the pronouns *his* and *he* appear. Not only does this create ambiguity (is the author talking about any student, or a particular male student?), but also the selection of the masculine pronoun as generic may communicate the subtle message that males are generally more highly valued in American society.

Linguist Robin Lakoff has observed that American women tend to use tag questions, such as in "We're going to the store. Aren't we?" instead of the more direct declarative "We're going to the store." In addition, American women tend to use more "hedges." Hedges are phrases indicating uncertainty, slight confusion, and indecisiveness. For instance, women are more likely to say, "That's what the book said, I think" as opposed to "That is definitely what the book said." Lakoff, Tannen, and other linguists working in this area of research maintain that differences in the ways men and women use language in North American society reveal differences in access to political, social, and economic power. In general terms, men tend to have more power across a wider spectrum of sociocultural domains (political and economic realms in particular) than do women. From the perspective of many feminist linguists, gender differences in language use, as revealed in cross-cultural studies of gender, provide a window for viewing fundamental societal inequalities between men and women.

Bogoras, Waldemar. (1922) *Chukchee.*

Eckert, Penelope. (1996) "The Whole Woman: Sex and Gender Differences in Variation." In *The Matrix of Language: Contemporary Linguistic Anthropology,* edited by Donald Brenneis and Ronald K. S. Macaulay, 116–138.

Haas, Mary. (1944) "Men's and Women's Speech in Koasati." *Language* 20: 142–149.

Lakoff, Robin. (1975) *Language and Woman's Place.*

Maltz, Daniel N., and Ruth A. Borker. (1996) "A Cultural Approach to Male-Female Miscommunication." In *The Matrix of Language: Contemporary Linguistic Anthropology,* edited by Donald Brenneis and Ronald K. S. Macaulay, 81–98.

Ochs, Elinor. (1996) "Norm-Makers, Norm-Breakers: Uses of Speech by Men and Women in a Malagasy Community." In *The Matrix of Language: Contemporary Linguistic Anthropology,* edited by Donald Brenneis and Ronald K. S. Macaulay, 99–115.

Sapir, Edward. (1929) "Male and Female Forms of Speech in Yana." In *Selected Writings of Edward Sapir,* edited by D. Mandelbaum, 206–212.

Shibamoto, Janet. (1987) "The Womanly Woman: Manipulation of Stereotypical and Nonstereotypical Features of Japanese Women's Speech." In *Language, Gender, and Sex in Comparative Perspective,* edited by Susan U. Philips et al., 26–49.

Tannen, Deborah. (1984) *Conversational Style: Analyzing Talk among Friends.*

———. (1986) *That's Not What I Meant!: How Conversational Style Makes or Breaks Your Relations with Others.*

———. (1990) *You Just Don't Understand: Women and Men in Conversation.*

Trechter, Sara. (1995) "Categorical Gender Myths in Native America: Gender Deictics in Lakhota." *Issues in Applied Linguistics* (6)1: 5–22.

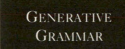

GENERATIVE GRAMMAR

See GRAMMAR.

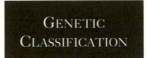

GENETIC CLASSIFICATION

See LANGUAGE FAMILIES.

GENRE The type or format of a communicative event is what linguists call genre. Examples include joke, narrative, lecture, riddle, and conversation. Sociolinguist Dell Hymes uses genre as a methodological tool for identifying and classifying various culturally recognized forms of communicative expression.

Hymes, Dell. (1972) "Models of Interaction of Language and Social Setting." In *Directions in Sociolinguistics: Ethnography of Communication,* edited by John Gumperz and Dell Hymes, 35–71.

GLOSSOLALIA Glossolalia is the technical term referring to the behavior more commonly known as speaking in tongues. Glossolalia involves the spontaneous use of verbal utterances and often excited physical gesturing in highly religious contexts. Most studies of glossolalia have concluded that its use corresponds directly with peaks of religiously charged emotional excitement. Thus, when a person who is known to "speak in tongues" feels an emotional surge coming on (typically produced as a result of interactions with fellow worshipers or as a result of religious thoughts), glossolalia can be triggered.

Glossolalia is attributed primarily to Pentecostal and charismatic Christian communities, although the linguist Felicitas Goodman has noted its use outside of North America in non-Christian communities. Goodman has observed glossolalia in small numbers of subcultural communities in West Africa, Europe, the Caribbean, and North America. In all of these communities the use of glossolalia is predicated on the belief that supernatural forces (God, the Holy Ghost, and so forth) are speaking through individual members of the community. In this sense speaking in tongues seems to provide worshipers with a tangible, concrete sense of God (or gods in some non-Western settings).

Glossolalia is not an actual verbal language; it is emotion conveyed through repetitive verbalizations and physical gesturing. General characteristics of glossolalia include the use of repetitive sounds (the same range of sounds found in parent languages: English, Bantu, and so forth), fluctuating prosodic patterns (rapid changes in pitch, tone, and intensity), and a reliance on driving mechanisms (singing hymns, chanting, drumming, and the use of various acoustic musical instruments).

———

Goodman, Felicitas D. (1969) *The Acquisition of Glossolalia Behavior.*

GLOTTOCHRONOLOGY Glottochronology is a method used by historical linguists to determine the time depth for the splitting off of a daughter language from a parent language. Glottochronology is subsumed under the more general approach known as lexicostatistics (using statistical tests to determine genetic relationships among languages). The method of glottochronology is based on an assumed 20 percent replacement of basic vocabulary words every 1,000 years from the time of separation from the parent language. Basic vocabulary words that derive from a parent language (cognates) are classified by linguists into word categories such as kin terms (mother, father, grandmother), body parts, numbers, and color terms. Linguists assume that these word types are more resistant to change or replacement through time and thus are useful for measuring the elapsed time of a language split. The mathematical expression used in glottochronology is in the formula $t = (\log C)/(2 \log r)$. In this formula r represents the constant (20 percent replacement every 1,000 years), C represents the percentage of basic vocabulary words in a language at any given time, and t is the time depth in 1,000-year increments.

The historical linguist who is most responsible for developing glottochronology is Morris Swadish. Swadish used the linguistic record for languages that had written histories, such as English, German, and Spanish, to calculate his 20 percent figure for cognate replacement. He then applied his approach to language history cases for which little or no writing existed. Perhaps the most famous of this type of case involved Swadish's analysis of an indigenous Mexican language called Huastec. Huastec speakers live in Mexico's Veracruz coastal region along the Gulf of Mexico. Linguists had previously determined that the Huastec language was related to Maya languages spoken in the Maya culture area farther south. Huastec is not mutually intelligible with any other contemporary Maya language; therefore most linguists assumed that Huastec must have split off from an early Maya language at some undetermined time in the past. Until Swadish developed his method, determining the time depth for the Maya/Huastec split would have been impossible. According to Swadish, using glottochronology, the Huastec separation from proto-Maya most likely occurred around 1600 B.C.

Not all historical linguists have embraced glottochronology as a reliable method. The linguist Dwight Bolinger, for example, has stated: "We cannot be sure that the social and historical forces of change have not been stronger in one epoch than in another, or that many items of supposedly basic vocabulary have not actually been borrowed rather than inherited." Other linguists have pointed out similar problems. For example, it is difficult to measure quantitatively the amount of prolonged cultural and linguistic contact a group of speakers might experience through an extended period. Moreover, it is also difficult to account for intangible variables that might influence language change. For instance, were relationships among groups speaking different languages who came into contact with one another amicable or hostile? Did extensive trade develop through time, thus influencing the rate at which basic vocabulary words might be replaced with foreign words? Although such problems have plagued glottochronology as a tool for historical linguists, it is still used as a way of indicating possible time depth figures for related languages, for suggesting possible migration patterns of related groups, and for determining general linguistic affiliations among languages.

See also COGNATE; LANGUAGE FAMILIES.

Bolinger, Dwight. (1968) *Aspects of Language*.
Swadish, Morris. (1955) "Towards Greater Accuracy in Lexicostatistical Dating." *International Journal of American Linguistics* 21: 121–137.

GOSSIP

Idle talk, generating rumors, and engaging in excessive chatter about friends, acquaintances, and others is called gossip. The term *gossip* derives from the Anglo-Saxon words *god sibb* (literally, God's relative) and was later modified in Middle English to *gossyp*. The term is also used as a noun for labeling people who are known for their constant gossiping.

Although few systematic cross-cultural studies of gossip have been conducted, ethnographers (field cultural anthropologists) have observed gossip in many societies and in numerous circumstances. It is quite possible, although not empirically verified, that gossip is a human universal (found in all societies).

GRAMMAR The linear arrangement of words into a logical or coherent pattern (a sentence) is grammar. Developing an understanding of grammar—or syntax, as it is sometimes called—is important to linguists because through grammatical organization language has coherence. Coherence refers to the logical binding together of word types (parts of speech) to produce low-level meaning. For example, consider the following sentence: "We took the kites out and flew them all day." For English speakers the arrangement of these words into a recognizable pattern (such as the noun phrase "the kite" and verb phrases "we took" and "flew them") allows listeners to obtain the general meaning of the sentence. If the word order is randomized, the sentence loses coherence: "Day and all we flew them out took kites the." Grammar, therefore, is the glue that holds sentences together as logical structures. The linguist Noam Chomsky illustrates the idea of coherence with his famous sentence: "Colorless green ideas sleep furiously." Although this sentence contains contradictions ("colorless green" and "sleep furiously") and thus has little practical meaning, the sentence still has coherence because the various parts of speech are arranged in a sequential logical manner.

Chomsky is also famous for his general theory of language, a theory in which grammar is central. For Chomsky, human language is essentially a process by which the human mind generates grammatical constructions; he calls this process *generative grammar*. Chomsky also notes that sentences can be organized in a number of ways and still maintain coherence. These variations of a single sentence are called *transformations* (variants of a single sentence). These two ideas, generative and transformation, together form the official label for Chomsky's theory of language: Transformational/Generative Grammar. To explain how these two levels exist, Chomsky makes a distinction between deep structure (the underlying logic of a sentence) and surface structure (the multiple ways in which a sentence can be organized and expressed). Understanding the difference between deep structure and surface structure is similar to developing an understanding of how things are made. For example, consider the following analogy: Building a house involves knowing the fundamental aspects of carpentry—laying foundations, forming wood frames, attaching various types of covering, and so forth. These fundamental underlying aspects (or rules) of carpentry are analogous to the deep structure of language. We know, however, that carpenters can build all sorts of houses; some houses are big, some are small, and floor plans can vary considerably. Variations at this level are analogous to surface structure. The simple sentence "Take the dog for a walk" can be transformed into "The dog take for a walk." Although the second sentence seems a bit awkward in standard English, grammatical constructions like this occur in many of the world's languages. The second sentence still has coherence.

Another important aspect of Chomsky's view of grammar has to do with language acquisition. Chomsky believes that human beings are born with the innate capacity for grammar. That is, human infants, as they grow older, bring grammar to the words they learn to speak. Language acquisition, from Chomsky's perspective, is a process guided by our innate human capacity for grammar, and our development and use of language generally follow universal patterns of human cognitive development. Therefore deep structure is not merely a product of precise logical limitations on grammar, but it may also be hardwired into the human brain. As proof for this stance, Chomsky has described the grammatical structure of a large number of languages. He discovered that there appear to be universal patterns (found in all languages sampled) of grammar, recurring grammatical patterns that Chomsky has dubbed UG (universal grammar).

Chomsky's theory of language is controversial. Some linguists have criticized his basic contention that universal features of grammar are the product of preexisting innate cognitive structures. These linguists have suggested that recurring patterns of grammar result more from logical constraints on language construction than from innate genetically "programmed" grammar. In other words, there are only a limited number of ways that something can be said and still make sense. Moreover, some linguists have pointed out that some of the grammatical features posited by Chomsky and

others as universal may not in fact be universal. Most comparative studies of language universals have relied extensively on Indo-European languages (English, German, and Italian, to name a few) for their samples. Most of these languages employ a general subject-verb-object (SVO) orientation for the grammar of simple sentences. Linguistic anthropologists have pointed out that some languages use general grammatical sequences other than SVO. Malagasy, the language spoken in Madagascar, relies on VOS (verb-object-subject) for the construction of simple sentences. The Maya languages, spoken in southern Mexico and in parts of the Guatemalan highlands, are also VOS languages. Thus, the simple sentence "He drank water" would literally translate into Maya as "Drank water [did] he."

Cross-cultural linguistic studies of grammar have revealed a significant degree of diversity in grammatical constructions across a wide sample of the world's languages. Linguists who have studied grammatical variation across language and cultural domains have raised questions regarding the mutual influences among language, culture, and perception (how people see the world). For example, in 1958 the linguists John Carroll and Joseph Casagrande conducted an experiment to determine whether or not grammatical differences influenced—or were influenced by—differences in perceptions of real objects. Five populations of children were used: only Navajo-speaking children, bilingual children (some dominant Navajo speakers, some balanced between English and Navajo, and some English-dominant), and English-only speakers. The experiment involved

Navajo or English verbs for "handling" (such as "I *picked* up the rock"). In Navajo, the correct verb is selected to match certain characteristics of the object being handled. Different verbs are used when describing the handling of hard round rocks, sticks, rope, or soft material. Different verbs could also be used if there were differences in the color of the object being handled. In each of the cases (for each population) the children were asked to match contrasting objects (yellow stick and blue rope) with a third object (yellow rope). Because each of these objects had two defining characteristics (shape and color), the children had to rely on subtle underlying mental tendencies in order to select matches. The results indicated that dominant Navajo-speaking bilinguals selected matches according to shape (blue rope goes with yellow rope). English-dominant bilinguals selected matches according to color (yellow stick goes with yellow rope). It was also noted that as the Navajo-dominant speakers got older a bias for color over shape emerged. Carroll and Casagrande have suggested that language actually frames how children in these various populations view specific objects. In other words, language preconditions speakers to see the world in a particular way because the use of a specific verb in conjunction with classes of objects forces speakers to focus on different salient characteristics of the objects in question. Other linguists feel that this conclusion is an overstatement, noting that there is no evidence that these speakers actually perceive the objects as being different because of the selection of certain criteria over others (shape over color and so forth). These speakers are, according to critics of the Carroll/Casagrande study, merely using learned grammatical rules for purposes of differentiation and reference among objects (merely using the conventions of grammar for indicating what is being referred to in a sentence).

Many of the theoretical issues surrounding grammar may never be fully resolved. However, the importance of grammar as an area for gaining insight into language and culture processes will persist as long as linguists and other social scientists raise issues pertaining to language structure.

See also LANGUAGE ACQUISITION.

Carroll, John B., and Joseph B. Casagrande. (1958) "The Function of Language Classifications in Behavior." In *Readings in Social Psychology*, edited by Eleanor E. Maccoby, Theodore M. Newcomb, and Eugene L. Hartley, 18–31.

Chomsky, Noam. (1957) *Syntactic Structures*.

———.(1965) *Aspects of the Theory of Syntax*.

Hanks, William. (1996) *Language and Communicative Practices*.

O'Grady, William D., and Michael Dobrovolsky, eds. (1993) *Contemporary Linguistics: An Introduction*, 2d ed.

GULLAH

See BLACK ENGLISH.

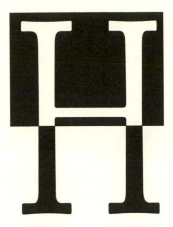

HEDGE

See GENDER DIFFERENCES.

HERMENEUTICS

Hermeneutics is an approach—or set of methods—used for interpreting written texts. In its earliest stages of development, hermeneutics was applied exclusively to the interpretation of religious texts (primarily the Old and New Testaments of the Judeo-Christian tradition). Hermeneutics subsequently was broadened to include descriptions and analyses of nonreligious texts.

Contemporary linguists, especially sociolinguists, employ hermeneutic methods for interpreting verbal discourse.

HEURISTICS

Heuristics literally means to explore, discover, or invent. As the term is used in conjunction with language and communication studies, it refers to the use of language by speakers to test or explore relationships between language (words, phrases, narration, and so forth) and events or things existing in the external world. Linguists who rely on heuristics as a conceptual model for language assume that language is not merely a symbolic system that is abstracted from reality. Moreover, language cannot be defined by a single set of principles because it is constantly undergoing change as speakers adjust to new circumstances. Thus, from the perspective of linguists who see heuristics as important, language is a nexus, inextricably connected to a wide spectrum of experiential domains.

Sociolinguists have used heuristics as a useful concept for describing how people employ language to mitigate ambiguous social situations. For instance, people who are uncertain of how to behave in specific social situations (for example formal dinner parties, creation ceremonies, or religious settings where prayer is being used) often listen to what is being said by more experienced participants in the hopes that what is being said will in some way be informative. In most situations like this, people do not come out and explain in explicit terms how one should behave; the inexperienced must derive the appropriate cultural norms through interpreting the indirect meanings of what is said. Being able to interpret meaning by exploring the possibilities behind subtle statements (in formal or informal social settings) is a function of heuristics.

That is, to learn what is proper, listeners try to discover clues in the statements made by others.

Heuristics has also been used as a conceptual tool for describing and analyzing language acquisition. Some researchers have observed young children associating words with things and actions (*wader* [water], *momee* [mother]). These researchers recognize that acquisition involves the use of language to construct and test propositions about the external world. Therefore language acquisition is viewed by some researchers as a trial-and-error "discovery" process.

See also ACQUISITION; CONVERSATION.

HIEROGLYPHICS

See WRITING.

HOLOPHRASE

Holophrases are one-word utterances (typically made by young children) that carry the dual function of referring to something while simultaneously communicating the intentions of the speaker. If a young child says, "Milk!" we recognize (especially if a glass of milk is within sight of the child) that the child is referring to the glass of milk. We might also recognize that the child is, with this simple utterance, asking for the milk. Thus, a reference to milk and the intention of the young child to obtain the milk have been communicated in a one-word utterance.

Linguists have noted that although holophrases are one-word utterances, they function as complete sentences.

HONORIFICS

In all human societies polite or formal forms of address are used when people of high status are being addressed. Highly formal and polite forms of address are called honorifics.

See also ADDRESS, FORMS OF.

HUMOR

Humor is the use of verbal discourse, pictures, and other media of expression with the intention of producing laughter in an audience.

The ways in which humor is constructed and carried out are highly culture specific. Keith Basso has spent years describing humor (specifically joking) among the Western Cibecue Apache (of the American Southwest). Basso has observed that a significant amount of Apache joking is about white tourists. Comments are often directed at how white tourists dress (shorts, T-shirts, the latest tennis shoes) and to other material possessions such as cameras, beer, soda, and children's toys. The Cibecue also make light of whites who, as the Apache see them, talk too much. In most greeting exchanges, for example, the Cibecue say very little. The fact that someone is present (after arriving) is enough knowledge to warrant a silent greeting (often only a head nod). When the Cibecue imitate whites greeting one another, the response on the part of Cibecue Apache hearing the sarcastic imitations is laughter. Basso recorded such "satirical routines": "You sure looking good to me, L. You looking pretty fat! Sure pretty good boots! I glad . . ." [laughter]. The Cibecue Apache produce humor by contrasting their Apache knowledge of how to greet someone with the way they perceive whites greeting one another. This is, in effect, a form of ethnic humor.

Among hunter-gatherer societies humor is often a response to overt arrogance. Hunter-gatherer societies are usually organized into cooperative hunting bands. If a hunter boasts or brags about a kill he runs the risk of severing social ties with other hunters. Moreover, if a hunter boasts, other members of the band can ridicule and make jokes about his kill. The anthropologist Richard Lee found this to be true of the !Kung (Ju/'hoansi) of the Kalahari Desert (of Botswana and Namibia, Africa). One year, while conducting research among the !Kung, just before Christmas, Lee purchased a large ox from a neighboring Bantu cattle herder. Lee wanted to give the ox to the group of !Kung he had been working with as payment for their cooperation.

When he gave the ox to the !Kung, Lee pointed out how large and healthy the animal was. Lee also boasted that the !Kung should be pleased with such a large and generous gift. The response Lee got was unexpected. Instead of praising, the !Kung mocked the gift. One !Kung hunter said, "Do you expect us to eat that bag of bones? . . ." [It's] old. And thin. Everybody knows there's no meat on that old ox. What did you expect us to eat off it, the horns?" Bursts of laughter followed this exchange. What Lee subsequently discovered was that he had violated a serious social taboo, bragging about a gift. Sharing among the !Kung is the expected norm. Calling attention to a gift is really a way of increasing the status of the gift giver. The cultural penalty for Lee's faux pas was to endure humorous ridicule.

See also AVOIDANCE; JOKING.

Basso, Keith H. (1979) *Portraits of "The Whiteman": Linguistic Play and Cultural Symbols among the Western Apache.*
Lee, Richard Borshay. (1969) "A Naturalist at Large: Eating Christmas in the Kalahari." *Natural History* 78: 10.

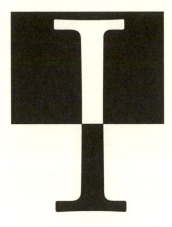

that carry special meaning. English examples of idioms (idiomatic phrases) include: "I've got a frog in my throat," for something in the throat that is preventing someone from speaking clearly; "Cat got your tongue?" to question why someone is so quiet; and "We were climbing the walls," a statement indicating extreme restlessness or anxiety.

Sometimes idiomatic phrases are expressed in proverbs (folk sayings). Proverbs are idiomatic in the sense that they often make little sense to people who do not share a common culture. For instance, the following examples of Hmong (an Asian society) idioms lose considerable meaning when translated into English: "If the leaves don't fall the woods are dark" or "To covet the corn whether it is early or late." The difficulty in translating idioms from one language to another can be recognized by imagining how English idioms such as "Ball hog!" (for a person who holds onto a basketball too long in a game), "Meat head" (an insult suggesting that a person is stupid), or "Bad!" (slang among many adolescent American English speakers for "good" [an inversion]) might be translated into other languages. In translation, often analogous idioms are used (idioms that carry a similar meaning) as opposed to using direct or literal translation. Thus, the Hmong idiomatic phrase mentioned above, "If the leaves don't fall the woods are dark," might be translated into the English idiom "Let nature run its course" (implying, for example, that overpopulation will be dealt with naturally). Note that the translation is not a word-for-word literal translation but rather the substitution of a complete idiomatic expression that

IDIOLECT A person's individual quality or distinctiveness of speech is what sociolinguists call idiolect. Elements of idiolect (tone, pitch, cadence) differentiate a single person's speech patterns from those of all other members of a speech community. Thus an idiolect is a personal dialect. It is through hearing idiolects that we as hearers can discriminate among speakers in crowds, over the telephone, or in any situation in which familiar speakers cannot be seen (but can be heard).

IDIOM Idioms are figurative phrases or expressions that carry culture-specific meanings. They are constructed from words obtained from common lexicons (vocabulary inventories) but placed together into specific recurring phrases carries a similar meaning to the original Hmong idiom.

See also FIGURATIVE LANGUAGE.

Heimbach, Ernest E. (1979) *White Hmong-English Dictionary.*

ILLOCUTIONARY ACT

See SPEECH.

IMMERSION

Immersion refers to situations in which language learners are surrounded by native speakers of a dominant language. When speakers of one language are immersed in a setting dominated by speakers of another language, given an ample amount of language contact, acquisition of the second language typically takes place in an easy, natural manner. Immersion, as an idea, has also been employed to describe the language acquisition process for infants who are learning their primary language. Most infants are surrounded by speakers of the language that predominates in the community of their birth and that is the language of their parents. Most infants will eventually acquire a comprehensive knowledge of the language they hear as they are growing up.

Some educational programs with bilingual/multilingual missions have adopted "immersion" as an instructional approach. In eastern Canada (particularly in Montreal) young English-speaking students were immersed in schools in which the entire curriculum (course offerings) was taught in French. As these students progressed through the various grades (first grade through high school) most became fully bilingual. English was spoken at home and French at school. Various versions of educational immersion have been adopted and used in the United States. In most cases these programs are based on partial immersion strategies. Double immersion, for example, is a type of partial immersion approach. Double immersion has been used by bilingual teachers as a means of periodically immersing students from differing ethnolinguistic backgrounds in speaking situations in which they must use a second language. This approach is usually set by taking primary speakers of one language (Spanish, for example) and teaming them with all English-only speakers. English-speaking students who are learning Spanish might be teamed with Spanish-only speakers. The central aim of double immersion is to force students to obtain basic conversational skills in a second language by having them converse with native speakers. Immersion programs such as these also facilitate positive social contact among students of differing cultural and language backgrounds.

See also ACQUISITION; BILINGUALISM.

Cohen, A., and M. Swain. (1976) "Bilingual Education: Immersion Model in the North American Context." *TESOL Quarterly* 10: 45–53.

Swain, M., and S. Lapkin. (1982) *Evaluating Bilingual Education: A Canadian Case Study.*

IMPLICATURE

Often when speakers are conversing, the messages behind their statements are implied—not directly or explicitly stated. Sociolinguists refer to this type of communication in verbal discourse as implicature (the use of implied meaning). To illustrate, consider the statement "Throw them in the corner." The only way that a listener will be able to interpret what the speaker is referring to is to know something about the context in which the statement was made. What is being referred to is implied (not overtly stated). Let us assume that the statement was made after a person had just taken off his or her shoes before entering a house. The context tells us that the speaker is most likely referring to the shoes: "Throw them [the shoes] in the corner." Implicature as an analytical tool is often used by sociolinguists who use discourse analysis.

See also CONVERSATION; DISCOURSE ANALYSIS.

INFORMANT

In ethnographic research (conducted by field cultural anthropologists) informants—or native consultants—are employed for the purpose of eliciting culture-specific data. Although anthropologists typically collect a wide range of ethnographic data, they sometimes employ native informants to obtain highly specific data on cultural patterns that influence language and communication behavior. Native informants can provide information on native systems of category (semantic classifications of plants, animals, kin organization, and other phenomena), cultural rules for organizing social interaction, and the structure of native languages (particularly grammatical structures). Linguistic anthropologists often make use of several key informants for the purposes of cross-referencing and increasing the overall sample size of the body of data collected. Informants represent an important resource in cross-cultural studies, but most researchers only use them in conjunction with other methods such as direct observation (describing what the researcher sees and hears) and participant observation (participating in the cultural activities of those being studied).

See also ELICITATION.

INTERCULTURAL COMMUNICATION

When two or more people of differing cultural backgrounds attempt to communicate, cultural barriers to communication often arise. This is often the case even when the communicators share a language. The study of communication as it is carried out among people of fundamentally different cultures is called intercultural communication. Intercultural communication has become an important applied (practical) field of study since the late 1960s. Concern about culture and communication barriers reached a critical stage when business personnel from Western industrial countries began to conduct business in other parts of the world (particularly in Africa and Asia). At that time executives

In the Middle East, conversing males can get quite close. As this photograph of two Bedouins demonstrates, they also tend to face one another directly as they talk.

of non-Western business firms also became aware of communication problems stemming from cultural differences. This growing awareness fueled the growth and expansion of intercultural communication. Since the late 1960s intercultural communication has extended its influence into such areas as education, international diplomacy, and various legal domains (court cases involving litigants of differing cultural backgrounds).

An early foundational study that established intercultural communication as an important applied field was conducted by Howard Van Zandt. Van Zandt conducted an extensive study of negotiation strategies used by Japanese business executives and middle-management personnel. Van Zandt contrasted the communicative styles of these Japanese businessmen (almost exclusively men) with the communicative styles of their American counterparts. He found that the Japanese prefer oral presentations supported by written documentation; they avoid argumentation; they prefer formal interactions over informal; and they take a considerably longer time to make decisions (concerning deals) than their American counterparts. As a result of this study and similar studies that followed, fewer business deals fell through between Japanese and American firms. Moreover, consulting firms specializing in intercultural communication began to appear as international business expanded.

Intercultural communication does not merely focus on differences in language structure. The emphasis in intercultural communication studies is on cultural rules for regulating communicative interaction and extralinguistic (nonverbal) patterns of communication. For instance, international students who attend public schools and universities in Canada and the United States often experience difficulties associated with communicative interaction in classrooms. These problems may persist even when these students are fluent in English. Problems often arise because of cultural differences in the way interaction is carried out. In the United States there exists an emphasis on informal interaction. In many other parts of the world, teachers are viewed as formal authority figures and it is proper that they be treated with respect. In most parts of Asia, for example, silence is used to show respect to authority figures. When Chinese, Japanese, and Korean students attend classes in the United States they usually sit quietly while American students interact openly and freely with teachers.

The problem involves more than just having international students adopt Western modes of interaction. In many cases international students feel uncomfortable with the discourse styles of American students. American students tend to emphasize incisiveness (brevity and going to a central point as quickly as possible); many non-Western peoples emphasize what intercultural communication specialists call "contextual style." In using contextual style in a narrative, no central subject or point exists; a series of related topics embedded in a comprehensive field of information is typically offered. In student introductions in classroom settings, individuals from West African countries are likely to describe how they are situated in their kin groups at home (this often involves discussing relationships among 20 or more people). In addition, they may discuss their families' possessions ("We own so many cattle, goats, rice fields . . ."). Whereas students from West African countries view this contextual form of discourse as normal, American students quickly become impatient with such lengthy introductions. Conversely, West African students sometimes complain that American students talk too much about trivial matters in informal contexts but do not provide ample information in formal introductions.

Analyses of communicative behavior that is culturally based also focuses on nonverbal styles. Some Chinese, in conversation, employ rapid, intense, terse bursts of verbiage. Non-Chinese who witness such conversations assume that an argument is taking place, when in fact the Chinese communicators are merely having a conversation. Thus, the nonverbal sound qualities (paralanguage) for one cultural tradition (in this case rapid, intense bursts of verbiage) do not carry the same connotative meaning that they might in another cultural setting.

Differences in cultural communicative style can often involve differential use of space (proxemics). The anthropologist Edward T. Hall has conducted numerous studies of differences in the cultural use of space and how these differences influence communication. In simple terms, Hall has observed that different cultural traditions regulate the distance between speakers according to culture-specific rules. These are what Hall calls "concentric circles of interaction." In the Middle East (primarily among Arab populations) males who talk to one another tend to get quite close (within a foot and a half). They also tend to face each other directly as they talk. North American men, in contrast, tend to maintain a wider distance when engaged in conversation. They also feel uncomfortable with direct face-to-face interaction. Problems arise when members of these different traditions try to converse. As Arab men talk, American men back off. American men are also quick to display their uneasiness with direct eye contact. Arab men, according to Hall, feel insulted when American men back off from a conversation.

Some critics of intercultural communication have pointed out that, to a significant degree, the discipline is based on generating broad generalizations for what are perceived to be recurring patterns of communicative behavior; however, these general patterns of communicative behavior may not be applicable to all members of the cultures studied. Not all Asians are quiet in formal settings. Not all Americans are talkative.

Intercultural communication specialists have answered these criticisms by pointing out that they describe only central points of tendency in communication while acknowledging that in any population there is likely to be a range of tendencies.

Hall, Edward T. (1968) *Proxemics*.
Samovar, Larry A., and Richard E. Porter, eds. (1991) *Intercultural Communication: A Reader*, 6th ed.
Van Zandt, Howard F. (1970) "How to Negotiate in Japan." *Harvard Business Review* 48(6): 45–56.

INTERLOCUTOR A person who is actively involved in conversation (dialogue between two or more people) is an interlocutor. The term *interlocutor* is used to describe participants in dialogue (conversation involving two people) or several people who are engaged in ongoing conversation.

ISOLATE An isolate is a language that does not appear to be related to any other known language. Kootenay, Beothuk, and Zuni are Native American languages that are classified by most comparative-historical linguists as isolates.

See also LANGUAGE FAMILIES.

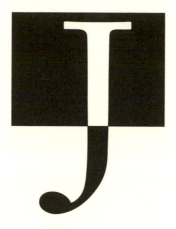

(communicative interaction must be limited, formal, or nonexistent). Among members of extended kin groups in which avoidance rules are absent, joking relationships often arise. Joking involves the use of verbal play for purpose of generating laughter, thus signaling informality of relations. Cross-culturally, joking behavior seems to occur among members of peer groups, cross-cousins, and across generational lines for members of the same sex. Exceptions to these recurring patterns can also be found in many societies.

See also AVOIDANCE; HUMOR.

JARGON

See ARGOT.

JOKES

Jokes are contrived forms of verbal play designed to produce laughter. Use of jokes indicates informality among members of a group of speakers.

See also HUMOR; JOKING.

JOKING

In many societies kin relations are defined by rules governing social interaction. In some circumstances in-laws of the opposite sex (mothers-in-law in particular) must be avoided

JUNCTURE

Varieties of sound qualities (changes in pitch, tone, and intensity) that delineate the ending of one word and the beginning of the next word in a sequence are what linguists call junctures. Junctures are particularly useful in separating the ends and beginnings of words that are homophonic (sound the same). In such cases junctures assist listeners in making proper distinctions among words with similar-sounding parts. For example, consider the following word pairs: "sea kelp" and "seek help." In the second word pair ("seek help") a juncture would occur after the *k* sound in the form of a pause to demarcate the words. Improper placement of a juncture can often cause confusion. Consider the following sentences based on these word pairs: "Sea kelp, if you can get it." "Seek help, if you can get it."

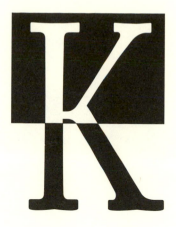

styles found in many Western funerals. Key therefore assists linguistic researchers in explaining why certain constraints are attached to the types of speaking styles that can occur in a given situation.

See also ETHNOGRAPHY OF COMMUNICATION; SPEECH.

Hymes, Dell. (1972) "Models of Interaction of Language and Social Life." In *Directions in Sociolinguistics: Ethnography of Communication*, edited by John Gumperz and Dell Hymes, 35–71.

KEY

Key, as the linguist Dell Hymes defines it, is "the tone, manner, or spirit in which the [speech] act is done." The concept of key, as a descriptive and analytical tool for describing speech situations, is analogous to the key or tone of a musical score. A minor key implies sadness and melancholy. A major 7th key might imply a positive or happy feeling. Hymes suggests that all situations involving speech interactions possess key. For example, funerals in most Western societies are sober, somber, sad events. The forms of speaking styles that tend to occur at these funerals reflect the overarching key of sadness and restraint. In many non-Western societies, funerals are more jubilant; funerals are viewed as a time for celebration. (On the island of Bali in Indonesia, for example, funerals are festive.) The styles of speaking that occur at funeral celebrations contrast sharply with those

KINESICS

Kinesics is the body language that people use to reinforce spoken language. Pointing, facial gesturing, and body positioning are all forms of kinesic expression. Some researchers have suggested that most kinesic gestures are universal (the same gesture carries the same meaning in all human societies). Although this appears to be the case for some gestures (such as smiling, crying, facial gestures showing pain), many linguists have observed that most nonverbal gestures are culture and language specific (the form and use of certain gestures vary considerably across cultures). In Thailand and throughout most of Southeast Asia, pointing directly at someone is considered an insult. In Greece, Turkey, and throughout most of the Arabian Peninsula, nodding the head up and down signals *no;* shaking the head laterally (side to side) signals *yes.*

Martin Luther King, Jr., speaks at a funeral for a youth killed during a civil rights protest in Marion, Alabama. Funerals in most Western societies are sober, somber, sad events. In many non-Western societies, funerals are viewed as a time for celebration.

In kinesics, meaning is contained in kinemorphs (physical signs that carry specific meaning, such as pointing or winking). However, as linguists have pointed out, kinesics cannot be fully understood simply by collecting an inventory of kinemorphs; kinesics must be correlated with spoken language. Physical gesturing tends to be carried out to support spoken language. Hand gestures and body position cues often indicate that talk is about to follow. All people unconsciously use facial expressions to hold a listener's attention and to emphasize and support what is being said verbally.

See also NONVERBAL COMMUNICATION.

Birdwhistell, Ray. (1970) *Kinesics and Context: Essays on Body Motion Communication.*

Saville-Troike, Muriel. (1989) *The Ethnography of Communication: An Introduction*, 2d ed.

KINSHIP TERMS Kinship terms are designated words in a language system that define relationships among members of a society or cultural group. Kinship terminology can be roughly divided into two general categories: consanguineal (blood) kin and noncon-

Pointing, facial gesturing, and body positioning are all forms of kinesic expression. These two Palestinian women flash the V-sign in support of hunger-striking Palestinians held in Israeli jails.

sanguineal (nonblood) kin. Kinship terms form a corpus of knowledge that, in traditional societies, establishes the basis for social organization. Linguistic anthropologists are interested in kinship terminology because kin terms define the underlying social organization for a culture. Kinship terminologies are organized into native semantic categories (and thus represent important cultural knowledge) and map the social/interactional patterns that can regulate communicative behavior.

Kinship systems vary somewhat cross-culturally. Anthropologists have recognized several recurring systems and have named them after the groups associated with particular kinship structures. These systems are the Iroquois, Crow, Hawaiian, Inuit (Eskimo), Omaha, and Sudanese. Variations of these systems can be found in many parts of the world. Criteria for further delineating kinship systems are employed on the basis of such characteristics as generational differences, same-generation relations, how immediate blood relatives are designated, gender, and descent (tracing lineage through either the mother or the father's side of a family).

The variability in kinship systems becomes apparent when one makes cross-cultural comparisons. The Hawaiian system emphasizes generational distinctions over specific terms for precise relationships. Hence, generic kin terms designate only differences in generation and gender. The same kin term for father is extended to all male members of one's father's generation. Terms for brother and sister (sibling terms) are extended to all female and male members of one's generation. However, specific qualifiers are sometimes added to mark more specific relationships.

In contrast to the Hawaiian system, the Indian system of southern Asia makes use of many different terms, each denoting highly specific relationships. *Pita*, for example, is the term used for indicating one's biological father. *Mata* is the term for one's biological mother. Different terms are used for one's father's brothers: *Tau* is the father's eldest brother and *Chacha* is his youngest brother. The terms *Nana* (grandfather) and *Nani* (grandmother) can be used only to refer to a person's grandparents on their mother's side of the family.

Understanding how kinship systems are organized and represented in language (in the form of semantic categories) provides anthropologists with a general sense of how individuals in various societies interact with one another. Knowing how specific kin terms are used to designate generational differences also communicates certain cultural rules for how members of differing generations should treat one another. In Hmong society, as an example, the term *txiv* literally means father. However, as in the Hawaiian system, *txiv* is often used to refer to male members of the father's generation. *Txiv* is also a term of respect, and so use of the term carries a powerful message for defining the formal and respectful relationship between fathers and younger members of Hmong society. Elder members of Hmong society often use generic kin terms to refer to younger members (particularly children). The term *menyuam* is used when referring to a group of children. The terms *tub* (son) and *ntxhais* (daughter) are typically used instead of personal names. This is even the case when mothers and fathers are referring to their own (biological) sons and daughters.

Most linguistic research on kinship has been concerned with describing cross-cultural/linguistic patterns for the semantic organization of kin terminology. The linguist and ethnographer Ward Goodenough, working with other ethnolinguists in the 1950s and throughout the 1960s and 1970s, developed a method for eliciting, sorting, and analyzing native semantic data. This method is called *componential analysis*. At the heart of many of these studies was the collection and analysis of kinship data. Goodenough and other linguists using componential analysis elicited from native speakers as many kin terms as these native speakers could remember. After collecting such data, the terms were organized according to semantic attributes (cousins are collateral, parents and offspring are generational, and so forth). What emerged from this type of research was cognitive (thought) maps that displayed native categories of knowledge (the *emic* perspective). Since the late 1960s componential analysis has been criticized for its lack of accounting for communicative dynamics (how people alter what they do in changing circumstances). The linguistic descriptions that Goodenough and other "ethnosemanticians" gathered in the form of kinship charts and cognitive maps are what some linguistic anthropologists call *static*—unmoving or not dynamic.

See also ELICITATION; EMIC AND ETIC; ETHNOSEMANTICS; LANGUAGE AND CULTURE.

————————

Findlay, Michael Shaw. (1994) "Structure and Process in Speech Subcommunities of Hmong Students at a Northern California High School." *Language and Education* (6)3: 245–260.

Fox, Robin. (1967) *Kinship and Marriage: An Anthropological Perspective.*

Goodenough, Ward H. (1956) "Componential Analysis and the Study of Meaning." *Language* 32: 195–216.

Heimbach, Ernest E. (1979) *White Hmong-English Dictionary.*

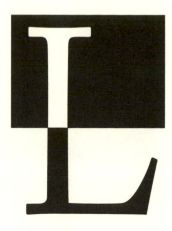

LA LA THEORY

See ORIGINS OF LANGUAGE.

LANGUAGE

A language is a symbolic system used by communicators to construct and convey information. Linguists generally agree that for a symbolic system to be considered a language it must contain minimal symbolic units that convey meaning (morphemes like *cat, dog,* or bound morphemes such as *pre* [*pre*game] or *a* [*a*typical]), a full grammar (rules governing the sequential ordering of words into a logical pattern), and ways of rearranging word patterns (recombining word phrases) to produce a wide variety of meanings (a function of semantics). Linguists who include spoken language as part of their definition point out that a

language must contain a useful range of contrasting sounds (vowels and consonants) before higher-level dimensions (morphology and grammar) of language can be constructed. The description and analysis of sounds incorporated into a language system is called phonology.

Linguists typically divide language into two general domains. First, language is seen as an abstract symbolic system (it resides in the minds of speakers). Second, language is recognized as speech (the overt verbal expression of language). Formal linguists tend to emphasize language as an abstract grammatical system of conventionally recognized symbols. Moreover, although formal linguists recognize that language is used for purposes of communication, they tend to de-emphasize its function as a system of communication, paying more attention to language structure. Linguistic pragmatists, in contrast, emphasize linguistic behavior (such as speech, conversation, nonverbal elements of communication, and so forth). Pragmatists tend to see language more in terms of its use and function. Linguistic pragmatists examine language structure as well, but its purpose (practical use and function) is a more central concern.

Theorists who attempt to explain various aspects of language tend to fall into two camps: formal linguists and linguistic relativists. Formal linguists, as mentioned above, describe and analyze language as separate from overt social and cultural patterning. Language for formal linguists is essentially grammar. For a person to know a language (to have *linguistic competence*) a comprehensive knowledge of grammar is essential. Language therefore must be described

In many African herding societies, such as the Masai in Kenya shown here, cattle are a valued commodity and occupy a special place in the culture. In Sudan, cattle are so important to the Nuer that cattle terminology is often extended to denote people's personal names.

and analyzed as a structured logical system that is organized and regulated by grammatical rules.

In contrast, linguistic relativists (in most cases linguistic anthropologists) view language as embedded in broader dimensions of the human experience. Linguistic anthropologists ("relational linguists" as they are sometimes called) do not separate language from the social and cultural contexts in which language is learned and used. The anthropologist E. E. Evans-Pritchard, for example, collected a significant amount of linguistic data from the Nuer, a pastoral (herding) society of Africa's Sudan. Evans-Pritchard observed that Nuer speakers used numerous metaphors that make reference to their cattle and to other aspects of Nuer culture. Cattle are perhaps the most important commodity to the Nuer and therefore occupy a special place in the culture of Nuer herders. The linguist Nancy Hickerson has analyzed Evans-Pritchard's linguistic data and has concluded that cattle are so important to the Nuer that cattle terms are often extended to denote people's personal names. For example, when young Nuer males go through their rite of passage into adulthood, they are given an adult name that is taken from some attribute of a prized ox that the initiate owns. A young adult Nuer might be named *Luthrial* (taken from *luth*, referring to a bell worn around the neck of an ox) or *Rial* (a term indicating the distributional pattern of colors on a particular ox).

Similarly, among American English speakers important cultural themes are found in language. Sports metaphors, for example, can be heard in many conversations ("He's coming from way out in left field"; "We are almost at the finish line"; "The ball is in your court"; "Give me a ballpark figure").

Differences in definitions of language generally follow the research and theoretical interests of particular linguists and communication specialists involved in language studies. Although many of the definitional and theoretical problems associated with language may never be fully resolved, enough agreement on what language is exists to allow scholars to continue to explore various aspects of the language process.

See also GRAMMAR.

Evans-Pritchard, E. E. (1948) *Nuer Modes of Address*.
———. (1968) *The Nuer*.
Hickerson, Nancy Parrott. (1980) *Linguistic Anthropology*.
Lakoff, George, and Mark Johnson. (1980) *Metaphors We Live By*.

LANGUAGE ACQUISITION

The process by which an individual acquires a comprehensive knowledge of a language is referred to by language and communication specialists as language acquisition. Language acquisition, as a field of inquiry, is concerned with observing the acquisition of primary languages (the first language learned) but can also be extended to include studies of second language acquisition.

Although a wide variety of methodological and theoretical approaches have been applied to language acquisition research, two schools of thought tend to dominate the field. The *innatists*, led by Noam Chomsky, Steven Pinker, and Derek Bickerton, believe that the acquisition of human language is guided primarily by internal, innate processes that are specific only to human beings. In other words, human evolution has provided a built-in human capacity for acquiring a full language. Chomsky has termed the innate capacity for human language acquisition the *language acquisition device* (LAD). Moreover, the innatists believe that a critical period exists (between birth and ages five to eight, with some variation among individuals) in which the language acquisition process occurs naturally, with little effort. According to Chomsky, as we get older our ability to acquire language diminishes. Language acquisition for adults therefore represents an extremely difficult and cognitively (thinking) demanding task.

In contrast, the *social interactionists*, led by Stephen Krashen and Tracy Terrell, believe that few if any internal barriers exist to language acquisition. Social interactionists assume that the barriers to subsequent language acquisition (languages learned later in life) are for the most part a product of external social and cultural factors. Krashen has noted, for example, that parents or caretakers tend to modify their speech

Many linguists believe that cultural differences in the way parents and caretakers communicate with their infants and children directly affect their children's process of language acquisition. Coddling and talking face-to-face with an infant tend to produce a talkative child.

when talking to infants and young children. Caretakers typically use simple words and phrases and tend to put a significant degree of emotion into their speech ("motherese"). According to Krashen, this allows young language learners to comprehend what is being said. This is called "comprehensible input." As more complex aspects of language are gradually introduced to young language learners, their ability to apply language to real-life situations increases until they are capable of using language fluently. Krashen and others have observed that when this process is replicated for adult second language learners, language acquisition unfolds as easily and effortlessly as it does for children. Therefore the main obstacles to second or subsequent language acquisition, according to Krashen, appear to be a product of how these languages are taught and acquired. For example, most conventional teaching methods for second language acquisition focus on rote memorization of grammar and vocabulary. With the conventional approach, classes that emphasize conversational use of language typically come after learning the basics of grammar and vocabulary. Following the "natural" approach to second language acquisition, a conversational use of language comes first (as it would for children). Thus vocabulary building occurs within the context of actual ongoing communicative events (conversation); grammatical rules are applied later, when a learner has some sense of the language. Ideally, for second language learners the natural approach should simulate the process by which first languages are learned.

Linguistic anthropologists and others interested in cross-cultural aspects of language and communication have been concerned with language acquisition as a function of learning the rules for language use (not merely learning language structure). Cross-cultural studies of language acquisition have therefore been biased toward describing and analyzing "language socialization" (learning the cultural rules for language use). The linguistic anthropologist Susan Philips, for example, has conducted extensive research on how Native American children living on or near the Warm Springs Reservation in north-central Oregon acquire the rules for using language across different social situations (including school, home, and other social environments). Philips has observed that Warm Springs children as well as Warm Springs adults tend to construct and regulate conversational interaction in fundamentally different ways from their Anglo-American counterparts. Warm Springs children tend to leave extensive pauses or periods of silence between changes in speakers (in conversation). Anglo-Americans tend to talk over one another and compete for "talk time." Anglo-Americans also tend to monopolize conversations; the competitiveness creates a situation in which Anglo-American speakers are constantly attempting to "keep the floor." Warm Springs children also tend to make extensive use of the visual channel (looking, using eye movement, and so forth) in ongoing communicative events.

Philips points out that contrasts in the conversational use of language between Warm Springs children and Anglo-Americans result from fundamental differences between the two communities in patterns of language socialization. For example, when taken to pubic events (usually community dances and ceremonies), Warm Springs infants are often wrapped in blankets and carried in cradle boards. These infants can look out over their mother's shoulders at activities carried out at various public events. Adults do not often directly talk to infants. The infants hear a great deal of adult speech, but most of it is not directed at them. As these infants become children and eventually adults they display behavior typical of passive observers. This, according to Philips, explains why their use of conversational strategies favors extensive use of silence, noncompetitiveness, and a generally negative view of speech monopolization (dominating conversation).

Similarly, the linguistic anthropologists Elinor Ochs and Bambi Schieffelin have described language socialization for the Kaluli of Papua New Guinea. In contrast to Anglo-American mothers, who pamper, coddle, and talk face-to-face with infants, Kaluli mothers seldom talk directly to infants. In general, Kaluli adults do not treat infants and younger children as capable of comprehending the world around them; therefore, from the adult Kaluli perspective, it is irrational to talk to the youngest members of society. As Kaluli children grow older they are expected to speak correctly and observe all of the appropriate social protocols (rules regulating respect) in their social interactions with adults. Ochs and Schieffelin point out that although infants and children are not often directly talked to by adults, they do grow up in a verbal environment that is extremely rich. The cultural emphasis in Kaluli society tends to be on engaging talk with members of society who are viewed as mature

enough for adult talk. Language and speech, from the perspective of the Kaluli, signal for members that they are growing older and thus should take part in the activities of the larger community. As is true for many small-scale traditional societies, becoming a member of society is emphasized in Kaluli society, as opposed to becoming an individual.

As a species we are obviously predisposed to acquiring full human language. Most experts agree the process involves both internal (genetic/mental) and external (the social/cultural environment) factors. The relative degrees to which internal and external factors influence language acquisition may never be fully understood, and it is becoming more and more obvious to researchers working in this area that the process of language acquisition is far more complex than previously thought.

See also ACQUISITION.

Bickerton, Derek. (1984) "The Language Bioprogram Hypothesis." *Behavior and Brain Sciences* 7: 173–221.

Chomsky, Noam. (1968) *Language and the Mind.*

Krashen, Stephen D., and Tracy D. Terrell. (1983) *The Natural Approach: Language Acquisition in the Classroom.*

Ochs, Elinor, and Bambi B. Schieffelin. (1982) *Language Acquisition and Socialization: Three Developmental Stories and Their Implications.*

Philips, Susan Urmston. (1993) *The Invisible Culture: Communication in Classroom and Community on the Warm Springs Indian Reservation.*

Pinker, Steven. (1994) *The Language Instinct: How the Mind Creates Language.*

LANGUAGE AND CULTURE During the first half of the twentieth century a significant number of cultural anthropologists ventured out to study a wide variety of the world's indigenous societies. As these anthropologists began to describe the lifeways of these primarily non-Western (non-European) indigenous peoples, they soon realized that comprehending the cultural logic (the knowledge and rules governing cultural behavior) of a given group of people involved learning the indigenous language. Moreover, these anthropologists recognized that language seemed to be the primary vehicle by which culture is learned. As cultural anthropology as a discipline has developed through the years, most anthropologists who do fieldwork (ethnographers) have asked important questions regarding the nature of the relationship between language and culture. The relationship between language and culture is complex and, as the numerous and vociferous debates on the subject attest, not well understood.

Perhaps the strongest statement favoring the view of a close relationship between language and culture is the Sapir-Whorf hypothesis. The name of this hypothesis is taken from the names of two famous linguists: Edward Sapir and Benjamin Whorf. In its most basic form the Sapir-Whorf hypothesis is the assumption that the language a person learns actually structures and organizes how that person views or perceives the world. Thus, culture (what a person has learned) is encoded (symbolically organized) into language; as a person acquires knowledge of a language, he or she also develops a particular view of reality.

Testing this hypothesis has proved difficult. In their attempts to uncover the relationships among language, culture, and perception, some linguistic anthropologists have focused on differences in the ways phonology (the sound systems of languages), word choice, and grammar are organized in different language systems. It was assumed that differences in language structure would influence differences in how people tend to see the world (comparing languages and worldview). For example, linguists have noted that bilingual speakers sometimes shift back and forth from one language to another (code switching) to select language elements that most closely express their thoughts. Other studies have focused on grammar and word choice. In 1958 the linguists John Carroll and Joseph Casagrande attempted to test the Sapir-Whorf hypothesis by comparing two populations of Navajo speakers. Their test was concentrated on dominant Navajo speakers who also spoke English as a second language, and English-speaking Navajos whose second language was Navajo. Speakers from each of the populations were asked to construct sentences selecting verbs that attach to the objects *blue rope* and *yellow rope*. Other objects, such as blue sticks, were included in the sample to control for both shape and color. Carroll and Casagrande concluded that primary Navajo speakers selected verbs for handling (Navajo terms for picking up, grasping, holding, and so forth) on the basis of the shape (the physical form) of the noun/objects. In other words, certain verbs were selected by the speakers on the basis of language-specific grammatical rules founded on verb association with classifications of

L 109

nouns according to shape. The English-dominant Navajo children tended to select verbs for the handling of the same objects according to color criteria. Carroll and Casagrande argued that the differences in grammatical rules and word choice between the two forms of Navajo (that is, the selection of a verb based on either the shape or the color of the object to be handled) predisposed speakers of these two populations to view aspects of the objects differently. The dominant Navajo speakers focused on shape as the most important feature of the objects. The dominant English speakers, although they were using Navajo for the test, focused on color as the most salient feature of the objects.

Critics of this test have suggested that differences in perception resulting from differences in language structure have not been proved to exist. Instead, the experiment demonstrates how, when constructing sentences, speakers use slightly different versions of the same language to select for somewhat different grammatical rules; members of both populations still see the objects in the same fundamental way. Therefore, if the critics are correct, language does not predispose speakers to see the objects differently; they all see the objects in much the same way.

Not being able to prove scientifically with absolute certainty the Sapir-Whorf hypothesis has not, however, dissuaded linguistic anthropologists from describing the important relationship between language and culture. The linguistic anthropologist Nancy Hickerson has suggested that, contrary to the central assumption contained in the Sapir-Whorf hypothesis (that language determines perceptual views of reality), language

merely reflects or mirrors a society's cultural patterns. Hickerson calls this idea *cultural emphasis*. Cultural emphasis refers to identifiable recurring patterns in language that reflect ongoing important cultural themes. For example, using cultural data collected years earlier by E. E. Evans-Pritchard, Hickerson notes how the Nuer pastoralists (cattle herders) of the Sudan, Africa, use cattle terms across a wide spectrum of social circumstances. Cattle terms (attributes of cattle) are given to young males who have passed through their rites to adulthood. Cattle terms are also used for particular forms of address. Moreover, cattle terms are often used as metaphors for describing a person's character, status, and wealth (measured in the number of cattle he owns). In the English-speaking world we might hear the metaphoric phrase "Time is money." Nuer speakers might say, "Don't waste time on another man's cattle," referring to a futile action. Thus, from Hickerson's perspective language reflects the overall cultural pattern for a group of people; language does not necessarily predispose people to see the world in a particular way.

Researchers interested in language and culture have also focused much of their research on describing patterns of language socialization. Language socialization refers to the process by which a person learns the cultural rules for using language as a form of social interaction. The anthropologist Shirley Brice Heath has described the language socialization for several different working-class communities of the Carolinas, on the southeast coast of the United States. One of the communities, composed of African Americans, had subtle ways of socializing the young to the usage of competitive verbal duels. These verbal duels represent a cultural form of verbal play in which speakers try to outdo one another through constructing clever insults. Generating quick and effective metaphors and analogies are all part of the word game. Speakers who could "turn" a clever insult gained in their overall status position within the group.

The development of language culture studies (conducted primarily in linguistic anthropology) has spawned new disciplines, one of which is intercultural communication. The central focus in intercultural communication studies is on describing, analyzing, and applying an understanding of how culture influences communication when people from fundamentally different cultures attempt to communicate. Intercultural communication specialists have observed that all people bring their culture to communicative events. For instance, when Japanese business personnel communicate with one another, strict formalities of address are adhered to (such as formal greetings, showing respect for age or seniority, and so forth). Americans engaged in business favor informality in their dealings with one another. Often, when American businesses attempt to conduct negotiations with Japanese business firms, communication (even when one language is being used) can be difficult. Americans tend to work quickly ("getting to the bottom line") and informally (for example, attempting to speak with their Japanese counterparts on a first-name basis). Japanese executives try to maintain a posture of formality and seriousness. These executives also tend to work slowly and methodically and do not make decisions in haste. Intercultural communication specialists often find ways to facilitate better communications in situations like this. Therefore intercultural communication is a field that lends itself to consulting (advising various parties of potential cultural barriers to communication).

See also INTERCULTURAL COMMUNICATION.

_____

Carroll, John B., and Joseph B. Casagrande. (1958) "The Function of Language Classifications in Behavior." In *Readings in Social Psychology*, edited by Eleanor E. Maccoby, Theodore M. Newcomb, and Eugene L. Hartley, 18–31.

Evans-Pritchard, E. E. (1968) *The Nuer.*

Heath, Shirley Brice. (1993) *Ways with Words: Language, Life, and Work in Communities and Classrooms.*

Hickerson, Nancy Parrott. (1980) *Linguistic Anthropology.*

Samovar, Larry A., and Richard E. Porter, eds. (1991) *Intercultural Communication: A Reader,* 6th ed.

Sapir, Edward. (1931) *Conceptual Categories in Primitive Languages.*

Van Zandt, Howard F. (1970) "How to Negotiate in Japan." *Harvard Business Review* 48(6): 45–56.

Whorf, Benjamin L. (1952) *Collected Papers on Metalinguistics.*

LANGUAGE BORROWING

See LANGUAGE CHANGE.

LANGUAGE CHANGE

All languages change through time. The forces that cause language change contribute to what linguists call "language variation." Linguists who are interested in studying language change have observed that several factors are primarily responsible for change: geographic isolation (when speakers of the same language become separated from one another for long periods), language contact (when speakers of one language come into contact with speakers of another or others), and language innovation (the invention of new linguistic forms).

Perhaps the most common forces leading to language change come when communities that speak one language split and become geographically separated or isolated from each other. The Austronesian languages of Southeast Asia and Polynesia, for example, represent the widespread diffusion and divergence of what was once a single language. Austronesian languages include all of the languages of New Guinea, most of the languages of the Malay Peninsula, and all of the Polynesian languages. These major language groups are made up of related but mutually unintelligible languages; a speaker of Hawaiian-Polynesian cannot understand a Samoan-Polynesian speaker, yet the languages are related. Approximately 8,000 years ago Austronesian speakers migrated from the mainland of Southeast Asia to the island regions of the South Pacific. These early Austronesian populations colonized the thousands of islands that are distributed throughout much of Oceania (the lands of the South Pacific). As the process of widespread migration and subsequent settling down occurred, these Austronesians became geographically and linguistically isolated from one another. As a result of this isolation, their languages developed along independent courses of change, eventually producing languages that could not be mutually understood across wide and diverse regions of the South Pacific. Linguists call this process *language divergence*.

Languages can also change as a result of language contact. For example, English contains a significant number of French words (chef, venison, poultry, and education are but a few examples). These words entered the English inventory of words during and shortly after the French-Norman invasion of Britain in the eleventh century. Sometimes the native terms of those who are colonized become part of the vocabulary stock of the conquerors. In Mexico, words from Nahuatl, the language of the Aztecs, have been incorporated into the Spanish lexicon (vocabulary). The word *metate* (milling stone for grinding corn) derives from the Nahuatl word *matatl;* the contemporary word *chipotle* (used in Spanish to refer to a smoked hot pepper dish) derives from the Nahuatl word *chipotl* (referring to the same dish).

Language contact and change can occur in *polyglot* situations (situations in which many languages are used). In the Caribbean during the seventeenth and eighteenth centuries, sugarcane plantation communities were composed of slave workers of African descent. The slaves spoke numerous West African languages that were not mutually intelligible. Moreover, the plantation owners spoke various European languages (English, French, and Spanish). The polyglot situation of the Caribbean region at that time produced several varieties of *pidgins* (simple new languages that allowed for basic communication across language barriers). These pidgins subsequently evolved into *creole* languages (new languages with full grammars). Thus, as a result of language contact in polyglot situations new "composite" languages were produced.

All languages show signs of gradual change. Focusing on subtle shifts in speech sounds, the linguist William Labov has observed English speakers on Martha's Vineyard (an island off the coast of Massachusetts) altering their vowels. Labov noted that changes in vowels were often stimulated by social mobility (moving up in social class). For example, in some contexts speakers from middle-class communities altered the vowel *a* to *ah* when in the company of upper-class people. In these situations the word *vase* (as in maze) was often shifted to *vahze* (as in Roz). Thus differences in socioeconomic class and social mobility, through motivating changes in vowel structure, contributed to ongoing language change.

Language innovation contributes to language change. Language innovation is the addition of new language forms, typically new words. In modern English, for example, the infusion of computer technology into everyday life has produced a significant distribution of technical terms that has become part of the common vocabulary. Words such as *byte* and its extended forms *kilobyte* and *megabyte*, for indicating the amount of computer memory and data storage space, are becoming words that many English speakers use. Compound words and new word combinations are also emerging as computers become more

important fixtures in our daily lives. Words such as *motherboard*, *hard drive*, and *diskette* are becoming commonplace terms. Computer-related language is also being used to construct new metaphors. "Let's *delete* that comment from our *memory space*" represents an example of the application of computer terms to human situations (not computer situations).

See also CREOLE.

Haugen, Einer. (1950) *The Analysis of Linguistic Borrowing.*

Holm, John. (1989) *Pidgins and Creoles.*

Labov, William. (1963) "The Social Motivation of a Sound Change." *Word* 19: 273–309.

———. (1972) "On the Mechanics of Linguistic Change." In *Directions in Sociolinguistics: The Ethnography of Communication*, edited by John Gumperz and Dell Hymes, 512–538.

Lehiste, Ilse. (1988) *Lectures on Language Contact.*

Trask, Robert. (1994) *Language Change.*

Voegelin, C. F., and F. M. Voegelin. (1977) *Classification and Index of the World's Languages.*

LANGUAGE DIVERGENCE

See LANGUAGE CHANGE.

LANGUAGE DOMINANCE

Language dominance occurs in situations in which one language is spoken more frequently by a larger number of people than is the case for other languages in a given region or country. The term *dominance* also implies that in such situations, minority languages can be viewed as less important by the dominant population. Expressions of language dominance range from folk beliefs about language superiority, such as when the language of the dominant population is viewed by the dominant population as superior to all other languages, to absolute legal domination, such as when a government makes a dominant language that country's official language.

LANGUAGE FAMILIES In the late eighteenth century Sir William Jones, a British magistrate working in India, noticed that some Hindi words (the dominant language of India) shared some similarities with English and other European languages. After carefully listing basic terms (such as number and kin terms) from numerous European and South Asian languages (mainly Hindi and Panjabi), Jones concluded that these languages were distantly related. For example, the English term for father resembled the same terms in other languages (*pater* in Latin and Greek and *pita* in Sanskrit [Old Hindi]). Other kin terms for these languages showed similar patterns. He also concluded that these languages must have emerged from some common linguistic source, an earlier first protolanguage. This earlier language Jones labeled "Indo-European." Throughout the century that followed, scholars who were stimulated by Jones's discovery

set about to find relationships among many of the world's languages. The linguistic approaches spawned by Jones and subsequent linguistic scholars who shared interest in describing language families eventually developed into contemporary historical linguistics. Historical linguists compare various languages in an attempt to determine whether or not relationships (historic/genetic) exist among the languages being studied.

Much of the initial groundwork for historical linguistics was established during the latter half of the nineteenth century (particularly from the 1860s on). At that time many American language scholars were concerned with the dying out of Native American languages. As Euro-American settlers moved west across the prairies to the Pacific coast and U.S. military forces engaged native peoples in a continuous series of violent conflicts, native culture and language use began to decline. As news of the displacement and decline of native cultures spread east, numerous linguistic scholars set out to record and curate (save) native languages. These incipient (first-stage) linguistic studies depended to a large extent on field methods based essentially on descriptions of words (vocabulary lists) and crude alphabets for describing phonetic elements. Through time these methods were refined. In addition, as these early linguists began to compare their findings they noticed recurring patterns in many of the basic terms for certain languages. On the basis of these observations (like Sir William Jones's organization of Indo-European languages) many Native American languages were grouped according to assumed historic relationships. These groupings are typically called "language families."

Language families are determined to exist when different languages share numerous recurring elements—sound, grammar, and particularly basic words. For example, the words for "stone" show similarities across languages subsumed under the Uto-Aztecan family: *tippi* (in Mono), *timpi* (in Shoshone), and *tibiri* (in Kawaisu). On the basis of these similarities, American linguists working early in the twentieth century proposed several large native language families. Working through such comparative methods historic linguists have been able to organize the indigenous languages of North America into recognizable language families. In the Northeast, Algonkian and Iroquoian languages dominate. In the Southeast, Muskogean, Iroquois, and Sioux are present. The Southwest, California, the Great Basin, and the Pacific Northwest coast have a wide variety of language families including: Athapaskan, Hokan, Penutian, Salish, Uto-Aztecan, and Wakashan. Most historical linguists interested in the original languages of North America assume that this high degree of linguistic diversity indicates a long period of development and linguistic divergence in the New World.

Although most historical linguists believe that a large number of native language families exist, some disagree. The linguist Joseph Greenberg, for example, who first became well known for his classifications of African languages, has posited three major language families (superfamilies) for the New World. Greenberg's analysis of basic vocabularies (composed of kin terms, body part names, and other basic word groups) indicates that all precontact New World languages can be grouped into Aleut-Inuit (Eskimoan), Na-Dene (all the Athapaskan languages), and Amerind (all other native languages). Greenberg's classifications for Native American languages are highly controversial. Critics of his classifications have pointed out that often languages seem to be related when in fact they are not, such as when language systems converge accidentally on similar linguistic forms. These critics have argued that much of Greenberg's linguistic data are made up of these coincidental similarities.

Most comparative historical linguists use methods that seek to discover similar elements in the languages being compared. This involves examining similarities in words (especially basic words that can be organized into semantic categories—words for body parts, personal pronouns, kin terms, color terms, and so forth), sound elements, and grammar. When the initial comparisons are worked out, linguists organize the sample languages according to their genetic (historic) relationships to one another. This process has involved the development of taxonomic categories for grouping languages. At the most general level (where old and distant relationships among languages are thought to exist) is the *phylum*. The linguist Edward Sapir, in 1915, proposed that many languages could be subsumed under this type of general heading. Sapir proposed phyla such as Na-Dene and Wakashan-Algonkian. Other phyla were subsequently proposed for New World languages: Macro-Penutian, Macro-Siouan, and Aztec-Tanoan. Classifying languages at the phylum level has not been embraced by many comparative linguists; most recognize the language *family* as the most useful level for organizing languages that appear to be related. A language family, sometimes called a language stock, typically is made up of languages for which substantial evidence of relatedness exists. Subsumed under language families are language *groups*. Language groups represent regional varieties of mutually intelligible languages (often referred to as regional dialects, for which there is mutual comprehension among speakers of these varieties, but differences in pronunciation are recognized). Comparative linguists also categorize language subvarieties according to differences in speech that result from class differences. Language varieties at this level are called sociolects.

Through using these methods and categories, comparative/historical linguists have grouped many of the world's languages. In Africa the dominant language families are Niger-Congo (of western-central and southern Africa), Khoisan (spoken by hunter-gatherer groups in the Kalahari Desert and Tanzania), Nilo-Saharan (spoken by many of the pastoral, cattle-herding groups of central-eastern Africa), and Afro-Asiatic (made up of languages spoken in northern Africa, extending into the Middle East). In Asia, Sino-Tibetan languages dominate (the Chinese languages make up most of this family). Also in Asia and the South Pacific are Austronesian, Austro-Asiatic, and Dravidian languages. In central-northern Asia, Ural Altaic languages are spoken (these extend into Persia [Turkic], Europe [Magyar of Hungary], Finnic [of Finland], and Lapp [of northern Scandinavia]).

Many of these classifications remain controversial. With the use of modern computers and through development of more comprehensive language databases, however, many of these controversial classifications may eventually be resolved. In the 1990s the linguist James Matisoff began compiling a large database composed of all known languages of the world. Through his "megalocomparisons" (comparing large numbers of words from different languages), he and his colleagues hope to refine and revise our classifications for many of the world's languages.

Campbell, George L. (1995) *Concise Compendium of the World's Languages.*
Greenberg, Joseph H. (1963) *The Languages of Africa.*
————.(1987) *Language in the Americas.*
Hock, Hans Henrich, and Brian D. Joseph. (1996) *Language History, Language Change, and Language Relationship: An Introduction to Historical and Comparative Linguistics.*
Jones, Sir William. (1786) *The Third Anniversary Discourse on the Hindus.*
Matisoff, James A. (1990) "On Megalocomparison." *Language* 66: 106–120.
Miller, Wick. (1983) "Uto-Aztecan Languages." In *Handbook of North American Indians*, vol. 10, *Southwest*, edited by Alfonso Ortiz, 113–124.
Sapir, Edward. (1921) *Language.*

LANGUAGE MAINTENANCE

Language maintenance, or language conservation, refers to efforts made to keep languages from disappearing. In the past, many languages have become extinct. The Yana and Yahi languages of northern California, for example, died out during the early part of the twentieth century. The linguist David Crystal estimates that by the end of the twenty-first century "one-half of the world's 6,000 or more languages may be extinct." Efforts are currently being made to preserve endangered languages. These efforts involve the development of bilingual educational programs, recording and curating native languages, and encouraging cross-generational use of native languages.

Most of the world's languages that are defined as endangered are associated with small-scale traditional societies; however, some languages spoken by members of relatively large modern populations are also in danger. For example, although a significant number of people in the British Isles speak several varieties of Celtic languages (Cornwall, Irish, Scot, and Welsh), large numbers of younger members of these speech communities speak English only.

In North America, the Native American Salishan family of languages is losing significant numbers of primary Salish speakers as well. At one time Salish languages dominated much of the Pacific Northwest and the plateau regions. Currently, only a small fraction of this original population speaks Salishan languages. Although the task is immense, many linguists feel that language maintenance projects can succeed if they are properly administered and funded.

Crystal, David. (1997) *Languages: When the Last Speakers Go, They Take Their History and Culture.*

LANGUAGE SOCIALIZATION

See LANGUAGE ACQUISITION.

LANGUAGE VARIATION

Differences in pronunciation, grammatical form, and meaning represent what linguists call language variation. Language variation is typically described through grouping language and speech at various levels of intelligibility (comprehensibility). For example, separate languages such as Spanish and Mandarin (Chinese) are not mutually intelligible. Therefore these two languages represent variety in the extreme. In contrast, variety expressed at the dialectical level is not extreme because intelligibility is not lost. For example, dialects of spoken British English vary somewhat from region to region. In most instances speakers of different varieties of British English can understand one another. In some cases, however, these differences in speech (varieties) can approach mutual unintelligibility. Cockneys who live in London's East End and who speak an archaic urban variety of English may not understand what someone from Yorkshire (in the north) is saying when conversing. Cockneys are also members of the lower working class, and hence their variety of speech is sometimes called a sociolect.

Currently, linguists prefer using the term *variety* over *dialect*. There has been much abuse of the terms *dialect* and *language* among linguists and others. For example, Scandinavian languages, although mutually intelligible, are often classified as separate languages. Conversely, many of the Chinese languages are referred to in historical literature as "different dialects," when in fact they are not mutually intelligible.

See also LANGUAGE CHANGE.

LINGUA FRANCA Languages that permit communication across linguistically diverse populations and regions are called lingua francas. Lingua francas, sometimes called trade or link languages, often allow widespread communication for the purposes of carrying out trade or international diplomacy. Swahili, for example, is a language used throughout a wide area of central Africa. The use of Swahili permits widespread communication for various African populations whose primary languages are not mutually intelligible. Other examples of lingua francas include Javanese (used as a trade language throughout much of Indonesia), Nahuatl (the language of the Aztecs), and English (which is rapidly becoming a global lingua franca).

LITERACY Having the ability to read, write, and generally comprehend written language is literacy. Sometimes the term *functional literacy* is used to refer to the minimal level of competence needed to read and write. Because literacy implies the existence of writing systems, the term is usually applied only to societies that have writing systems. Recently, however, some linguists (specifically sociolinguists) have used literacy as a conceptual tool for describing the construction and use of verbal texts in strictly oral societies (societies without writing).

Conventional studies of literacy have focused on the role that written materials have played in the education of members of society. Since the 1970s this general concern has been extended to include cross-cultural studies of literacy. Cross-cultural studies have tended to focus on literacy socialization, that is, the ways in which culture prescribes subtle uses for written materials and how those cultural rules are imparted to younger members of society. For example, the linguistic anthropologist Shirley Brice Heath has researched differences in the ways in which working-class whites and blacks (African Americans) from the Carolinas (both North and South) use written materials in their respective households. She found that the working-class whites used a relatively wide range of written materials as part of their household communication. Parents left notes for their children, Bibles were often left out, and storybooks were used to tell and retell children's narratives. Written materials were also used in the working-class African American communities, but written sources of information were typically used less than oral forms of communication.

According to some researchers, many societies that are traditionally oral have experienced difficulties in acquiring literacy skills. Robert Shuter, an intercultural communication specialist, has observed American Hmong (a Laotian

Despite their household and maternal duties, these Latin American women apply themselves to the important task of learning to read and write.

immigrant population) learners having difficulty with literacy. Shuter attributes this difficulty to what he calls residual orality, the retention of cultural traits exclusive to oral societies. In this case American Hmong retain some cultural characteristics of the more traditional oral traits associated with strictly Laotian Hmong. Shuter points out that traditional patterns of Hmong communication are based on *situational* and *narrative* formats; moreover, these cultural patterns conflict with Western patterns of literacy, which he describes as "categorical, detailed, and, at times, ab-

stract and conceptual." The author of this volume disagrees with Shuter's assessment. Findlay has observed that although the traditional Hmong pattern for communication is essentially oral, the Hmong have had a significant history of exposure to various writing systems, including the use of a romanized script system developed for the Hmong by missionaries in the early 1950s. Findlay has also observed that when American Hmong students are engaged in either oral or written communication, they are as "categorical," "detailed," and "abstract" as their non-Hmong classmates.

Moreover, Findlay has noted that most American students (from various ethnolinguistic backgrounds) are largely oral in terms of their overall orientation to communication (talking in the halls, playgrounds, and at home); it is only during actual school hours in class that a literate orientation dominates.

Observing that stark differences between oral and literate societies may have been exaggerated by some scholars does not, however, suggest that culture plays no role whatsoever in the acquisition of literacy skills. Much educational policy regarding literacy is still based on the assumption that most children acquire literacy skills in much the same way. Many anthropologists working in educational research challenge this notion, favoring the view that culture plays a significant role. These anthropologists point out that literacy itself is a culturally based phenomenon that to some degree regulates how literacy skills are acquired. Anthropologists such as Shirley Brice Heath, mentioned above, are interested in describing how writing is used across a variety of cultural and situational circumstances, recording people's perceptions of writing (especially whether or not they view writing as important), and observing how culture influences the process by which literacy skills are acquired.

Findlay, Michael Shaw. (1992) "American Hmong High School Students: An Ethnographic Study of Communication and Cultural Adaptation." Ph.D. dissertation, University of Oregon.

Heath, Shirley Brice. (1993) *Ways with Words: Language, Life, and Work in Communities and Classrooms.*

Shuter, Robert. (1991) "The Hmong of Laos: Orality, Communication, and Acculturation." In *Intercultural Communication: A Reader*, 6th ed., edited by Larry A. Samovar and Richard E. Porter, 270–276.

| MEANING | Meaning generally refers to the content of messages |

conveyed through language or some other form of communication. Linguists describe and analyze meaning at two levels. First, linguists describe a language's morphology. Generating a description of morphology involves isolating minimal units of language that carry recognizable meaning. These units are called morphemes. In English, for example, the words *house, dog,* and *tree* are all morphemes because they carry meaning. Some morphemes cannot stand alone and carry meaning, and only obtain meaning when they are attached to specific words. *Pre,* for example, only makes sense in English when it is attached to the front of certain other words (such as *pregame, preview,* and *prejudice*). Morphemes that have meaning only when they are attached to other words are called *bound morphemes.*

Morphemes that can stand alone as single words (such as *house, dog,* and *tree*) are called *free morphemes.*

The second and more complex level of description and analysis of meaning is semantics. Semantics is the study of meaning as it emerges through understanding content relationships among words and how words are used in either sentences or longer strings of discourse such as paragraphs, narratives, and so forth. To illustrate, the word *cat* can be defined by definitions typically found in dictionaries. However, if someone says, "That *cat* can really play piano," the person speaking is not literally referring to the feline mammal that is usually associated with the word *cat.* The speaker is using a vernacular form of the word to refer to a jazz musician (a term more common during the late 1950s and the 1960s). In this example the word *cat* has an extended meaning.

Semantics also involves describing how words relate to one another by way of general to specific dimensions of meaning. For example, the word *tree* is a general cover term; more specific terms such as types of trees—*oak, maple, pine*—are subsumed under the more general term. Taken together (cover terms and more specific terms), these words make up a *semantic field.* The ways in which semantic fields are structured vary considerably cross-culturally. Kinship systems, for instance, are organized into semantic fields. In some cultures many kin terms are used to indicate members of the same sex and generation. Many Southeast Asian and Polynesian societies use kin terms in this manner. Thus, the term for father is extended to all male members of one's father's generation (with qualifiers added to indicate differences in specific relationships). These kinship systems and their Western counterparts (such as European and North American) are essentially organized into semantic constructions (fields) that convey meaningful relationships among words—in this case kin terms.

Some semanticists are interested in metaphors. Metaphors are expressions (or words) that convey meaning figuratively (not concretely). The linguists George Lakoff and Mark Johnson have observed that all human languages use metaphors to communicate meaning at various levels of abstraction from concrete reality. English speakers, for example, use prepositions as metaphors when the prepositions do not approximate the physical realities of the objects or conditions being referred to. In the statement "We were *on* the dole" (meaning taking monetary assistance), the preposition *on* implies that the "dole" is a surface (like a table or shelf). In reality the dole is not literally a surface, and therefore the preposition *on* functions as a metaphor (an abstraction or figurative expression rather than a statement of concrete physical reality) by implying that the dole has a physical surface. The preposition *in* often has metaphoric properties. When, for example, someone says "I am *in* trouble," the preposition *in* implies that "trouble" is a container. In concrete or real terms, *trouble* is a set of problematic circumstances for the individual in question, not a container, as the metaphor implies.

Studying the extensive use of metaphors in language has implications for cross-cultural studies of communication as well. For example, Lakoff and Johnson have observed that in some

language systems speakers do not include themselves as departure points (primary datum points) for referring to objects in the immediate environment. Hausa speakers of West Africa might say, "The ball is on the other side of the rock" even though, in physical terms, the placement of the ball is between the speaker and the rock. This cultural difference, contrasting with most European languages, in which speakers are the primary reference points, assumes another reference point, one other than the speaker, for referring to objects. Thus, the use of referential markers, like prepositions, have metaphoric properties. These differences are important to note because mistranslations can emerge when Hausa texts are translated into languages that discuss objects in relation to the person doing the speaking.

Linguists recognize that meaning is essentially culturally constructed. The relationship between meanings and the symbolic verbal patterns (spoken words, phrases, and narratives) to which they are attached is *arbitrary*. Arbitrariness in language means that it makes no difference what sounds are used to denote something (such as *house* in referring to structures that provide shelter); a language and cultural system could have just as easily incorporated sounds like *glop* to refer to shelters. We use *house* in English because that particular configuration of sounds has become the conventional pattern for referring to shelters in English. Arbitrariness is the central aspect of language that accounts for the fundamental sound/word differences among languages. The word for house in Spanish is *casa;* in Maya the word for house is *na.* Meaning, in this sense, is purely a function of learning the correct set of verbal symbols that are specific to a particular language. Meaning is not inherent in the form of the words themselves; it is always attached.

Arbitrariness is also apparent in the way various language systems divide reality into semantic categories. For example, Japanese speakers use the same color term for *blue* and *green*. English speakers use *blue* to refer to a single focal color and *green* for another focal color (focal colors are recognized as separate colors as opposed to gradient or in-between colors, e.g., yellow-orange or blue-green). The semantic boundaries that are made by both English and Japanese speakers (representing their respective languages) are for the most part arbitrary. Color differences between green and blue can be plotted along a color continuum (spectrum), and therefore the semantic boundary set up by the words *blue* and *green* (in English) is arbitrary.

Finally, linguists often distinguish denotative meaning (the precise meaning of words, statements, and so forth) and connotative meaning (where meaning is implied). In English, for example, the statement "The trash sure has been sitting there for a long time" denotes a factual claim. In contrast, the statement may also carry a connotative meaning: "Would you take out the trash!"

See also CONNOTATION; DENOTATION; ETHNOSEMANTICS.

Burling, Robbins. (1964) "Cognition and Componential Analysis: God's Truth or Hocus Pocus?" *American Anthropologist* 66: 20–28.

Gleason, Harold. (1961) *An Introduction to Descriptive Linguistics.*
Lakoff, George, and Mark Johnson. (1980) *Metaphors We Live By.*
Lewis, David. (1972) "General Semantics." In *Semantics of Natural Language,* edited by Donald Davidson and Gilbert Harman, 169–218.

MESOLECT

See CREOLE.

METALANGUAGE

Linguists use language to discuss language process. The language used to describe language is metalanguage (literally, language about language). Thus any terms that denote parts of language (verb, noun, sentences, and so on) or the dynamics of language (conversation, rapping, yelling, joking) are parts of a metalanguage.

METAPHORS

Metaphors are figurative forms of language that link concrete to abstract conceptual meanings. For instance, in the statement "The debate was heated," the term *heated* is used to indicate high levels of emotion; in this instance it does not literally mean hot or warm (as in physical temperature).

See also MEANING.

MNEMONIC

Linguistic or symbolic formulas employed to facilitate memory, often in the form of rhymes, are called mnemonic devices. The modern word *mnemonic* derives from the ancient Greek word *mnemonika*, which literally means "to sing." The association with memory was made when singing rhymes were used as tools for remembering specific information. Perhaps the best-known examples of mnemonic devices in English are the ABCs (the alphabet sung in a musical melody), "Every Good Boy Does Fine" (for lined notes in musical notation), and spelling out FACE (for spaced notes in musical notation). Mnemonic devices are often used to assist in tabulating large sets of numbers. For example, the use of tick marks (four ticks and a diagonal tick for units of five), according to the linguists Hans Hock and Brian Joseph, may be a conventional mnemonic device that has been in use for 10,000 years. The Incan quipu system of using color-coded knotted cordage to represent numerical information is an example of a complex mnemonic device.

In Japan specially constructed words are often used to remember highly specific information. For instance, words that label businesses are sometimes organized in such a way that the last four digits of the establishment's telephone number can be remembered. Anthropological folklorist Thomas Johnson has collected several examples of this type of mnemonic device. For instance, the spelling for the Japanese word for butcher shop *(nikuyasan)* becomes modified to indicate the last four digits of the butcher shop's telephone number: 2983 is represented as *ni* (which means 2), *ku* (9), *ya* [*yattsu* or *hachi*] (8), *san* (3), or, all together, *nikuyasan*. Thus, potential clients can use the unusual spelling to remember the butcher shop's number.

Hock, Hans Henrich, and Brian D. Joseph. (1996) *Language History, Language Change, and Language Relationship: An Introduction to Historical and Comparative Linguistics*.

Johnson, Thomas Wayne. (1997) "Japanese Mnemonic Devices." From the Folklore Archives at California State University, Chico.

MORPHOLOGY

See MEANING.

MOTHERESE

See LANGUAGE ACQUISITION.

MULTILINGUALISM

Having the ability to speak several languages is sometimes called multilingualism. The term *polyglot* is sometimes used to describe a person who speaks several languages fluently. Multilingualism has also been used as a guiding concept in conjunction with bilingualism to refer to educational approaches and philosophies pertaining to the teaching of second languages or to the teaching of linguistically diverse populations.

See also BILINGUALISM.

MYTHOLOGY

Mythology refers generally to the comprehensive body of knowledge held by a society or cultural tradition regarding their world-view—their descriptions of how the world (or the universe) came into existence and how the world works. Mythology is typically conveyed through extensive oral narratives and shorter stories. Myths, stories that convey mythic knowledge, can be divided into two general categories: cosmogonies, which are stories of creation, and cosmologies, which are stories about how the universe is structured and how it works.

The scholar Joseph Campbell has, through his many books on mythology, suggested that themes common to all of humanity are contained in myths found throughout the world. According to Campbell, themes such as "fire-theft, deluge, land of the dead, virgin birth, and resurrected hero have worldwide distribution." The constant recurrence of such themes suggests that either diffusion (spreading of thematic elements) has occurred or that storytellers tend to converge on themes that are common to the human experience in most parts of the world. Through cross-cultural analyses anthropologists, while recognizing that diffusion does occur, tend to support the idea that similarities in mythic stories arise independently. In other words, recurring themes result because storytellers react to conditions common to all or most human societies. For instance, Campbell has observed that many societies have stories about journeys to the world below. Individuals in the stories (presented as animal characters or as human beings) sometimes visit the underworld and return to the real (surface) world. This is the basic theme of the Greek myth of Orpheus. Orpheus strikes a deal with the gods so that he can go to the underworld and retrieve his wife, who is imprisoned there. Orpheus is informed that his wife, upon leaving the underworld, must not look back. Unfortunately for Orpheus, the moment before he and his wife emerge into the surface world, Orpheus's wife looks back and is condemned to live out eternity in the underworld. Orpheus, on the other hand, is allowed (at least for the time being) to remain in the world above. The Maya creation story, the *Popol Vuh*, has a similar theme. In the *Popol Vuh*, two boys who are described as twins are cast into the underworld. The underworld is governed by nine evil lords (the "lords of the night"), whom the twins must engage in a war of wits if they are to make their way out. One of the twins succeeds and is "brought back into the world of light." Although on the surface the story of Orpheus and that of the Maya twins are different—the characters are not the same, and the descriptions of the underworld are dissimilar—it is clear that a single thematic element is shared. In each of the stories an individual visits the underworld and returns. The presence of shared themes such as these suggests that shared elements serve a common function. Here it is quite possible that having characters return from the underworld serves a legitimating function in that "eyewitnesses"

Many societies have myths about journeys to the underworld. In many cases, individuals will visit the underworld and return to the real world. This is the case in the Greek myth of Orpheus, depicted in this seventeenth-century copper engraving, who tries to save his wife, Euridice, from Hades, but loses her when she looks back.

are needed to substantiate the belief in the existence of an underworld. Although the thematic elements in stories such as these are symbolic in nature, they are often interpreted as literal (referring to actual places and events). Having characters who have visited the underworld and returned provides a kind of proof (albeit in story form) of the existence of the underworld.

Some folklorists have observed that mythic stories sometimes function to reinforce existing cultural institutions. Amazon stories, for example (stories of past societies ruled by large women), may function to reinforce male dominance. Most Amazon stories point to a time in the past when women ruled over men; at some later time women were unsuccessful in maintaining power and the men took over. It is interesting to note that it is typically the men who tell such stories. Folklorists point out that the stories tend to reinforce male dominance because men can, through telling these stories, point out that the women had their chance but could not hold onto public power, and therefore men should retain this power. Folklorists call this type of story a "male-dominance ideology."

The Mehinacu, a horticultural group (they practice simple agriculture) who live in the Amazon Basin, have a set of Amazon stories that are told by the men. In these stories, there was a time in the mythic past when women controlled life in the villages. The women had control of the sacred flutes (long wooden flutes) and played them in their sacred houses. The men came to realize that the women did not play the flutes properly, so the men revolted and took the flutes away from the women. This, according

to Mehinacu men, is why men own and control the sacred flutes today. In fact, the women are not allowed to view the flutes; viewing the flutes might bring serious harm to the women who do so. Of course these are only stories, but they reflect the cultural attitudes held by the people who tell them.

Some mythic stories explain how human beings came into existence. These are cosmogony stories because they are concerned with creation. The Haida, northwest coastal Native Americans who live on the Queen Charlotte Islands off the coast of British Columbia, Canada, describe the emergence of humanity into this world as the result of the actions of a giant raven. In the beginning, Raven was flying high over the earth looking for food when he spotted a giant clam. Raven landed next to the clam and opened it with his powerful beak. Inside the clam was all of humanity. These original human beings crawled out of the clam and subsequently populated the earth. There is an element of cynicism in the Haida version of the story. It is often told as a form of social criticism. The release of humanity is viewed as a major event that has caused the world to be imperfect and full of strife and conflict. In this light, the story of the raven and the clam is similar to the Greek story of Pandora's Box, in which Pandora unknowingly releases chaos into the world.

Anthropological folklorists have sometimes interpreted various folk stories as containing mythic themes (mythic themes generally refer to ideas that address profound or fundamental ideas common to many people). The Paul Bunyan stories, for example, have been examined in terms of how North

Americans value work, their relationship to nature, creativity, and technological advancement. Paul Bunyan is seen as an archetypical North American hero because he has a vigorous work ethic, is able to control the whims of nature, is creative (he made the Grand Canyon), and uses tools effectively to exercise his control over nature. The author suggests that the Paul Bunyan stories tend to function to legitimize North American economic, political, and religious values. These themes might emerge out of a kind of Euro-American "manifest destiny."

Campbell, Joseph. (1969) *The Masks of God: Primitive Mythology.*

Findlay, Michael Shaw. (1989) *Paul Bunyan and the North American Ethos.* (unpubl.)

Gregor, Thomas A. (1969) *Social Relations in a Small Society: A Study of the Mehinacu Indians of Central Brazil.*

Swanton, John R. (1905) *Haida Texts and Myths.*

Tedlock, Dennis. (1985) *Popol Vuh: The Definitive Edition of the Mayan Book of the Dawn of Life and the Glories of Gods and Kings.*

All societies provide for ways of naming individual members. Names are given to people according to cultural rules, and these rules vary considerably across cultures. Cultural rules for naming can establish when names are given, who provides the names, how names are chosen, how the names are to be used in certain circumstances, and what types or forms of names can be used.

Naming, from a cross-cultural perspective, appears to serve a number of functions. First, naming is a form of referencing. Using names simply allows members of a society to identify other members. Names can also indicate how a person is situated in the overall social system of a society. Clan names, for example, mark a person's membership in a particular clan. Clan membership in many societies carries certain rules and obligations for social behavior. The exogamy rule (a person must marry out-

side of one's clan) is regulated by knowing the clan names of potential spouses. Clan names therefore serve the dual function of marking clan membership and facilitating marriage rules. Moreover, in some societies many names are gender specific—they are given either only to males or only to females. This generally allows a listener to know the gender of people being referred to before actually meeting them. In contrast, some groups use a high number of names that are not gender specific—names that may be given to both males and females. Among the various Apache groups of the American Southwest, interchangeable names tend to dominate. Some names can be conferred only on individuals who belong to particular age sets. Terms of respect, for example, may be added to existing names to indicate a person's status as an elder. English terms such as "Ma'am" and "Sir" serve this type of function. The use of such devices assists in setting up the appropriate modes for interaction across age, gender, and status dimensions. Using formalities such as "Ma'am" and "Sir" implies that a certain degree of respect is observed when younger individuals address elders. In contrast, nicknames and common names might imply social closeness (such as the way friends, peers, and close family members address one another). Some societies believe that names will determine the deeds or predispositions of an individual in life. Native American scholar Scott Momaday has observed that for his own group (the Kiowa) it is believed that names carry magical significance and that life will flow from the name. Momaday recounts that the storyteller who gave Momaday his name believes

Among the various Apache groups of the American Southwest, interchangeable names tend to dominate. Some names can only be conferred upon individuals who belong to particular age sets. Terms of respect, to illustrate, may at times be added to existing names to indicate a person's status as an elder.

that "a man's life proceeds from his name, the way that a river proceeds from its source."

Through a cross-cultural study of naming practices, Richard Alford has discovered that in 75 percent of the 60 societies included in the study infants are named at the time of birth or shortly thereafter. Nicknames may also be acquired by members of some societies. Typically, nicknames are given informally and are used more frequently in informal and mundane circumstances. In contrast, some societies confer personal names only after members pass through rites to adulthood or when individuals are inducted into special groups or secret societies (such as hunting cults and fertility cults of the Ndembu of Zambia, Africa). These rites often involve some form of significant trial; going through the rite and receiving a new name signals a culturally sanctioned change in a person's status.

In some societies a person can have several names at various times in his or her life. Among the Laotian Hmong, for example, a person receives a clan name at birth. The clan name is always passed down through the father's side of the family (patrilineal descent). A Hmong youngster sometimes receives a second name if he or she undergoes a curing ceremony when ill. Often the second name is associated with the village where the curing ceremony took place; in cases of serious illness the Hmong often seek the help of shamans (traditional healers) outside of their own villages. New Hmong names are also conferred on some when individuals get married (Hmong males typically receive a new name).

Among the Cheyenne of the American plains various names were given at different times in a person's life. Young Cheyenne males might receive a new name after they had their first "war path" (the first time they went into battle). The name given to a young warrior was usually selected by the family and often was derived from the name of an "outstanding predecessor." Before receiving an adult male name, kin names indicating parent-offspring relations (linguists call these *teknonyms*) were

used, especially when referring to infants. For example, phrases such as: "son of," "niece of," or "daughter of" could be used to refer to specific individuals who had not yet received their adult names or when kinship relations were being emphasized (as in the case of "son of . . ."—a father most likely has an adult name, so a son can be specifically identified through association with his father's personal names).

The Yanomamo of Venezuela and Brazil have a strict taboo on using the personal names of relatives who have died. In addition, courtesy and respect are demonstrated through avoiding the use of the personal names of living relatives (especially close relatives). The anthropologist Napoleon Chagnon had to throw out a year's worth of Yanomamo kinship data because his native informants (consultants) were inventing names to avoid the use of personal names associated with their close relatives.

Among the Ndembu of northwestern Zambia, Africa, individual members receive names through being incorporated into gender-specific cults (societies within societies). Males are given their adult names when they are inducted into the society of Ndembu hunters. Before receiving these names inductees must pass through a ceremony called *Mukanda*. This rite of passage into adulthood involves ceremonial circumcision and marks the individual as a full male adult in Ndembu society. Females pass through the "milk tree" ceremony *(Nkang'a)*. In this ceremony girls must lie still for long periods of time; any movement is considered a bad sign. After going through various stages of this rite of passage women may marry. Through all of this the women keep their family names because descent (tracing lineage) among the Ndembu is matrilineal. Public displays, by way of ceremonial dancing around a sacred milk tree, along with various forms of dress, mark these women as adult members of society. Thus overt public displays function much like implied categorical names in that the social status of these young women is being communicated to the larger community.

The Inuit (Eskimo) of the Arctic of North America provide names for infants within one month of birth. The names given are typically taken from recently deceased relatives or from dead nonrelatives who were highly respected in life. From the Inuit perspective naming a child in this manner allows the qualities of the deceased person to be transferred to the infant. Traditional naming practices among the Inuit are in decline. Many English names were introduced to the Inuit at the turn of the century, and today many Inuit receive Christian names after they are baptized.

Alford, Richard D. (1988) *Naming and Identity: A Cross-Cultural Study of Personal Naming Practices.*

Chagnon, Napoleon A. (1992) *The Yanomamo*, 4th ed.

Chan, Sucheng. (1994) *Hmong Means Free: Life in Laos and America.*

Chance, Norman A. (1966) *The Eskimo of North Alaska.*

French, David H., and Kathrine S. French. (1996) "Personal Names." In *Handbook of North American Indians*, vol. 17, *Languages*, edited by Ives Goddard, 200–221.

Hoebel, E. Adamson. (1960) *The Cheyennes: Indians of the Great Plains.*

Momaday, Scott. (1976) *The Names.*

Saville-Troike, Muriel. (1989) *The Ethnography of Communication: An Introduction*, 2d ed.

Turner, Victor. (1967) *The Forest of Symbols: Aspects of Ndembu Ritual.*

NARRATIVE

Extended forms of discourse, often oral stories, that convey information about past events or fictional events are called narratives. Narratives represent a communicative genre that exists in all human societies. Descriptions of battles, feasts, and communications with spirits and gods, as such themes emerge in various cultural settings, are often conveyed in narratives. The *Popol Vuh*, the creation story of the highland Maya of Guatemala, was told to Spanish translators in narrative form. Typically, narratives are lengthy, comprehensive stories that can communicate a wide variety of cultural themes.

Cross-cultural studies benefit significantly from narratives collected from native informants. Narratives provide extensive accounts of real and perceived events that are presented in context (the cultural context here is constructed by the informant through the telling of the narrative). Historians also make use of narratives for the purpose of reconstructing historical events for which few written accounts exist. For instance, the mass exodus of Southeast Asian refugees from Cambodia and Laos was not covered extensively by the Western media. What information we have comes largely from refugee accounts conveyed through narratives.

See also MYTHOLOGY.

Tedlock, Dennis. (1985) *Popol Vuh: The Definitive Edition of the Mayan Book of the Dawn of Life and the Glories of Gods and Kings.*

Tenhula, John. (1991) *Voices from Southeast Asia: The Refugee Experience in the United States.*

NATURAL APPROACH

See LANGUAGE ACQUISITION.

NONSTANDARD LANGUAGE

See STANDARD LANGUAGE.

NONVERBAL COMMUNICATION

Communication that is not conveyed in verbal language (that is, not in spoken words, sentences, and narratives) is called nonverbal communication. This form of communication includes not only physical gestures, such as using hands, arms, body posture, and facial gestures, but also alterations in the sound qualities of speech. Altering the sound qualities of speech is not considered verbal communication because communication at this level relies on changes in pitch, tone, intensity, and pause, and not on the words that are actually said. The manipulation of sound qualities as a form of nonverbal communication is sometimes called "paralanguage" or "prosody."

Communication specialists are interested in nonverbal communication for several reasons. First, a significant proportion of communication is carried out through nonverbal channels. Second, nonverbal communication reinforces ongoing verbal communication. For instance, while talking, people often use their arms, shifts in body posture, and facial gesturing to emphasize what is being said verbally. Moreover, nonverbal cues often reveal the emotional state of mind of a person who is talking or ready to talk. Finally, nonverbal communication varies considerably across cultures; intercultural communication specialists are interested in describing such variations for the purpose of enhancing communication across cultural and linguistic boundaries.

The most common form of nonverbal communication is physical gestures. Human beings and other primates often use their arms, hands, and fingers to convey basic information. Fingers, for example, are often used to indicate direction, to indicate numbers, and to signal upcoming verbal communication (raising a finger to obtain an audience's attention). Fingers (and in some cases toes) can also be used as forms of insult. In many parts of Southeast Asia—Thailand in particular—pointing fingers and toes at others is considered not just rude but highly insulting.

Many physical gestures carry culturally specific meanings. Culture influences the types of gestures selected for communication and constructs the meanings that are attached to specific gestures. For example, in Saudi Arabia and many other parts of the Middle

N 133

It's not difficult to figure out how 1961 baseball great Stan Musial feels about winning a trophy from a sports magazine. Nonverbal communication cues like Musial's include physical gestures and alterations in the sound quality of speech.

East, shaking the head laterally (from side to side) signals the affirmative *yes,* and nodding the head up and down signals *no;* these are exactly the opposite messages for head movements in Europe and North America as well as much of the rest of the world. Differences in meaning that are attached to recognizable physical gestures can, across cultural boundaries, produce a significant degree of miscommunication. For visitors to Saudi Arabia, who are not familiar with the local cultural rules for communicating through physical gestures, communication might be difficult and confusing.

Eye contact, or the avoidance of eye contact, is another form of nonverbal communication that is often influenced by subtle cultural rules. Among many Latinos (Spanish-speaking Americans from Mexico) direct eye contact with someone who is not a close relative or friend is considered disrespectful. Euro-American teachers sometimes demand that eye contact be established when a student is being reprimanded. From a Latino student's perspective, maintaining eye contact with a formal authority figure while being reprimanded constitutes a double offense. Among many Southeast Asians (such as the Hmong, the Mien, and the Vietnamese) eye contact with strangers is difficult to maintain because social ties between the individuals involved have not yet been defined. Many schoolteachers in the United States have reported that many Southeast Asian immigrant children in their classes will not initially look a teacher or other students in the eye. After these students become more comfortable in their new setting, as teachers have noted, eye contact is typically established more easily.

The anthropologist Edward T. Hall has observed that *proxemics* (spatial distancing among communicators) and body posturing and movement *(kinesics)* are, to a significant degree, organized by cultural-specific rules for interaction. Hall has observed that in many Arab countries a relatively close spacing between communicators is tolerated. In many parts of Europe and North America, in contrast, a greater distance between communicators is expected. Problems arise when members of these cultural groups attempt to communicate with one another. Those with an Arab background will attempt to get closer to those with whom they are interacting;

North Americans will back off, seeking to maintain a distance that is "comfortable" for them. Most people, as Hall points out, fail to recognize that the spatial distancing tolerated (or not tolerated, as the case may be) by people interacting is based on subtle differences in cultural rules. Each person participating assumes that his or her understanding of how distance should be maintained is what is normal.

The employment of alterations in sound qualities such as pitch, tone, pause, intensity, and extension (such as extending a vowel) is also considered to be a function of nonverbal communication. Use of such nonverbal sound qualities to reinforce what is said verbally or to communicate a hidden message is called *paralanguage*. Among British and English speakers, sarcasm is often communicated through manipulations of the conventional sounds that make up recognizable English words. For instance, if an English speaker wants to make fun of a person's car they might say: "Nice caaar . . ." extending the vowel to indicate that the person doing the talking does not think much of the car. In tonal languages (languages that mark literal changes in meaning through changes in tones at the ends of words) the use of paralanguage is seriously constrained; a shift in a single tone will literally change the meaning of a word. All Chinese languages (such as Mandarin and Cantonese) are tonal. Hence, in order to communicate, sarcasm speakers of Chinese languages rely on intensifiers—nonverbal paralinguistic cues that use stress (amplifying the volume)—or on words that subtly connote a sarcastic message. The same utterance used by English speakers ("nice car"), translated into English but with paralanguage noted, might be constructed by a Chinese speaker as "NICE car"; or using a different set of words: "This is the car that you will be using for a short time?" Without directly stating that the car is not a good one, the speaker has communicated sarcasm by suggesting that the person who is going to use the car will only be using it for a "short time."

The linguistic anthropologist Susan Philips has noted that nonverbal communication serves essentially three functions. First, as mentioned earlier, nonverbal communication imparts information regarding the emotional states of participants. Second, nonverbal communication indicates social relationships among participants (markers such as dress, hairstyles, body posture, and so on tend to serve this function). Finally, nonverbal cues facilitate the subsequent carrying out of talk; it signals that talk is about to begin and secures the attention of potential listeners.

See also COMMUNICATION; PARALANGUAGE.

Bliatout, Bruce, Bruce T. Downing, Judy Lewis, and Dao Yang. (1988) *Handbook for Teaching Hmong-Speaking Students.*

Hall, Edward T. (1959) *The Silent Language.*

———. (1963) *A System of Notation of Proxemic Behavior.*

———. (1966) *The Hidden Dimension.*

Malandro, Loretta A., and Larry Barker. (1983) *Nonverbal Communication.*

Philips, Susan Urmston. (1993) *The Invisible Culture: Communication in*

Classroom and Community on the Warm Springs Indian Reservation.

Samovar, Larry A., and Richard E. Porter, eds. (1991) *Intercultural Communication: A Reader,* 6th ed.

NOSTRATIC

Nostratic is the hypothetical language that some linguists believe is the mother tongue of all or most Old World languages. These linguists believe that Nostratic gave rise to the great language families of the Old World such as Indo-European, Altaic, Afro-Asiatic, and others. Linguists who subscribe to the idea that a Nostratic language existed and can be proved to have existed point to a few shared ele-

ments found in some modern languages. Most linguists, however, feel that if such a mother language existed—though all admit that it is possible—because of its assumed great antiquity, its existence and therefore its form (structure) could be scientifically reconstructed. These skeptics point out that shared linguistic elements can appear as a result of real historic relationships among contemporary languages and as a result of mere coincidence. Despite the overwhelming skepticism among linguists, a small group of Russian linguists still hold to the theory of a Nostratic language.

See also LANGUAGE FAMILIES.

and function of oratory varies across cultures; however, oratory generally functions to communicate public messages either to special groups (such as councils) or to entire communities.

Throughout New Guinea speech making is considered high art. Big Men (important men) in many New Guinean societies often deliver speeches at public gatherings to muster support for a wide variety of festivals. Among the Enga of the central highlands of New Guinea, speeches are used to settle disputes, organize gatherings, and, most important, to negotiate treaties and peace between warring groups. Among the Enga oratory can also be used as a kind of verbal warfare that serves the dual function of stating opposition as well as stating the terms (usually gift giving) of peace. The anthropologist Mervyn Meggitt has observed that "Big men of each force make speeches touching on the day's events and their outcome (a drawn match) and listing the dead. In these orations, aimed at their opponents as well as their own followers, they also set the scene for future exchanges of valuables between the two sides."

Among the traditional Iroquois of upper New York State and southern Ontario, Canada, speech making was extremely important. Most political persuasion, carried out in councils, was conducted through speeches designed to influence a speech maker's council peers. Joseph Brant (Thayendanegea was his Mohawk-Iroquois name) was famous for his oratory skills. Through the use of clever metaphors, logical argumentation, and a keen sense of politics (both Iroquoian and Euro-American), Brant was able to convince the

ORAL TRADITION

The passing down of cultural knowledge from one generation to the next through spoken forms of expression such as myths, folk stories, poetry, and sagas is what historians and anthropologists call oral tradition. It is generally assumed that throughout human history spoken forms of expression have been the primary means by which cultural knowledge is transferred across generations.

ORATORY

Oratory is the art of speech making. The ability to construct and deliver a comprehensive and articulate public speech is generally defined as having oratory skills. In many societies, especially those that do not rely on writing, oratory is the most important form of public address. The form

137

Oratory generally serves to communicate public messages either to special groups or to entire communities. Here, 1940 G.O.P. presidential nominee Wendell L. Wilkie addresses a gathering of well-wishers from the rear of a train.

Mohawk to remain on the side of the British during the American Revolutionary War. He is reported to have been able to deliver speeches in English, French, and in several of the Iroquoian languages.

Kehoe, Alice B. (1992) *North American Indians: A Comprehensive Account,* 2d ed.

Meggitt, Mervyn. (1977) *Blood Is Their Argument: Warfare among the Mae Enga Tribesmen of the New Guinea Highlands.*

ORIGINS OF LANGUAGE

Anthropologists and linguists have for many years wondered about the evolutionary conditions that might have stimulated the emergence of human language. Although no definitive explanation has been developed, paleoanthropologists, linguists, and evolutionary biologists have pointed to several key factors associated with human evolution that may, at least in part, explain how human language emerged. Perhaps the most important factor may have been the need among early hominids (early human beings) to communicate information at a level that was more detailed and differentiated than is the case for animal communication. For instance, early hominids might have had to use language to differentiate among various types of threats posed by different types of predators. Knowing the type of immediate threat from a particular predator and being able to communicate specific information about the nature of the threat might have provided a selective advantage for some early hominids, especially if they could not as individuals defend themselves.

This need for communicating more differentiated information (having words for a considerable range of objects and contexts in the world) stands in sharp contrast to the call systems of communication used by other animals. Call systems are closed systems of communication in which one sound (a call) carries only one general meaning (an alarm, a signal for bonding, and so forth). Other factors include the possible need among early hominids to communicate information about events that had not yet occurred (thinking and communicating in the future tense). Using language to refer to things, actions, and events in the future tense could be viewed as a selective advantage because early hominids could rely on linguistic structures to plan strategies for foraging. Moreover, having language capabilities that imply an awareness of the future suggests that language could have been used to refer to things not in the immediate visual field. In sum, human language, as it emerged at some point in human evolutionary history, provided its speakers with a significant degree of referential flexibility, since early hominids

were not limited to single calls that referred only to immediate time-bound events. These hominids could refer to things not immediately visible and they could talk about events yet to occur.

Various theories on the origins of language have been offered through the years. Early theories put forth in the nineteenth and the early twentieth centuries focused on single causes. For example, the *Ding-dong theory* assumed that human speech arose as a result of early human beings imitating various sounds in nature. This has sometimes been called the *onomatopoeia theory* of language origins. The English word *jay* (as in *jaybird*) denotes not only the bird but the recurring sound made by the bird as well. The *La La theory* is based on the assumption that human language emerged from singing. The *Yo-he-ho theory* holds that human language resulted from rhymes, in the form of sequences of sounds, performed by early communal societies while they worked. These theories are not based on empirical observation and contain obvious contradictions. With regard to the La La theory, for example, what could have been the possible linguistic content of the songs before language actually emerged? The Yo-he-ho theory does not tell us what the actual causal relationship is between work and the evolution of language; what force might cause language to result from work-related situations? Even in the mid–twentieth century simplistic models have been proposed. The linguist Charles Hockett proposed in 1960 that human language began to emerge when early hominids started "blending" calls. Blending occurs when two or more calls (from a call system) are combined to form an entirely new call. Hockett had observed blending among gibbons. The new calls supposedly allowed early hominids a greater degree of linguistic flexibility by providing a wider range of linguistic choices. Although these early theories are naive, they do suggest that people have been interested in the question of language origins and have, for a long time, spent considerable effort to produce explanations (although these explanations have often been somewhat misguided and provocative).

Since the 1960s more complex theoretical models have been developed to address the question of language origins. The most prominent theory, developed by the linguist Gordon Hewes in the early 1970s, is called the *gestural hypothesis*. The central assumption of the gestural hypothesis is that primates, and therefore early hominids, used finger, hand, limb, and facial gestures to communicate basic messages. Through time the use of the tongue became an extended part of this system of articulated gesturing. Eventually human beings became capable of using the tongue in conjunction with the rest of the vocal tract to articulate a wide range of contrasting sounds in the form of consonant and vowel alternations. This ability to articulate contrasting sounds, according to Hewes, is merely an extension of the gestural systems used by other primates. The significant difference between human and nonhuman language (communication) is that human articulated sound allows for an infinitely wider range of communicative cues, ultimately in the form of spoken words. Coupled with the mental ability to construct complex word relationships based on grammar and semantics, the ability to produce and use a wide range of contrasting sounds allows the production of what is essentially human language.

Human beings have the same set of organs in their vocal tracts as other primates. However, the arrangement of specific organs (tongue, glottis, and vocal cords) in humans is such that humans can, in general, produce a wider range of sounds than can other primates or animals. Perhaps the most important feature of the human vocal tract is the facility for producing consonants (the concise, distinctive sounds that contrast with vowels). The production of consonants provides a significant degree of flexibility in language and what is sometimes called "contrastive power." Contrastive power—using sounds that are markedly different from one another—provides human communicators with a sound system that makes it easy for listeners to hear differences in words. Other primates can produce only vowel sounds, which starkly limits their ability to rely on vocalization for purposes of communication. Most linguists concerned with the question of human language origins find it difficult to reconstruct how the human vocal apparatus evolved. These linguists can with some degree of certainty, however, suggest that the human vocal tract most likely emerged as the need to communicate more specific and complex information became more crucial for survival.

In general, the evolution of human language represents a trade-off of instinct for cognition (thinking). Human beings, unlike many other animals, are not capable of using the olfactory sense (the sense of smell) at a practical level to read the immediate environment around them. Moreover, human beings are not particularly fast runners compared to most other animals. The fastest human sprinters are at the slow end of the scale when compared to other animals (including other primates). These limitations may have created a selective pressure to maintain individuals in the population who could reason or think through critical problems. Thus, not having a keen sense of smell and being vulnerable to predators because of slowness might have selected in favor of creatures (early hominids) that could solve critical problems of survival through flexible thinking. The facilitation of problem solving on this order most likely required the development of an increasingly sophisticated means of communication. It is quite possible that human language evolved out of a more general evolutionary process favoring cognition over instinct.

Another possible factor in the evolution of human language may have to do with subsistence (how organisms get food). Some archaeological evidence suggests that early hominids (*Homo habilis* in particular) were scavengers, not hunters. If this was the case a community of these early hominids might have had to compete with predators and other scavengers for food. Lacking a keen sense of smell, not being able to run fast, and having insufficient strength to overpower their competitors made scavenging an extremely dangerous occupation for these early hominids. It is quite possible, therefore, that *Homo habilis* had to learn to read the environment to predict when and where food could be obtained safely. Strolling in on several large predator cats immediately after a kill might have proved fatal. Hence, reading variable conditions in the environment must have been crucial. For example,

viewing vultures in flight over a kill carries information about when and where the kill occurred. The particular pattern of the vultures' flight thus had symbolic content as long as there were creatures who could interpret the signs. Decoding symbolic systems—in this case natural signs—is a central function of language use. It is possible that for these early human beings, having the ability to decode events occurring in the environment served to select for an increased ability to process symbols, an important facet of human language.

When and where human language first evolved has not been determined with certainty. Scientists may never be able to answer this question precisely. The hominid fossil record, unfortunately, does not provide much information on this subject because evidence of language does not survive in material form unless it is written. Some paleoanthropologists (anthropologists who examine human fossil remains) have described and analyzed some indirect lines of evidence. Ralph Holloway, for example, has obtained endocranial casts (casts of the inside of the skull, showing the form of the brain) of a variety of early hominids and has attempted to reconstruct the organization of early hominid brain function by measuring the contours of the casts. In casts obtained from *Homo erectus* specimens (an early member of our genus), evidence of Broca's area, an area of the brain that is crucial for language production, is present. This evidence does not prove absolutely that *Homo erectus* had developed language on the order of *Homo sapiens* (us); it does, however, indicate that the *Homo erectus* brain was evolving in a direction that favored human language production. Some paleoanthropologists believe that human language is exclusively the domain of modern human beings *(Homo sapiens)*. Philip Lieberman has analyzed the bone forms of Neanderthals (an early form of human being) and has concluded that Neanderthals were not capable of producing full human speech. Lieberman's argument is largely based on his reconstruction of Neanderthal vocal tracts, which he claims could only produce a limited number of sounds (too few to produce complex human language). Critics of Lieberman's thesis have argued that his reconstruction of the Neanderthal vocal tract is flawed, pointing out that it is nearly impossible to reconstruct soft tissue forms solely on the basis of fossil bone materials. Moreover, these critics point out that even if Neanderthals could only produce a small range of sounds they still could have produced an infinite number of words and phrases as long as the sounds they used had contrastive power—that is, as long as the Neanderthals were able to produce consonants and vowel sounds. Lieberman's critics have pointed out that some contemporary languages have in their inventories only a small range of sounds (the Khoisan language, for example), yet speakers of these languages can generate an infinite variety of phrases and sentences.

In viewing the emergence of human language as an important part of human history, one fact is clear. As human groups began to spread throughout the Old and New Worlds, geographical isolation among human communities produced a significant degree of linguistic diversity. Today thousands of human languages are spoken throughout the world (although many languages associated with small-scale societies are disappearing). Although we may never have an accurate description of how human language evolved, we can study how contemporary human language families continue to diversify.

See also ANIMAL COMMUNICATION; COMMUNICATION.

_____

Armstrong, David F., William C. Stokoe, and Sherman E. Wilcox. (1995) *Gesture and the Nature of Language.*

Hewes, Gordon. (1973) "Primate Communication and the Gestural Origin of Language." *Current Anthropology* 14: 5–24.

Hockett, Charles F. (1960) "The Origins of Speech." *Scientific American* 203(3): 88–96.

Holloway, Ralph. (1985) "The Poor Brain of Homo sapiens neanderthalensis: See What You Please." In *Ancestors: The Hard Evidence*, edited by E. Delson, 319–324.

Lieberman, Philip. (1971) *On the Speech of Neanderthal.*

———. (1984) *The Biology and Evolution of Language.*

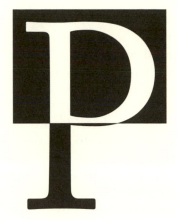

PARALANGUAGE Paralanguage comprises the nonverbal elements of speech, including intonation, pitch, intensity, and pause. Changes in intonation, for instance, can signal subtle changes in meaning. For example, sarcasm is often communicated in this manner. The term *prosody* is also sometimes used to refer to these paralinguistic cues. Prosodic cues (alternations in intonation, pitch, and so forth) are considered nonverbal elements because by themselves they carry no meaning; they are merely changes in sound contours that can signal subtle hidden messages such as sarcasm, doubt, sadness, and a wide range of human intentions and emotions.

See also NONVERBAL COMMUNICATION.

PATOIS

See DIALECTS.

PEJORATIVE Words or phrases that carry negative or insulting meaning are said to be pejorative (as in "pejorative language"). Whether a word or phrase carries a pejorative meaning or not usually depends on the intention of the person using the language and, to a significant degree, on the history of the pejorative use of a word or phrase. For instance, the Naskapi Cree (a Native American group) of northern Quebec Province, Canada, used the word *Eskimo* to refer to Arctic peoples who lived to the north of the Cree. Eskimo literally means "eaters of raw meat." Because during traditional times relations between the Naskapi Cree and the Arctic Inuit (Eskimos) were strained, the Cree use of the word *Eskimo* was intended to be pejorative.

Some words carry more pejorative meaning than others. Words that stigmatize various ethnic groups can often be considered so offensive that uttering them in most social situations is discouraged. Some words, such as *pushy* (for someone who is aggressive), although containing pejorative meaning, do not carry the same insulting power of other words. Moreover, the degree to which a word is considered pejorative can often be determined by context. The word *bitch*, for example, is often used in animal shelters to refer to female dogs. The term can also carry an extremely offensive (pejorative) meaning when it is used across a variety of social situations to describe female behavior. Some linguists have argued that although the word *bitch* might carry a different connotative meaning at an animal shelter, it still retains its pejorative attributes no matter what the situation might be and, unless it is used for purposes of linguistic analysis, should not be used at all.

PERFORMANCE

See DRAMA.

PHONOLOGY

See SOUNDS.

PHYLUM

See LANGUAGE FAMILIES.

PICTURE WRITING

Picture writing, using pictorial representations to convey linguistic information, is thought to be the most basic and perhaps the earliest form of writing in human history. Picture writing has been observed in many societies. Plains Native American groups used pictures painted on bison hides to convey basic information regarding clan labels, calendrics (calendar cycles), and hunting/war magic. True picture writing involves the use of pictorial representations that correspond to the word for the object being represented. A pictorial representation of the moon, for example, denotes the word used in a given language for "moon." Pictorial writing systems therefore are extremely limited in that symbols (pictures) can, with a few exceptions, be used only to denote objects; it is nearly impossible to find direct pictorial representations of most words in a given language. Although verbs can sometimes be indicated through pictorial representations of actions, other word types such as pronouns, some prepositions, and connectives are difficult to display through the use of pictures.

Historical linguists have observed that many of the world's written languages may have evolved from early pictorial writing systems. Overcoming the limitations of a purely pictorial system of writing must have involved the use of *rebus* constructions. A rebus construction involves the use of a pictorial representation to refer to other words or parts of words that sound identical to, but carry a different meaning from, the word associated with the object being represented. A drawing of a human eye, for instance, might be used as the first-person pronoun *I* in English. The picture symbol corresponds to a homonym for the picture/object. Rebus constructions can also be used to make up segments of compound words (complex words made by combining two or more words). A drawing of an eye combined with the drawing of a sickle could be used to denote the English word *icicle*. Rebus constructions are called *logographs* (sometimes *logograms*). Some of the world's great written languages are logographic in nature: Chinese, Japanese, and Maya spoken languages have been organized into logographic systems of writing.

Plains Native Americans used pictures, such as the ones depicted on this robe, to communicate basic information regarding clans, calendars, hunting, and war.

See also WRITING.

Salzmann, Zdenek. (1993) *Language, Culture, and Society: An Introduction to Linguistic Anthropology.*

PIDGINS Simple languages that emerge in multilingual situations are called pidgins. Pidgins have simple grammars and limited vocabularies. Most pidgins quickly evolve into *creoles* (composite languages with full grammars and complex vocabularies). Pidgins and creoles usually contain linguistic elements from the parent languages. Pidgins are spoken in such places as New Guinea (where they function as trade or link languages), Africa, the Caribbean, and many other parts of the world.

See also CREOLE.

PLAY LANGUAGE

Using language and speech creatively and for purposes of entertainment, through such expressive forms as poetry (verse), riddle making, improvisation, and joking, is play language (sometimes called *word play*). These basic forms of verbal expression—or *genres*—appear to be universal; however, the structure, contextual use, and cultural functions of play language vary across cultures.

Perhaps the most common type of word play found cross-culturally is verse (poetry). Using verse requires clever constructions of rhyme, meter (pacing), and metaphor. For some language systems verse is closely associated with everyday vernacular speech. Many of the Polynesian languages, for instance, when used in mundane or everyday settings, are spoken in verse. Therefore using creative metaphors, exaggerating descriptions of events, and generally organizing verbal language into aesthetic, artistic verse is part of normal speech throughout Polynesia.

In many cases the use of verse in non-Western societies differs significantly from its functions in European societies. The mixing of verse with domains of knowledge not normally combined in verbal and written texts in Western societies is found in many parts of the world. In India, for example, the ancient Hindus wrote their science in verse. Among some Native Americans calendrics (calendar cycles) were often expressed in verse form. Among the Hopi of the American Southwest the simple act of planting corn required the ritual use of verse in the form of praying.

The anthropologist Robbins Burling has suggested that various aspects of children's verse may be universal. Burling has observed that a 4/4 time signature (as in musical measures of beat) appears to recur in many societies. Burling notes that the four-beats-per-measure pattern can be found in children's verse (rhymes recited to children) among the Serrano (a native group of the desert regions of southern California), the Benkula of Sumatra (Indonesia), the Yoruba (Nigeria), the Trukese (South Pacific), and throughout many parts of the Arab world. The widespread distribution of this recurring verse-time pattern strongly suggests its universality, although this cannot be confirmed scientifically.

Word play can sometimes be expressed in the form of *argots* (secret or hidden languages). British Cockney prisoners being sent to Australia for imprisonment often used *Flash language* (named after a famous British prisoner) to hide messages from their jailers. Some linguistic historians have suggested that the Flash language evolved over time on board the prison ships as prisoners were being transported to Australia. Linguists have noted that much of the words (lexicon) of the Flash language derived from the Cockney variety of English. Its use among prisoners, however, extended beyond the Cockney population in the prisons, indicating that an extensive period of language experimentation must have occurred.

The use of language and speech as a form of informal competition also has been noted by linguists, anthropologists, and historians. The Inuit (Eskimo) of the Arctic, during traditional times, were observed engaging in song duels. Song duels were carried out by males who invented insulting verses, which they sang. The songs were typically directed at others, who were expected to reciprocate by delivering insulting songs in turn. The primary goal of song dueling was to create verses that might have an impact on a listening audience. A clever verse usually produced laughter. Although no official score was kept, an audience usually had a sense of who the winner was and acknowledged their approval through laughter and by observing which of the participants eventually backed down and conceded.

Doublespeak is also considered a form of word play. Doublespeak occurs when individuals construct utterances that seem to make sense but are actually nonsensical (illogical). Politicians in many societies sometimes seek to avoid public embarrassment by using doublespeak, especially when they must address topics in which they are not well versed. If the subject at hand involves a significant degree of technical terminology, a speaker can create the illusion of coherence by placing technical terms into cohesive sentences and using speech performances that imply a high degree of confidence (using nonverbal cues that imply that the speaker knows what he or she is talking about).

One of the most common forms of word play cross-culturally is punning. A pun is a humorous ending to a joke or story (sometimes called a punch line). Cross-culturally there may be a general tendency to use puns in conjunction with taboo language. Often puns are made through references to sexuality or fecal waste, insults to members of other ethnic groups, and other taboo topics.

Among the Southern Pomo (a native group of central northern California) puns were often used to ridicule their non-Pomo neighbors. One pun, recorded by the linguist Wick Miller, was (translated to English) "The south have shriveled testicles." What made this pun particularly humorous was that it was sung to the song of a meadowlark, although as puns are language and culture specific, the humor may be lost in translation.

See also ARGOT; AVOIDANCE; DOUBLESPEAK; JOKES; SONG DUELING.

Burling, Robbins. (1966) "The Metrics of Children's Verse: A Cross-Cultural Study." *American Anthropologist* 68: 1418–1441.

Chance, Norman A. (1966) *The Eskimo of North Alaska.*

Farb, Peter. (1978) *Word Play: What Happens When People Talk.*

Hock, Hans Henrich, and Brian D. Joseph. (1996) *Language History, Language Change, and Language Relationship: An Introduction to Historical and Comparative Linguistics.*

Miller, Wick R. (1996) "The Ethnography of Speaking." In *Handbook of North American Indians*, vol. 17, *Languages*, edited by Ives Goddard, 222–243.

POETRY Language that is organized into verse and is generally used as a form of artistic expression is called poetry. Poetic forms include short measured verse, long narrative verse, and highly abstract (sometimes unmeasured) verse found in modern Western societies (free verse). Across cultures poetry typically is presented in two basic forms: epic poetry and lyrical poetry. Epic poems are long oral narratives (typically mythic stories) told in verse form: the *Odyssey* and the *Iliad* of the ancient Greek tradition are examples of epic poems. Lyrical poems are relatively short verse recitations that possess a songlike quality. Sonnets, limericks, short poems like Japanese haikus, and song lyrics are a few of the types of lyrical poetry found cross-culturally.

Poetic forms of expression are designed to create new, insightful perspectives on topics that may or may not be conveyed through vernacular (everyday) language. Attention to rhyme, choice of special words, and use of abstract-metaphoric language help create the "specialness" of poetic language. Across a variety of cultural contexts, poetry might be used to communicate with supernatural forces, to consecrate marriages, to tell stories of epic proportions, to sing children to sleep, or to communicate the internal emotional state of the poets who recite verse.

Epic poems have been recited by storytellers in many parts of the world throughout human history. When writing systems arose in some parts of the world many of these epic stories were recorded in inscribed texts. The creation story of the highland Maya of Guatemala, the *Popol Vuh*, is an example of an extended epic verse that was recorded on ancient Maya pottery and has subsequently been translated into several modern languages, including Spanish and English. Because the original oral versions were recited in poetic verse, much of the aesthetic quality of the narrative has been lost. The anthro-

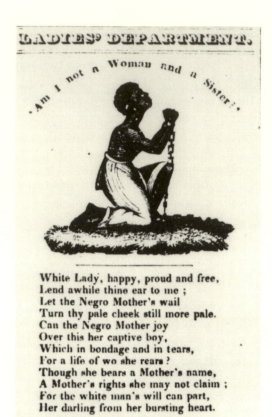

LADIES' DEPARTMENT.

"Am I not a Woman and a Sister?"

White Lady, happy, proud and free,
Lend awhile thine ear to me ;
Let the Negro Mother's wail
Turn thy pale cheek still more pale.
Can the Negro Mother joy
Over this her captive boy,
Which in bondage and in tears,
For a life of wo she rears ?
Though she bears a Mother's name,
A Mother's rights she may not claim ;
For the white man's will can part,
Her darling from her bursting heart.

From the Genius of Universal Emancipation.
LETTERS ON SLAVERY.—No. III.

Through the ages, poetry has played a significant role in communicating ideas. This poem, which appeared in the Ladies' Department of William Lloyd Garrison's The Liberator, *was intended to rouse antislavery sentiment by appealing to mothers' emotions.*

pologist Dennis Tedlock has translated the *Popol Vuh* and has tried to maintain the poetic quality of the story. Unfortunately, Tedlock has had to rely on older Spanish translations of the *Popol Vuh*, making some of the poetic reconstructions questionable. Tedlock has also attempted to translate contemporary Zuni (a Native group of the American Southwest) epic poems based on recitations obtained through actual written transcriptions and audio recordings. In these poetic texts much of the aesthetic qualities of the verse style have been maintained. For these translations Tedlock relied on transcribing the pacing, intensity (loudness), intonation, and rhetoric (internal logic) of the poems, thus keeping to some degree the aesthetic qualities of the originals.

Lyrical poetry has been observed and recorded by linguistic anthropologists and other scholars in many parts of the world. Dale Kinkade and Anthony Mattina, for example, have transcribed Salish (a set of linguistically related native groups of the Pacific Northwest and the plateau regions of North America) lyrical verse and, like Tedlock, have attempted to maintain the poetic qualities of the poems. Through placement of the verse in particular line and indentation formats, linguists interested in poetic style attempt to communicate the original intention of the speaker. The Salish verse "Chipmunk and Owl" is an example:

Oh, all right,
you take along that little basket
and you pick.
Pick
until you fill it.
Don't eat it
until you get back,
and we pray over it;
and afterwards we will eat it. . . .

Japanese haikus, as a concise form of lyrical poetry, do not focus on extensive, drawn-out abstract metaphors, as do many other types of lyrical poetry; instead, the emphasis in haiku is on short rhythmic verse (15 to 17 syllables) and on figurative language intended to cre-

ate a momentary—yet profound—response in the listener. The great seventeenth-century Japanese poet Basho used the haiku form to convey the Japanese sense of simplicity and conciseness of composition:

How still it is!
The cries of the cicadas
Stab into the rocks.

Poetry, in its many formats and through its use across a wide spectrum of cultural contexts, has played a significant role in communicating cultural ideas. Poetry has been used to communicate romantic love (particularly, although not exclusively, in Western societies), to send the dead to the spirit world, to provide emotional impact to political decrees (as in Thomas Jefferson's Declaration of Independence), to communicate cultural values to a society's young, and, more recently, to distribute ideas associated with contemporary popular culture (often through lyrics contained in popular music).

See also PLAY LANGUAGE.

Kinkade, Dale M., and Anthony Mattina. (1996) "Discourse." In *Handbook of North American Indians*, vol. 17, *Languages*, edited by Ives Goddard, 244–274.

Tedlock, Dennis. (1972) *Finding the Center: Narrative Poetry of the Zuni Indians*.

———. (1985) *Popol Vuh: The Definitive Edition of the Mayan Book of the Dawn of Life and the Glories of Gods and Kings*.

Welty, Paul Thomas. (1971) *Pageant of World Cultures*.

POLITENESS

Behavior that is courteous and respectful of others is polite. Politeness is reflected in language and communication in forms of address, in using inoffensive language in conversational interactions, and in generally avoiding taboo language. Politeness is sometimes used as a synonym for *euphemism*. Euphemistic language is acceptable in public use, whereas taboo or harsh language is less acceptable. In North America, for example, euphemistic terms for *bathroom* such as *rest room* and *little boys'/girls' room* are often substituted for *bathroom* and other, harsher terms.

All languages have terms and phrases that are considered polite or acceptable in public use; all languages also have taboo or avoidance terms and phrases. Sometimes in bilingual settings polite terms from one language may resemble taboo terms in another. The anthropologist Peter Farb has noted that the Creek (a Native American group of the southeastern United States) tend to avoid using the terms *fakki* (earth) and *apissi* (fat) because these terms resemble taboo English terms.

See also ADDRESS, FORMS OF; AVOIDANCE.

Farb, Peter. (1978) *Word Play: What Happens When People Talk.*

POSTURES

Body positions that communicate nonverbal messages are what sociolinguists call postures. The manner of stance, position of limbs, and use of fingers and toes to make gestures constitute posturing. Although it is difficult to substantiate scientifically, some basic postures appear to be universal in form and meaning. For example, standing up straight indicates respect and formality, and slouching (bending over in a relaxed position) indicates the opposite. Most posturing, however, is culture specific. The Hadza, a hunter-gatherer group of Tanzania, Africa, use certain postures when recounting a hunt. Hadza men strike a particular pose where their hips are pushed forward, and the back is curved (in the shape of a question mark) when they reenact the shooting of an arrow. This position is often struck when Hadza men tell such hunting stories.

Sometimes body posturing is used to demonstrate religious adherence. Orthodox Muslims, for example, kneel and bow toward Mecca (in Saudi Arabia); Mecca is considered to be the geographical and spiritual center of the Islamic world. In Japan, Shinto worshipers kneel before outdoor altars before they make offerings and prayers.

Barnard, Alan. (1992) *Hunters and Herders of Southern Africa: A Comparative Ethnography of Khoisan Peoples.*

Bradley, David G. (1963) *A Guide to the World's Religions.*

Malefijt, Annemarie de Waal. (1968) *Religion and Culture: An Introduction to Anthropology of Religion.*

Woodburn, James. (1968) "An Introduction to Hadza Ecology." In *Man the Hunter,* edited by Richard B. Lee and I. Devore, 49–55.

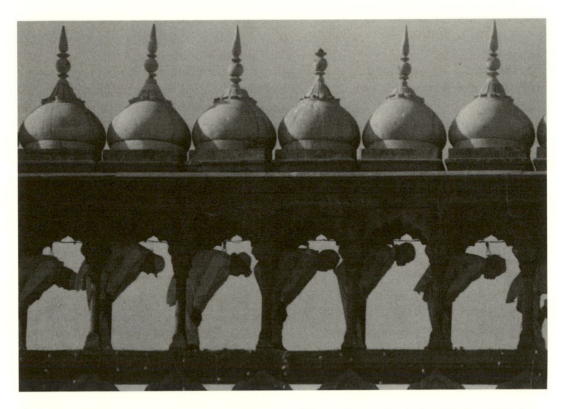

Sometimes body postures are used to demonstrate religious adherence as depicted by these Moslems praying on the occasion of Eid al-Fitr, which celebrates the end of the holy fasting month of Ramadan, the ninth month of the Muslim year.

PRAGMATICS

Pragmatics is a branch of linguistics that is dedicated to the study of language use. Pragmatics contrasts with formal linguistics, which focuses more on language form than on use. To illustrate, consider the following utterance: "The trash basket is full." On the surface the utterance appears to be a direct neutral observation. From the perspective of pragmatic analysis, however, the utterance may be an indirect way of suggesting that someone take out the trash (because it is full). The emphasis in this example is thus on the subtle use of language, not necessarily on the specific grammatical form of an utterance. Ethnographic studies of communication, sociolinguistics, and discourse analysis are all approaches subsumed under linguistic pragmatics.

PROSE

Written language that reflects mundane, common speech (vernacular speech) is called prose. Prose contrasts with poetry in that the former lacks the aesthetic qualities of poetry. The term *prose* comes from the Latin *prosa*, which literally means "straightforward."

PROSODY

The various features of paralanguage such as intonation, pitch, tempo, loudness, rhythm, and pause are called prosodic features (taken together, *prosody* or *paralanguage*). Prosodic cues, as they are sometimes called, are used to generate subtle messages. Sarcasm, exaggeration, and the emotional state of a speaker can be communicated through manipulating prosodic elements of speech. Prosodic cues and paralanguage in general are considered nonverbal elements of speech.

Linguists working cross-culturally or with single languages have found that describing how speakers utilize prosodic features to alter messages is an important part of understanding human communication. The form and functional use of prosodic features vary considerably across cultures, and in fact the use of prosodic features may be limited by the structure itself of the parent language. For example, tonal languages (languages in which the concise meaning of a word will change according to changes in ending tones) cannot make use of changes in tone as prosodic features. In tonal languages the change of a tone signals a real or explicit semantic change. In nontonal languages, such as English, the prosodic use of tones can be used to change implied meanings (for conveying sarcasm, doubt, joy, and so forth), but in tonal languages such as Chinese, Vietnamese, and Hmong, the only prosodic cues that can be used are loudness, tempo, pause, and whispers.

See also NONVERBAL COMMUNICATION; PARALANGUAGE.

PROTOLANGUAGES

Protolanguages are early singular languages that gave rise to subsequent related languages. For instance, approximately 8,000 years ago a group of people living in the northern region of the Middle East (present-day Iran) spoke a language we now call Indo-European. This protolanguage gave rise to most languages now spoken in Europe and beyond, including German, English, and Latin- and Slavic-based languages. Indo-European is also the source of many languages found in India (such as Panjabi and Hindi).

See also LANGUAGE FAMILIES; ORIGINS OF LANGUAGE.

PROVERBS

Proverbs are short sayings that make use of figurative language to convey a general truth or conventional wisdom. Unlike riddles, in which answers are not provided, proverbs provide both questions and answers.

The anthropologist Peter Farb, in his book *Word Play* (1978), describes a West African Yoruba proverb. A mother laments that her son is "young and foolish and therefore should be indulged." The father counters with the Yoruba proverb: "Untrained and intractable children would be corrected by outsiders." Translated into a recognizable English idiomatic form, the Yoruba proverb means: "If we can't raise our children with discipline the community will have to do it."

Proverbs are quite common across cultures. Moreover, proverbs function to convey basic cultural values. Among English-speaking Americans, for example, proverbs are often used to reinforce cultural values: "The pen is mightier than the sword"; "Don't cry over spilt milk"; "Idle hands are the devil's workshop." In these proverbs several recurring cultural themes are communicated. The first conveys the idea that it is wiser to collect one's thoughts and challenge an opponent through writing and civil discourse than to be hasty and brash. The second suggests that for problems that cannot be corrected a person must learn to move on, to get beyond the problem. The third proverb stems from a long Protestant tradition in parts of Europe and in the United States that values hard work (the "Protestant work ethic").

PROXEMICS

In communication studies the description and analysis of the spatial-physical relationships among communicators is called proxemics. Proxemics generally refers to the actual distance between speakers as well as such spatial patterns as angle and direction. For example, the sociolinguist Deborah Tannen has noted that Euro-American men do not typically face one another directly when they are talking. Instead, American men tend to face outward, away from one another and only occasionally glance at each other. According to Tannen they are careful to avoid excessive direct eye contact. The anthropologist and linguist Edward T. Hall has noted that people from various Arab countries, especially the men, tolerate a much closer distance when talking than do Euro-American men. Moreover, Arab men often look directly at one another when they are conversing. Hall has noted that proxemics provides insight into the subtle cultural rules that regulate communicative interaction. Hall has also noted that when people of differing cultural backgrounds come together and attempt to communicate, the cultural rules for spatial patterning can often cause a significant degree of confusion and frustration for the participants.

See also NONVERBAL COMMUNICATION.

Hall, Edward T., and Mildred Reed Hall. (1994) "The Sounds of Silence." In *Conformity and Conflict: Readings in Cultural Anthropology*, edited by James Spradley and David McCurdy, 61–72.

Tannen, Deborah. (1990) *You Just Don't Understand: Women and Men in Conversation*.

PUN

A pun is the humorous use of a word that sounds like another word (a homonym) but carries a different meaning. In general, puns are clever, surprise endings to riddles and jokes. They are found extensively across cultures and are language specific (they generally make sense only in the language of their origin).

See also PLAY LANGUAGE.

deep reflection," the word *deep* qualifies the word *reflection*. The type or quality of reflection was qualified to suggest a profound reflection at this somber occasion. All language systems make use of qualifiers.

Most qualifiers are adjectives (such as *gracious, impolite, rough, smooth,* and so forth). However, in some languages adjectives—and therefore qualifiers—may function more like verbs of being. This is the case for many Southeast Asian languages. In Hmong (a highland Laotian language), for example, the statement "He is tall" literally translated into English would be "He is talling" and would mean essentially "He is in the state of being tall." Thus, the adjective *tall* qualifies the subject *he* but does so as an irregular verb.

QUALIFIER A qualifier is a word or phrase that influences the meaning of other words or phrases. In the sentence "The funeral was an occasion for

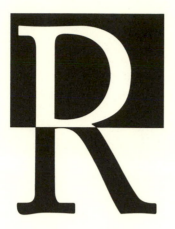

Most reconstructions have been conducted through descriptions and analyses of early writing systems. This is the case for Old English, Old Persian, Sanskrit (ancient Hindi), Egyptian, and Classical Maya. At the time that Old English was spoken (from A.D. 850 to A.D. 1100), the spelling of words had not yet been standardized. Although spelling was often inconsistent, the letters used for constructing words corresponded more closely to the manner of everyday pronunciation than contemporary standardized spellings do in English. In some cases the modern spelling closely resembles the original pronunciation. The English word *boat* was originally pronounced *bo-aht;* both the *o* and *a* vowels were pronounced in the Old English version. Some historical linguists even claim it is possible to reconstruct regional varieties of Old English by noting differences in spelling from region to region.

Finally, some reconstructions are made by describing modern languages that have not undergone significant linguistic change through the years. Fresian, a language spoken by a group of people living on islands off the coast of the Netherlands, is thought to be closely related to Middle English. The Fresian pronunciation of such words as *cow, boat, milk,* and *cup* corresponds closely to Middle English spellings for those words.

Hock, Hans Henrich, and Brian D. Joseph. (1996) *Language History, Language Change, and Language Relationship: An Introduction to Historical and Comparative Linguistics.*

REBUS

See PICTURE WRITING; WRITING.

RECONSTRUCTION

Reconstruction refers to the methods and outcomes associated with describing preexisting languages. Languages that are no longer spoken can, according to some linguists, be reconstructed through analysis of early writing systems and by comparing existing languages that are related to earlier protolanguages. In the field of linguistics reconstructions of early languages are controversial. Many linguists feel that reconstructions are not obtainable, that what some linguists call reconstructions are merely the results of guesswork.

REGIONAL DIALECT

See DIALECTS.

RIDDLES

A riddle is a type of oral folklore expressed in the form of a puzzle question. Riddles are similar to proverbs in that they convey general truths associated with the general folk knowledge of a given group of people. They differ from proverbs in that riddles are always stated in the form of a question, the answer to which is typically supplied through a reply from a listener (although the answers to many riddles are supplied rhetorically by the person initiating the riddle). A common English riddle is as follows: "When is a door not a door? When it is ajar." Riddles are a common form of word play across cultures. In many societies riddles are used mainly by children; however, cross-cultural studies have also indicated that riddles are often used by adults in many societies.

Riddles always contain two basic elements. First, riddles are always offered in the form of a question. Second, riddles draw analogies between literal meaning and figurative (abstract) meaning. In the riddle mentioned above, the question "When is a door not a door?" forces the listener to imagine a *door* literally. The question is also a paradoxical contradiction ("a door not a door"), which leads the person who has to solve the riddle to a more abstract level of interpretation (a figurative level). The answer "When it is ajar" represents a clever play on words by implying two possible interpretations, one literal and one figurative: the door is *a jar* (as in a glass container), and the door is slightly open (*ajar*).

Linguistic anthropologists have observed that riddles function to assist children as well as adults in sharpening their linguistic and communicative skills. Sociolinguists (linguists who study language as a form of social interaction) have noted that riddles are sometimes used as a form of verbal dueling and thus function to influence status differences among members of a community of speakers. Among the Bantu of sub-Saharan Africa riddles can even be used as an oral form of team competition. Members of two teams compete through rapid exchanges of riddle question-and-answer volleys. These riddles are typically cryptic (short and brief) in nature. For example, questions are often conveyed through simple statements such as:

> Statement: "Invisible."
> Reply: "Wind."
> Statement: "Little things that defeat us."
> Reply: "Mosquitoes."

In southern Africa riddles are traditionally used to show off a person's knowledge of the natural surroundings. Among many southern African societies bird riddles are common. The person offering the riddle will name a bird and then produce a clever analogy with a known person. Listeners must try to guess to whom the riddle maker is referring. This type of riddle demonstrates a person's knowledge of birds as well as his or her skill at constructing an inventive riddle.

See also Play Language.

Farb, Peter. (1978) *Word Play: What Happens When People Talk.*

Salzmann, Zdenek. (1993) *Language, Culture, and Society: An Introduction to Linguistic Anthropology.*

clops, tries to avoid romantic temptations, and throughout must combat the constant mutinous tensions among his crew.

Sagas are also told in many non-Western societies. Among the Kaguru of eastern Tanzania, Africa, saga stories are used to explain their migration histories. Kaguru storytellers speak of ancient times when they lived in the northwest of Africa. Before settling in Tanzania they were wanderers who encountered numerous conflicts. The highland Maya of Guatemala use saga-like stories to tell their version of creation. In the *Popol Vuh*, the Mayan creation myth, hunter twins do battle with the evil lords of the underworld. Like Odysseus, they must show courage and use their wits to survive. In one episode the twins trick a helper of one of the evil lords by using light obtained from fireflies to create the illusion of lit cigars. The evil lord mandated that the twins had to smoke powerful cigars for a long period of time before they could pass upward to the next level of the underworld. By tricking the evil lord with the artificially lit cigars the twins were permitted to continue their journey and eventually reach the real world above.

Historians and scholars dedicated to the study of extensive narratives (sagas) have suggested that this type of story serves the people who tell them in numerous ways. Sagas often present fictional histories, which typically portray the storyteller's society in a favorable way. Moreover, through the recounting of the challenges in the stories, sagas also tend implicitly to convey the idea that life is full of obstacles to overcome. Thus sagas serve to communicate cultural values associated with work, perseverance,

SAGAS A saga is a long narrative story that describes major ongoing events such as wars, blight, famine, and the extended reigns of despotic and noble kings and queens. Sagas are usually stories that take place over long periods and always include the exploits of central hero figures who engage many of the challenges just mentioned. In the Western tradition the most famous sagas are the *Odyssey*, the *Iliad*, and the *Aeneid*. The *Odyssey*, originally told by the Greek storyteller Homer in the eighth century B.C., contains all the basic elements of a saga. Odysseus, the central hero of the saga, is victorious in the Trojan War (the story of which is told in the *Iliad*). After the war, the gods punish Odysseus for his excessive pride. Odysseus spends the next ten years trying to find his way home (Ithaca, Greece) by sailing from place to place without a clear sense of direction. On his journey he fights a Cy-

Homer's eighth-century Greek epic, the Odyssey, *contains all the basic elements of a saga. In this seventeenth-century copper engraving, Odysseus's ship passes the Island of Sirens, whose sweet song had the power to lure sailors to their death.*

and industry and present role models based on the personal integrity of the culture hero(s).

Obeidelman, T. O. (1971) *The Kaguru: A Matrilineal People of East Africa.*

Sandy, J. E. (1921) *A History of Classical Scholarship.*

Tedlock, Dennis. (1985) *Popol Vuh: The Definitive Edition of the Mayan Book of the Dawn of Life and the Glories of Gods and Kings.*

SAPIR-WHORF HYPOTHESIS

The assumption that language structures and organizes the way a person views the world is called the Sapir-Whorf hypothesis. This hypothesis is also called the *Whorfian* or the *linguistic relativist hypothesis*. The name of the hypothesis is taken from the linguists Edward Sapir and Benjamin Whorf.

The Sapir-Whorf hypothesis is a controversial idea, for it has been difficult to prove scientifically. The problem in obtaining scientific verification is that it is difficult to prove in concrete terms that people who speak fundamentally different languages actually perceive reality differently.

See also LANGUAGE AND CULTURE.

SARCASM

In communication, speaking negatively about someone or something through subtle forms of ridicule is generally called sarcasm. Because the construction of sarcastic messages often relies on subtle shifts in communicative cues (alterations in pitch, tone, pause, and so forth), interpreting sarcasm across cultural and linguistic boundaries is usually problematic. Hence, interpreting sarcastic messages sometimes depends on a person's ability to make sense of slight discriminating differences in communicative cues—cues that are often language and culture specific.

See also NONVERBAL COMMUNICATION; PARALANGUAGE; PROSODY.

SECOND LANGUAGE

See LANGUAGE ACQUISITION.

SEMANTICS

Semantics refers to the study of relational meaning (content) in language. Semantics does not necessarily refer to the specific meanings of words as they are defined in dictionaries (although the definitions of words are said to have "semantic attributes"). Rather, semantics describes and analyzes meaning in language as it exists in relationships among words, in sentences, paragraphs, and other extended forms of discourse. For example, the English cover term *house* represents the starting point for a "semantic field" composed of more specific terms for types of houses. Attempting to understand the meaningful relationships among general terms (such as *house*) and more specific terms (such as types of houses) is a function of semantics. All language systems construct meaning through semantic relationships.

See also MEANING.

SEMIOTICS

The study of signs (symbols) is called semiotics. Semioticians—people who study symbolic systems—are primarily concerned with describing and understanding the meaningful relationships among symbolic icons, their conventionally attached meanings, and the cultural use of specific symbols. The relationship between a sign and its meaning is in most cases arbitrary; there is no *inherent* meaningful connection between a sign and its meaning unless the icon is representational. For example, the Spanish word for apple is *manzana*. The English word for this type of fruit is *apple*. The two sets of sound symbols that make up these two words, although they refer to the same thing, are completely different. This explains in part why there exists a great deal of variation in pronunciation across different language systems. Icons for which inherent meaningful relationships exist (representational icons) are found in such symbolic representations as directional symbols (arrows pointing to the left or right), pictures of an outstretched hand for *stop*, and pictures of people working if road crews are at work on a particular stretch of road.

The assumed inherent relationship between signs and their meaning, however obvious, are still the result of human decision making; sometimes an assumed obvious connection between a sign and its meaning may lead to misinterpretation. For example, westerners (people from Europe and North America) assume that nodding the head up and down denotes *yes*, while lateral head waving denotes *no*. In many parts of the Arab world this assumption would be wrong; the exact opposite is true.

Semioticians are also concerned with social dimensions of symbolism. For example, the arrangement of desks into straight rows in a classroom carries the connotative meaning of formality. Arranging the same desks in the same classroom into a large circle or several smaller circles carries an implied meaning suggesting informality. Semioticians have also noted that the use of colors as symbolic communication is highly culture specific. For instance, in Korea black is worn at weddings because Koreans feel that black symbolizes life (black contains all of the colors). White, in contrast, is empty of life and therefore is worn at funerals.

See also SIGNS.

Hodge, Robert, and Gunther Kress. (1988) *Social Semiotics*.

Saville-Troike, Muriel. (1989) *The Ethnography of Communication: An Introduction*, 2d ed.

SIGN LANGUAGES

Sign languages, sometimes called signed languages, are systems of communication based on manual gestures. The gestures are primarily made with hands and fingers, although other parts of the body, such as arms, legs, and the

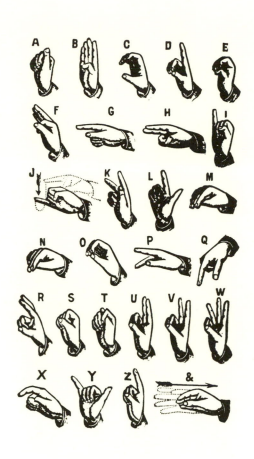

Sign languages are communication systems based on manual gestures. As this chart of the American Sign Language shows, gestures are primarily made with hands and fingers.

face, are sometimes used as well. Each gesture or sign corresponds to a word or a singular idea. This gestural system contrasts with manual alphabets and finger spelling, where gestures are used to represent written language. However, sign languages are not always related to the spoken language of the dominant surrounding community. For example, American Sign Language (ASL) is not related to spoken American English. In fact, ASL derives from a signed system of communication developed in Paris during the latter part of the eighteenth century by Abbé Charles-Michel de l'Epée. ASL is therefore related to French Sign Language (FSL), not to spoken English.

Sign languages are found in many parts of the world and appear to have been in use among early human societies. Cross-cultural studies include descriptions of sign language systems in Africa, Asia, and Australia as well as throughout major regions of the Americas.

Perhaps the most well known example in the anthropological literature is that of the signed system of communication used by Native American groups of the Great Plains and the American Southwest. This general sign language, with some variations (similar to dialects), involved using hand and finger gestures in conjunction with differences in the placement of the hands at high, middle, or low positions. For example, the sign for snow was made by extending both hands out with all ten fingers extended. The fingers were pointed toward the ground while the hands and arms were whirled in circular motions. Sign languages such as those used by Great Plains Native Americans functioned as link languages. Through the use of signed languages, trade, peace negotiations, and general communication could be carried out despite differences in the spoken languages of the various indigenous groups of the American West. Hence, the Native American sign language was essentially a lingua franca (a trade or go-between language).

See also LINGUA FRANCA.

Hock, Hans Henrich, and Brian D. Joseph. (1996) *Language History, Language Change, and Language Relationship: An Introduction to Historical and Comparative Linguistics.*

Salzmann, Zdenek. (1993) *Language, Culture, and Society: An Introduction to Linguistic Anthropology.*

SIGNALS

A symbol (sign) that carries a simple, direct meaning is a signal. Traffic lights, stop signs, and similar symbols that convey simple information are culture-bound signals.

The use of signals, for purposes of rudimentary communication, is extensive and varied across cultures. Among traditional Native American societies of the Great Plains and the Southwest, smoke signals were used to relay messages over long distances. Fires made from green kindling and leaves were lit, and dampened blankets were used to cover the flames momentarily to produce separate (discrete) puffs of smoke. This form of distance communication was performed on visible bluffs and promontories. Smoke signal communication was limited in terms of the form and content of messages being sent; only basic information (such as "someone is coming," "we are moving," and so forth) could be communicated. The advantage of smoke signal communication, however, was that it allowed for the communication of messages over long distances.

The Romans used fire towers as a means of sending messages over long distances. Large towers of wooden scaffolds were built and filled with dry brush. On the order of military officers in charge, the towers were lit. These towers could be seen from distances of several miles, thus signaling for other towers to be lit. Again, there were tight constraints on the form, type, and nature of the messages that could be sent. The Roman military used fire towers to signal the movement of troops, to warn of invading forces, and to mark the coming of an emperor.

Archaeologists working in the American Southwest have suggested that the ancient Anasazi may have used fire towers as a means of signal communication. Although these researchers are not completely certain as to whether or not the Anasazi actually used fire towers for purposes of communication, some archaeological evidence, in the form of stone towers located on the edges of mesas and bluffs and along ancient roadways, suggests that it is possible that they did. Most of these relic towers, or "shrines" as they are sometimes called, are in plain view of one another. Fires lit at night would have been highly visible over relatively long distances. When the Anasazi tradition was flourishing around A.D. 1200, people living at various sites, such as those at Chaco Canyon, Aztec, Mesa Verde, and Salmon (among others), could have sent messages via fire signaling, generating a regional communication system that might have linked various segments of the Anasazi world.

In many parts of the world flags, placards, and other visible markers have been used to identify clan, tribal, and national affiliations. Throughout much of Europe flags were used to herald regional, ethnic, and national identities. These "logos" or visible labels helped to identify members of different groups in the heat of battle. They also became

In many parts of the world, flags and other visible markers have been used to identify clan, tribal, and national affiliations. Here, a white youth holds up a small Confederate flag intended to magnify the insults he yells at civil rights marchers.

symbols of loyalty. In many cultures defiling a flag or cultural logo is considered a serious offense. In Scotland clan markers have evolved into the current system of emblems ("coats of arms") used to identify family surnames. In the past these same emblems were used to differentiate clan groups on the battlefield and were, as they are today, a great source of pride for each of the respective groups.

See also SIGN LANGUAGES.

———————

Devereux, Eve. (1994) *Flags.*
Hayes, Alden C., and Thomas C. Windes. (1975) *An Anasazi Shrine in Chaco Canyon.*
Jones, A. H. M. (1964) *The Later Roman Empire.*
Taylor, Allan R. (1996) "Nonspeech Communication Systems." In *Handbook of North American Indians*, vol. 17, *Languages*, edited by Ives Goddard, 275–289.

SIGNS All communication systems are composed of symbolic forms that, taken together, make up messages. Symbolic forms at their most basic level are signs. Linguists organize signs into three categories: symbolic signs, in which the relationship between the sign and its meaning is arbitrary (that is, the sign does not in any way resemble what it refers to); indexical signs, which display emotional states such as crying, screaming, cooing, and so forth; and iconic signs, which resemble in some way what they refer to, such as an outstretched hand for stop, or the icons used in computer menus.

The structural linguist Ferdinand de Saussure was the first linguist to emphasize the arbitrary relationship between signs and their attached meanings. Most contemporary linguists, however, point out that the relationship between signs and what they refer to is not always entirely arbitrary. With iconic signs, a recognizable relationship, usually in the form of graphic representation, is apparent. Thus iconic signs are easier to understand than symbolic signs. In most cases iconic signs are self-evident. Directional arrows, images of people walking (signaling "Watch out for pedestrians"), and signs warning to watch for falling rocks appear to some to be universally understood. However, the anthropologist Edward T. Hall has observed that many signs and symbolic patterns assumed to be universal may not be universal. Cross-cultural studies such as those carried out by Hall and others indicate that more arbitrariness across cultures and language systems exists than might be expected. Among North American males, for example, closeness (in physical proximity) with other males is generally viewed negatively. Most North American males see closeness as a sign of intimate affection, implying that the two males may be romantically involved. In many parts of the Arab world, in contrast, closeness among males is merely a sign of friendship and trust. Using fingers to point at someone or something in one society

may be acceptable for directing the attention of another; however, pointing a finger at someone in some other cultures, particularly among various Southeast Asian societies, is considered a serious insult.

Cross-cultural studies focusing on the variable use of signs as they are embedded in larger symbolic systems suggest that beyond iconic and indexical signs (which carry apparent or obvious meaning), specific culture-bound meanings of many signs must be learned for comprehension to occur. Merely assuming that all signs are basic or fundamental to human understanding might produce a significant degree of cultural misunderstanding.

Hall, Edward T. (1981) *Beyond Culture.*
Hodge, Robert, and Gunther Kress. (1988) *Social Semiotics.*

SLANG

The frivolous use of language involving such nonstandard forms as obscenities, special group-specific language (jargon), and terms and phrases that generally conflict with the acceptable speech of a society is sometimes referred to as slang. On the basis of cross-cultural studies, linguistic anthropologists have noted that slang has a tendency toward rapid change in form. Moreover, slang use is more prevalent among adolescents and young adults than it is among adults and small children. Sometimes slang is mistaken for nonstandard dialects or language varieties. For instance, some Euro-Americans assume that African American English is a form of slang; by definition it is not slang. Thus, slang is not a dialect or a complete subvariety of any language. Slang speech is composed of nonstandard elements of speech (terms and short phrases) that almost always derive from a parent language.

Use of slang has been observed across numerous cultural and linguistic groups. Its use has been observed, for example, among the Zuni of the American Southwest. Zuni men sometimes use the phrase "a spring of water" to refer to "a woman." The connotation that underlies the slang statement refers to the Zuni male's view of women as desirable in sexual terms. In Zuni culture use of such a phrase is limited to informal male gatherings. Use in most other contexts would be unacceptable.

The anthropologist Peter Farb has suggested that slang functions to set apart or define various segments of a larger society, especially subgroups that are not necessarily concerned in most cases with maintaining societal norms. Hence, jazz musicians, adolescents (in many societies), countercultural groups, and other nonmainstream segments of a society might make use of slang as a means of marking their group identity as different from that of mainstream society. Slang therefore shares some basic functions with argots (jargon and cants).

See also ARGOT; CURSING.

Farb, Peter. (1978) *Word Play: What Happens When People Talk.*

Miller, Wick R. (1996) "The Ethnography of Speaking." In *Handbook of North American Indians*, vol. 17, *Languages*, edited by Ives Goddard, 222–243.

Newman, Stanley S. (1955) "Vocabulary Levels: Zuni Sacred and Slang Usage." *Southwestern Journal of Anthropology* 11: 345–354.

SOCIOLECTS

The way in which a person speaks that reveals that person's membership in a particular socioeconomic group or class is what sociolinguists call a sociolect. In stratified or class societies, members of the same general society may make use of different forms of speaking according to differences in economic and social class. Members of different castes in India, for example, although they may speak the same parent language (Hindi or Panjabi among others), speak different dialects of the parent language. Dialectical differences based solely on class differences are sociolects.

See also DIALECTS.

SOCIOLINGUISTICS

The branch of linguistics dedicated to the study of the social dimensions of language and communication is called sociolinguistics. Sociolinguists are interested in describing and analyzing how people rely on cultural rules for regulating social interactions. Sociolinguists generally want to know how people's social backgrounds influence their speaking and interaction patterns. Moreover, sociolinguists try to describe how perceptions and societal attitudes shape social-communicative interaction.

Sociolinguistic methods and forms of analysis have often been applied to cross-cultural studies of language and communication. Susan Philips, for example, spent a year studying sociolinguistic patterns of behavior among the Native Americans on the Warm Springs Indian Reservation in Oregon. Philips concluded that a significant degree of underlying cultural differences between Native Americans (at Warm Springs specifically) and their Anglo counterparts contributed to ongoing miscommunication. These persistent miscommunications, described largely in classroom settings, led to persistent problems of cultural conflict. In her conclusion, Philips recommended that only Native American teachers be allowed to teach on this reservation because Native Americans knew how to organize and carry out the multifaceted social-interactive behaviors required for effective communication.

In a similar study that was intended as a follow-up to Philips's study, the anthropologists Frederick Erickson and Gerald Mohatt described and analyzed classroom interactions among a group of Native Americans on the Odawa Reservation in Ontario, Canada. As in the Warm Springs case all or most of the students were Native American. Many of the teachers were also Native American, but some were nonnative (Euro-Canadian). The results of this study were similar to those of the Warm Springs study. In general, Native American students brought a different set of cultural rules to school for how people should interact and use language than did their Anglo teachers (when Anglo teachers were present). Like Philips, Erickson and Mohatt noted that native teachers were better able to work and communicate with their native stu-

dents than were their Euro-Canadian counterparts.

These case studies represent classic sociolinguistic description and analysis. For sociolinguists a great deal of emphasis is placed on describing how people "use" language as opposed to how language is structured (structure usually refers to grammar). Moreover, sociolinguists will describe how people alter or shift their communicative behaviors as social situations change. For instance, most people, despite their cultural backgrounds, behave differently in formal situations than in informal ones. The choice of words, body posture, and use of space (proxemics) differs across these situational contexts. Among the Warm Springs and Odawa Native American groups the behavior of native students varied according to who was teaching the classes (native versus nonnative), how in-class lessons were organized, and in the ways that more spontaneous behaviors emerged as participants interacted. In all cases, individuals relied on a range of cultural rules (hidden or tacit rules) that assisted them in regulating ongoing social interaction. The sociolinguists who conducted these studies generally described how the participants (both native and Anglo) made variable use of cultural rules as social situations changed.

The approach of sociolinguists contrasts slightly with that of the more conventional linguistic anthropologists (ethnolinguists) in that sociolinguists do not see cultural rules as highly rigid. Ethnolinguists, especially in the past, have tended to describe the specific grammar and semantic features of various languages and have typically only paid minor attention to language use as it occurs across social dimensions of a community of speakers.

See also ETHNOGRAPHY OF COMMUNICATION.

Erickson, Frederick, and Gerald Mohatt. (1988) "Cultural Organization of Participation Structures in Two Classrooms of Indian Students." In *Doing the Ethnography of Schooling: Educational Anthropology in Action,* edited by George Spindler, 133–174.

Giglioli, Paolo, ed. (1973) *Language and Social Context.*

Gumperz, John, and Dell Hymes, eds. (1972) *Directions in Sociolinguistics: The Ethnography of Communication.*

Labov, William. (1970) "The Study of Language in Its Social Context." *Studium Generale* 23: 30–87.

Philips, Susan Urmston. (1993) *The Invisible Culture: Communication in Classroom and Community on the Warm Springs Indian Reservation.*

SONG DUELING

The use of improvisational song verse in competitive situations—typically involving put-downs and insults—is known in the anthropological literature as song dueling. The most well known example of song dueling, as it is represented in the cross-cultural record, is found among the various Inuit (Eskimo) groups of North America's Arctic region.

According to the anthropologist Norman Chance, Inuit song dueling is an extension of other local competitive activities (such as "foot, boat, and dog races, tests of strength, . . . dancing, and storytelling"). These forms of competition are not socially disruptive in most cases and tend to facilitate social solidarity for each Inuit group. However, Inuit men sometimes use song duels to settle disputes. In such cases a challenge to a song duel is made by one party against another. If the challenged party accepts, the two participants will meet at an agreed time and, after an audience gathers, the duel will begin. Song dueling among the Inuit involves exchanges of short verses that are based on turn taking, audience response, and capitulation in a final set of verses that informally decides the winner (typically indicated by an enthusiastic audience response favoring one of the duelers). Emphasis is placed on quickness of response to an insulting verse and on generating clever metaphors in return that in some way ridicule the opponent. Often these metaphors make indirect reference to a person's physical appearance, to a man's wife, or to an embarrassing event associated with the opponent.

An expressive form similar to Inuit song dueling can be found in many African American communities. Currently, terms such as "snapping," "chopping," and "playing the dozens" are used to describe this type of verse dueling. Verbal dueling of this type originated on the streets in African American communities in many parts of large cities in the eastern United States. As in the Inuit case, the exchanges are short and constructed through the generation of clever metaphors; these metaphors often make insulting allusions to an opponent's mother, wife, or other close relatives. Sociolinguists have described African American verbal dueling as an urban expressive art form that provides the participant with an informal means of raising his or her (though participants tend to be male) perceived status in the group. A person who exhibits a high degree of skill in verbal dueling is generally perceived as smart, clever, and a valuable member of the group.

Sociolinguist Roger Abrahams has observed that a kind of "metalanguage" (talk about language) typically accompanies African American verbal competition. Terms and phrases such as "styling," "having a flash," "on someone's case," "all over him," and "getting shot through the grease" describe how an individual may be subjected to effective verbal abuse. Terms that generally ridicule a person's style of verbal dueling are "jiving," "shucking," and "lame." Abrahams also points out that participants who appear to be losing an exchange may produce verbal expressions designed to get out of the contest, which Abrahams calls "disavowal techniques." Disavowal techniques involve utterances such as "playing [I was only playing]." As Abrahams notes, the speaker who finds himself in a difficult verbal situation may have to select even more extreme verbal responses if his initial "I was only playing" does not work. When an individual is unsuccessful at saving face, the crowd may use phrases such as "copping a plea," "gripping," or "eating cheese" to further ridicule the person. As part of the metalanguage of verbal dueling these last utterances serve two purposes: they effectively ridicule the individual who wishes to get out of the contest, and they signal the potential end of the overall exchange.

See also PLAY LANGUAGE.

Abrahams, Roger D. (1977) "Black Talking on the Streets." In *Explorations in the Ethnography of Speaking*, edited by Richard Bauman and Joel Sherzer, 240–262.
Chance, Norman A. (1966) *The Eskimo of North Alaska*.
Hoebel, E. Adamson. (1974) *The Law of Primitive Man*.
Kochman, T. (1970) "Toward an Ethnography of Black American Speech Behavior." In *Afro-American Anthropology: Contemporary Perspectives*, edited by Norman E. Whitten and John F. Szwed, 145–162.

SONG STYLE

The multiplicity of elemental forms and functions that singing songs has across cultures is generally termed song style. Songs have been used across a wide spectrum of sociocultural settings and contexts. Songs have been used to embellish myths and rituals, for vocalizing children's verse, as curing songs for shamans (traditional healers), as a means of carrying out courtship, as chants at funerals, and simply for entertainment.

The stylistic elements of song include the use of verse, figurative language (such as metaphors and similes), rhymes, and rhythmic patterns. Style is also a function of how songs are expressed and used in specific cultural contexts. For example, among the Inuit (Eskimo) songs are sometimes used to establish social bonds between two male hunting partners. The Inuit also

Songs always contain some form of verse and convey cultural information in a public context. In this Sambura tribe dance, it is clear that song is being used to enhance the ritual.

use songs as a form of competition among rivals, which is called song dueling. Songs may also be used to cure sickness, call on spirits, send a dead relative safely into the afterlife, and, most important, to tell folk stories. Thus style is composed of both the elemental features of the songs themselves and how the songs are used for purposes of cultural expression.

The Lakota of the American plains use songs as a form of verse play. Songs used in this manner are typically associated with children, but adults often take part. These Lakota songs are often nonsensical in the way they are constructed;

many of the words are jumbled, and syllables from some words are mixed or combined with those from other words. Thus for Lakota participants the overall effect produced through these nonsensical songs is laughter.

Among the Upper Chehalis, a Native American group of the Pacific Northwest coastal region, songs are often embedded in mythic tales. In fact, lengthy Chehalis narrative myths usually contain a series of songs. For example, the Upper Chehalis tell a long mythic story called "The Contest for the Length of Night and Day." This extensive narrative contains more than 20 songs. The songs work to embellish parts of the story through character development. Various characters within the story sing songs that reveal to listeners the motivations and personal attributes of the characters who are doing the singing. It is interesting to note that this format is not very different from American Broadway musicals (including film versions of musicals, such as "The King and I" and "The Music Man"). Singing occurs sporadically at carefully planned times during the story. A major difference, however, can be found in the Upper Chehalis' use of these songs in conjunction with ritual. Many of the mythic stories are acted out in important rituals and are performed throughout the cycle of the Upper Chehalis year. As such, many of these songs cannot be performed outside of their ritual/mythic contexts.

The Canela, a horticultural group of the Amazon Basin of South America, perform what is best translated into English as a "sing-dance." During traditional times sing-dances, according to the anthropologists William and Jean Croker, took place quite frequently in Canela society. The dances typically begin with the Canela women lining up facing uphill, facing men who sing and play rattle gourds. This form of singing, performed in association with dancing, seems to serve a recreational function. It is not normally associated with any specific ceremonial or sacred institution. From an anthropological perspective the sing-dance most likely functions subtly to reinforce traditional male and female roles as they are defined in Canela culture.

The Navajo (Dine) of the American Southwest have an internal society of healers called "singers." The singers are charged with the responsibility of cur-

ing members of the Navajo community who suffer from mental disorders. The ceremony they perform—a "sing"—lasts nine days and involves the singing of numerous ritual songs designed to comfort the patient and the family of the patient. Navajo singers only cure problems of the mind; other shamans cure physical and spirit-based disorders. As a form of cultural expression, the songs used by the singers serve the specific purpose of bringing an individual back into the mainstream of Navajo society. The songs are not sung for purposes of mere entertainment or for the retelling of myths (although references are made to mythic characters).

Sometimes songs are sung at funeral ceremonies. The Hmong of Laos sing "death songs" designed to soothe the soul (spirit) of the deceased. The songs always contain warnings of hazards that might exist along the journey of the dead. The deceased are warned that the ghosts of dead enemies or other evil spirits might lie in hiding, waiting to injure or steal from an unsuspecting victim. Many of the songs make reference to what the deceased should take with them into the world of the dead, items such as food, clothes, and protective charms.

Song style varies considerably across cultures. However, some general recurring patterns have been noted by anthropologists. Songs always contain some form of verse; they always convey cultural information; and they are usually performed in public contexts (the only exception is songs performed in secret religious ceremonies). As forms of cultural expression, a significant degree of cultural information is contained in songs. For instance, in the United States patterns for courting lovers and attitudes toward politics and social issues are echoed in popular music. Although many people do not recognize song music as something ancient and universal, the appeal of song verse can be found in all parts of the world and across all cultural traditions.

See also PLAY LANGUAGE; SONG DUELING.

Bergman, Robert. (1993) "A School for Medicine Men." In *Magic, Witchcraft, and Religion: An Anthropological Study of the Supernatural,* edited by Arthur C. Lehmann and James Myers, 153–157.

Chance, Norman A. (1966) *The Eskimo of North Alaska.*

Croker, William, and Jean Croker. (1994) *The Canela: Bonding through Kinship, Ritual, and Sex.*

Johnson, Charles, and Se Yang. (1992) *Myths, Legends, and Folk Tales from the Hmong of Laos,* 2d ed.

Kinkade, Dale M., and Anthony Mattina. (1996) "Discourse." In *Handbook of North American Indians,* vol. 17, *Languages,* edited by Ives Goddard, 244–274.

Powers, William K. (1992) "Translating the Untranslatable: The Place of Vocable in Lakota Song." In *On the Translation of Native American Literatures,* edited by Brian Swann, 293–310.

SOUNDS All human verbal languages are built from sounds produced by the human vocal system. The human vocal system is composed of various organs that provide contrasts among sounds (such as the different vowel and consonant sounds). The human ability to produce a wide range of contrasting sounds, especially consonant sounds, is an important feature that sets human language and verbal communication apart from all nonhuman forms of verbal communication. Chimpanzees, our nearest relatives, may have the ability to comprehend simple human utterances; however, they are incapable of producing consonants and thus lack the ability to produce something like human speech.

The study of sounds used in human language is called *phonology.* Linguists who concentrate on phonology have developed systems of notation for describing and analyzing the full range of sounds that human beings are capable of making with their vocal systems. Linguists who describe sounds have observed that humans have the capacity to make approximately 250 distinct sounds. Linguists have also pointed out that no human language makes use of all of these sounds. Instead, each language makes use of a smaller number of sounds in different combinations. The sound inventory of a given language—the number of sounds used and the sounds incorporated into the language—also varies among languages. For instance, most varieties of English use between 40 and 45 sounds (factoring for dialectical differences). Hmong, an Asian language, has between 80 and 85 sounds. Khoisan, the language spoken by Ju/'hoansi (!Kung), a hunter-gatherer group of Africa's Kalahari Desert, incorporates about 20 sounds. All of the world's languages, however, contain both vowels and consonants.

These 250 or so minimal physical sounds that human beings can produce are called *phones*. Phones range across all vowel and consonant forms but can also be distinguished according to more specific criteria. For example, in the English word *more*, the *m* sound is unvoiced (the vocal chords only slightly vibrate). In the English word *man*, the *m* sound is voiced (the vocal cords vibrate considerably). Linguists describing phones at this level have developed a simple scheme for categorization. First, they note the *manner* associated with the phone. Manner refers to the sound quality of the phone (such as voiced versus unvoiced, aspirated versus unaspirated [the *p* in *push* is aspirated because air blows out; the *p* in *spin* is unaspirated because no air is expelled when *spin* is pronounced]). Second, linguists describe the *point of articulation* as a means of labeling certain phones. The point of articulation refers to the precise point where the tongue is placed in relation to the rest of the vocal system at the moment a sound is produced. Thus, descriptive linguists (linguists who describe all aspects of language, including sounds) can note any sound made by the human vocal system according to how the sound is situated within the manner/point of articulation matrix.

Contemporary descriptive linguistics has shifted the description of phonology to sounds specific to particular language systems. The phones or sounds associated with a particular language are called *phonemes*. Phonemes are essentially phones but differ in definition because they refer only to the specific range of sounds that are used by speakers of a particular language. Linguists are more interested in phonemes because these contrasting sounds have ba-

sic properties that link up with larger dimensions of language (such as *morphology*—minimal language units that have recognizable meaning—and grammar). For example, the English word *pit* differs minimally from the English word *bit* by only one sound or phoneme. Thus, an English speaker, hearing the difference between *pit* and *bit*, knows what is being referred to based on the difference between the *p* and the *b* sound (phoneme). By themselves *p* and *b* have no meaning, but when they are attached to the front of *it* they can indicate what the meaning should be. Because phonemes have this property of having no meaning by themselves but being able to alter meaning, linguists have moved away from describing languages at a purely phonetic level.

There is another reason for the shift away from pure phonetic transcription (describing phones in language). In the 1920s the famous linguist Edward Sapir was working with several Navajo (Dine) consultants. During the process of gathering linguistic information on the Navajo use of sounds, Sapir noticed that the native speakers were often inconsistent in their use of sounds in words. If they were speaking fast they appeared actually to change some sounds (not merely saying the correct sounds faster). Moreover, Sapir noticed that as contexts or situations changed, some changes in sound (phonemic) representation also occurred. When Sapir asked these native speakers for clarification as to why they were changing sounds, they appeared dumbfounded. They were unaware that they were changing the sounds. A simple example in English will demonstrate the problem. Most English speakers, when they are speaking slowly, pronounce the word *baseball* correctly by making the second *b* sound as it should be made. However, when English speakers speak rapidly they often (without realizing it) shift the second *b* to a *p*, and hence are actually saying *basepall*. They are of course unaware that they are using the *p* sound, because in their minds they—and usually their English-speaking listeners—hear the correct *b* sound. Noting this kind of inconsistency in sound representation is extremely important for descriptive linguists because merely describing the actual sounds (phones) might lead to confusion. Thus descriptive linguists have to describe what native speakers think they are saying as well as what they actually say. Sapir noted that describing sound systems in language (describing phonemes) takes into account how sounds are psychologically perceived by the speakers who make the sounds.

On the basis of Sapir's work, linguists have been able to generate four properties of phonemes. First, by themselves phonemes have no meaning. Second, they are linguistically significant because they can alter meaning (as in the *pit* and *bit* example). Third, phonemes are sounds that are language specific (they are the range of sounds associated with a particular language). Fourth, as Sapir observed, phonemes are psychologically perceived sound as well as physically produced sound (as English speakers we know that the second *b* sound in *baseball* is the correct sound). These four properties of phonemes, by definition, distinguish them from phones.

Sapir and other linguists also observed that the sounds that often get substituted for one another are closely related in terms of how they are produced by the vocal system. They also sound similar when a listener hears them. Phonemes that are closely related are called *phonemic pairs*. When phonemic pairs are likely to get substituted for one another in ongoing talk, linguists call them *suspicious pairs*. Thus, an important aspect of describing sound systems associated with particular languages is to identify all suspicious pairs. Examples of phonemic pairs are *t* and *d*, *g* and *k*, and *p* and *b*.

In describing the variable use of sound across language systems, linguists are also interested in how sounds are used to convey subtle, suggestive meaning. In English, for example, a rising tone can indicate doubt or even sarcasm, depending on the situation. A falling tone followed by a pause might indicate closure and signal that it is someone else's turn to talk. Use of sound differences at this level is called *paralanguage*. The sound contours, as they are sometimes called, are described by linguists as *suprasegmental* sounds or, more commonly, *prosodic cues*. Prosodic cues are changes in pitch, tone, intensity, and pause. These aspects of sound are not part of the actual language; they represent subtle alterations that are often used by speakers to modify what is being said; for example, the difference between saying "nice car" (and meaning it) and "nice ca:r" (and being sarcastic [the colon indicates an extended vowel]).

Some languages are tonal. Tonal languages employ ending tones (such as rising, falling, high-level, medial-level, and low-level intonations) to signal actual changes in meaning. These tones are different from prosodic cues. They do not suggest sarcasm or emotion and so forth; they change the actual meaning of words. Hence, tones in tonal languages function in the same way that phonemes do (they can alter meaning, but by themselves they have no meaning). Linguists have labeled tones that are phonemically significant *tonemes*. All of the Chinese languages (Cantonese, Mandarin, and so forth) are tonal languages. In such languages, a speaker who gets a tone wrong might be saying something that makes little sense. For people who grew up speaking nontonal languages (like English), understanding and learning tonal languages is extremely difficult. People who are attempting to learn a tonal language have to develop an ear for hearing the subtle changes in tone that occur at the ends of words.

The linguistic study of sounds (phonology) is a significant part of descriptive linguistics. It is the starting point for linguists who want to describe a particular language system. Once a solid understanding of how the sound system for a particular language is established, a linguist can move on to describing higher-level dimensions of language such as morphology (the description of minimal linguistic units that carry meaning), syntax (grammar or how words are organized into sentences), and semantics (how content is derived from relational meanings among words, sentences, and larger bodies of linguistic texts).

See also DESCRIPTION; PARALANGUAGE.

Eastman, Carol M. (1978) *Linguistic Theory and Language Description.*

O'Grady, William D., and Michael Dobrovolsky, eds. (1993) *Contemporary Linguistics: An Introduction*, 2d ed.

Sapir, Edward. (1933) "The Psychological Reality of Phonemes." In *Selected Writings of Edward Sapir*, edited by David G. Mandelbaum, 46–60.

SPACE

Researchers who focus on intercultural communication (the comparative study of communication across cultures) generally use the term "space" to refer to the physical distance among communicators. Space, or proxemics as it is sometimes called, is an important aspect of cross-cultural studies of communication because differing cultural rules are often applied for the use of space across cultures.

See also PROXEMICS.

SPEECH

Spoken language behavior in the form of audible utterances is what linguists call speech. Speech is sometimes viewed as a separate domain from language because some linguists assume that language is knowledge and speech is behavior. Most linguists, however, view speech as the outward representation of language. Therefore language and speech are closely integrated phenomena. The linguist Ferdinand de Saussure marked a sharp difference between language and speech and labeled these differences with his concepts *langue* (language) and *parole* (speech). From Saussure's perspective this distinction is crucial for linguistic analysis because speech is merely an imperfect representation of ideal linguistic knowledge. Saussure therefore viewed speech as highly variable and inconsistent, and language as a more stable ("structured") symbolic system (and thus more worthy of study).

Sociolinguists (those who study language as social behavior), in contrast, assume that speech use—like language, which is governed by rules of grammar—is governed by social and cultural rules for proper use. For sociolinguists, speech is not considered a product of random, inconsistent, or irregular behaviors. Hence, from a sociolinguistic perspective, speech can and should be studied as an important aspect of human language and communication.

Speech has been studied from a variety of disciplinary perspectives. Anthropologists who are interested in describing and analyzing speech have examined it as behavior that is situated in various cultural and situational contexts. For example, the way in which speech forms might change among the Balinese (an island society in Indonesia) as situations change from informal to formal. Anthropologists who conduct such studies are doing what is called the ethnography of communication or of speaking. Sociologists have also described speech behavior. Sociologists tend to emphasize the role of social context in speech use.

Cross-cultural studies of speech suggest that it is often used more to manipulate existing social situations than to communicate explicit information. The sociolinguist Karl Reisman, for example, has described a form of speech called "making noise." Speech behavior of this sort is used on the island of An-

tigua in the West Indies of the Caribbean. Making noise is a speaking style that signals changes in talk turns (who can talk to whom, and when they can talk). Making noise also communicates subtle differences in the general social relationships among those in a community who talk. Reisman has observed that these relationships are essentially communicated through three basic genres of making noise: "boasting, cursing, and argument." Boasting, for example, can signal a person's relationship to others in the immediate peer group or in other segments of Antiguan society. The following boast indicates how a speaker views his relationship to the rest of his peers as well as to the views his peer group share with regard to the local police force (as spoken in Antiguan English/Creole):

"Mi no ka wa mi do" [I don't care what I do].
"Kuz mi big, bad an mi buos" [Because I am big, bad and I am the boss].
"An mi jain di polis fuos" [And I am not afraid of the police force].

By boasting to his peers this individual is subtly manipulating his overall status in the group. Moreover, by boasting about his indifference to the police, he is communicating the fact that relations between his peer group and the local police are not particularly friendly.

Judith Irvine, in a similar study, described how the Wolof of West Africa use various forms of greeting to reinforce existing status differences (degrees of perceived social importance) among individuals. The Wolof are a society that is highly structured and status conscious. Thus, a person's social position is known to every other Wolof person and is marked by differences in dress, economics, and the way an individual speaks. Irvine has observed that, although the Wolof class system is rather rigid, the various ways in which individuals greet one another leaves some degree of latitude open for "maneuvering for position." Irvine has also observed that status differs according to age and gender differences. Predictably, all of these perceived differences in social rank provide for the variable use of speech as greeting situations arise.

In contrast to the Wolof, the Polynesian Maori of New Zealand have tended to standardize their greeting rituals. The anthropologist and linguist Anne Salmond describes these social contact rituals as "rituals of encounter." Much of Maori history is made up of continuous conflicts with neighboring groups (typically in the form of warfare). When competing groups came together to form peaceful relations, the interactions among competing participants was almost always highly formal. During more recent times the practice of warfare has subsided. Group interactions, however, have remained formal. Salmond describes speech forms used in such ritual encounters as oratorical contests. Speakers attempt to outdo one another in terms of duration of speech, use of clever metaphors, and skill in persuasive art (rhetoric). Thus, speaking is an extension of other competitive activities and seems to be one type of substitute for warfare.

Among many Native American groups formal speeches were used as a means of conducting political decision making. Among the Iroquois of the upper part of New York State, speech

making was the primary means by which political agendas were communicated. Each speech maker delivered his (they were always males) to a council. Sometimes these speeches lasted for hours. Speeches of this kind were designed to argue for particular positions on important issues and to persuade others to adopt the views of the speaker.

See also ETHNOGRAPHY OF COMMUNICATION.

Irvine, Judith. (1977) "Strategies of Status Manipulation in the Wolof Greeting." In *Explorations in the Ethnography of Speaking,* edited by Richard Bauman and Joel Sherzer, 167–191.

Reisman, Karl. (1970) "Cultural and Linguistic Ambiguity in a West Indian Village." In *Afro-American Anthropology: Contemporary Perspectives,* edited by Norman E. Whitten and John F. Szwed, 129–144.

Salmond, Anne. (1977) "Ritual Encounter among the Maori: Sociolinguistic Study of a Scene." In *Explorations in the Ethnography of Speaking,* edited by Richard Bauman and Joel Sherzer, 192–212.

Saussure, Ferdinand de. (1966) *Course in General Linguistics.*

Speck, Frank. (1945) *The Iroquois: A Study in Cultural Evolution.*

STANDARD LANGUAGE Languages that have either formally or informally agreed-upon standards for grammar, spelling (in the case of written languages), and pronunciation are standardized languages. Standardized languages are often confused with dominant languages. Dominant languages are those spoken language systems that are used by a dominant population. Standardization refers specifically to the development of consistent rules for language structure and use. For example, Yoruba and Ibo have been the dominant languages of Nigeria for many years, yet they have only become standardized in the past 40 years. English has been the dominant language of the British Isles since the ninth century, but it was finally standardized only during the latter half of the eighteenth century, when many of the formal rules for English grammar were established. Agreement on spelling, some agreement on pronunciation, and lexicography (definitions in dictionaries) were established as well.

Controversy has followed the development of standardized languages. Some feel that language is like art. Its expressive power can be found in the many ways that speakers manipulate and alter its structure and use. From this perspective, standardization tends to eliminate or constrain many of the creative aspects of language. In contrast, others point out that standardization increases the overall effectiveness of communication because confusion over language form and use is generally reduced. Through the years, because of tensions produced by such controversies, compromises have been worked out for English and many other standardized languages. Contexts have been developed (such as literary or poetic license) in which poets, writers, and playwrights are given a significant degree of latitude in their use of lan-

guage. In other contexts, however, standardized language is the rule (such as for legal documents, writing research papers, for news media copy, and so forth).

Standardized languages have arisen in many parts of the world. In Africa, many of the trade or link languages, such as Swahili or Sierra Leone Creole, have become standardized because so many people used them. They represent dominant languages that became standardized out of necessity. Other standardized languages were engineered (the result of actual language planning). Nynorsk, a language spoken in Norway, was altered or reorganized in such a way as to facilitate its use as a standard language.

See also LINGUA FRANCA.

Hock, Hans Henrich, and Brian D. Joseph. (1996) *Language History, Language Change, and Language Relationship: An Introduction to Historical and Comparative Linguistics.*

SWEARING

See CURSING.

SYMBOLISM   The relationship between symbols (signs) and their cultural meanings is called symbolism. Spoken and written languages are essentially symbolic systems because they are constructed from basic symbols. Spoken language, for example, is made up entirely from sounds. The sounds are used in various combinations to form words and more lengthy units such as sentences and narrative texts. Spoken languages are symbolic systems because meaning is attached to these combinations of sounds. Meaning is also attached to combinations of written symbols; thus, written languages are symbolic systems.

Some symbols are discrete—that is, they can stand alone and carry meaning. The swastika of the Nazis, the yin and yang symbol of Chinese Taoism, and the American flag are discrete symbols that carry culture-specific meanings. Because some discrete symbols are fairly simple in their geometrical design, they recur across a wide variety of cultures. Sometimes the distribution of similar symbols results from diffusion (the spreading or trading of symbolic patterns from one region to others), but in most cases differing cultures converge on similar symbolic configurations because the patterns are made up of basic geometrical patterns common to all peoples. The swastika, for example, is found in several variant forms in many parts of the world. It has been displayed on Hopi and Anasazi pottery in the American Southwest; it has turned up on rock paintings in Australia's outback, and, more recently, Hitler used it as his logo before and during World War II. The cultural meaning or significance of the swastika of course varies considerably cross-culturally. Its general meaning among Western societies, however, is closely linked with Nazi Germany and the Holocaust and it therefore usually carries a highly negative meaning.

Many theoretical perspectives have been used to make sense of symbolism. The neurologist and psychologist Sigmund Freud thought that symbols were the outward manifestation of inward psychological tensions. Freud believed that all individuals form their personalities through a combination of the relationships they form with their parents and from internal erotic sexual motivations. The form and use of symbols, from Freud's perspective, developed from these human psychological patterns operating deep within the human psyche. The psychologist Carl Jung, who worked with Freud for some time, believed that symbols emerge as a result of internal neurotic fantasies. Although anthropologists admit that symbols may often reflect internal psychological patterns, cross-cultural studies of symbolism (typically conducted by anthropologists) suggest that the form and function of most symbols is culture specific and therefore highly variable across cultures. The simple cross pattern, for example, shows up in many parts of the world across a wide variety of cultural and social circumstances. In Europe, a cross pattern usually carries meaning associated with Christianity. In southern Mexico, particularly in the Maya area, the cross signifies "the tree of life" and may derive from an older cross pattern associated with the back of the caiman (an alligator-like reptile). Among the ancient Maya, caimans may have been symbolically linked with intensive agriculture. The association of life with agricultural

These Arizona Native Americans are banning the use of the swastika—traditionally a symbol of friendship among southwestern Native Americans—from all their craft designs due to its relatively recent link to the horrors of Nazi Germany.

production was and still is important to the Maya.

In some parts of the world the landscape takes on symbolic importance. In Bali, Indonesia, for example, rice terracing is carried out as an art form. The arrangement of the fields, the placement of shrines, and the regulation of water through the entire system have symbolic meaning for the Balinese. The Balinese are primarily Hindu. The terraced rice fields reinforce the Balinese Hindu idea that there is an underlying unity to all things. This "cosmic unity" is such an important idea to the Balinese that its symbolic representation permeates all aspects of Balinese life, including the way the countryside is sculpted.

See also SIGNS.

Firth, Raymond. (1997) "An Anthropologist's Reflections on Symbolic Usage." In *Magic, Witchcraft, and Religion:*

An Anthropological Study of the Super-natural, edited by Arthur C. Lehmann and James E. Myers, 53–56.

Schele, Linda, and Mary Ellen Miller. (1986) *The Blood of Kings: Dynasty and Ritual in Maya Art.*

Syntax

See Grammar.

the use of tag questions might indicate doubt or uncertainty on the part of the person using them. Lakoff, however, maintains that tag questions are used to level social distances among speakers by avoiding more assertive—and therefore aggressive—language associated with direct or "blunt" statements. Lakoff also points out that males tend to be more direct and do not use tag questions as often as females. This, she says, is due to the male preoccupation with assertiveness. Furthermore, males tend to use language to establish status differences; hence, in contrast to female use, males use language to create and maintain social distance.

The ideas of Robin Lakoff have sometimes been criticized by other linguists, especially those interested in cross-cultural studies of language and communication. One major criticism has focused specifically on tag questions. There is little evidence that tag questions are used more by females when their use is examined cross-culturally. The frequency of tag question use among females in the United States appears to be high, but there is no good evidence that this pattern can be generalized to other parts of the world. Even in parts of the United States the frequency of tag question use varies. In some parts of the United States and across a spectrum of social dimensions and individual predispositions, some males tend to use more tag questions than do other males. In contrast, in some parts of the United States, and again depending on differences in social contexts and individuality, women can be as direct and assertive as males.

See also GENDER DIFFERENCES.

TABOO LANGUAGE

See AVOIDANCE; CURSING.

TAG QUESTIONS

Questions that follow statements are called tag questions. Consider, for example, the English sentence "This is a good paint job, isn't it?" The question "isn't it?" after the statement "this is a good paint job" is a tag question. Tag questions have been studied primarily as an aspect of gender and language patterning. The linguist Robin Lakoff has suggested that females use tag questions more often than males because females tend to employ language to ease or reduce social distances. Superficially,

Lakoff, Robin. (1975) *Language and Woman's Place.*
———. (1990) *Talking Power: The Politics of Language.*

One of the most famous non-Western examples of tattooing is found among the Maori, a Polynesian people of New Zealand. Note this young Maori woman's tattooed chin.

TATTOOING Permanent markings made by inserting (punching) indelible pigments into the skin are called tattoos. The word *tattoo* derives from the Polynesian-Tahitian word *tatu*, which means mark. The cultural purposes of tattooing vary somewhat across cultures. In most cases tattoos communicate the social status of individuals relative to other members of a society. In some cases tattoos mark clan membership. Clan totems (such as animals or abstract symbols) are sometimes embossed on the skin to signify a clan association or family crest. In other cases tattoos may mark a person as an adult or as a member of a traditional internal society, such as a society of shamans (traditional healers). In some societies the cultural functions of tattoos are only vaguely defined. In such cases tattoos are considered art, and their purpose is open to subjective interpretation.

Perhaps the most famous non-Western example of tattooing is found among the Maori, a Polynesian people of New Zealand. For the Maori, tattooing is a highly embellished art form, but its specific cultural functions remain unclear. However, tattooing was extremely important to the Maori because they invested significant time and energy engraving them on the bodies and faces of Maori men and women. Many traditional Maori men had tattoos covering their faces. The designs were primarily curved or spiraled and did not typically depict recognizable objects. Sometimes the men had tattoos on their buttocks and thighs. The women usually had their ankles, lower jaws, and lips tattooed. Maori tattoos were and still are made by using tattoo chisels made from sharp pieces of bone. The chisels are placed against the skin and lightly struck with a wooden mallet. Small puncture marks are made in the skin, and black pigment made from soot is rubbed into the punctured skin regions until the markings are deep enough to last. The blood is then wiped away, and a permanent tattoo remains.

The underlying cultural functions of tattooing are somewhat vague. Most Maori males will tell you simply that tattoos, especially elaborate ones, are beautiful. In fact, the Maori tell a story that reveals their aesthetic appreciation of fine tattooing. Briefly, the story describes a man who, through jealousy, alienates his wife, whereupon she leaves and returns to the underworld. The man, feeling guilty and lonely, follows her to the underworld, where he discovers his father-in-law carving a tattoo onto a man's face. The blood was flowing, but when the father-in-law was finished the *moko* (design) was beautiful. The man asked his father-in-law if he could have a tattoo done as well. The father-in-law agreed and engraved an elaborate tattoo on the man's face. The wife heard that her father had given her husband a tattoo and the two were reunited. The couple returned to the upper world, where they continued to live happy lives. The man was extremely proud of his tattoo and often commented on its intricate designs and overall beauty. Implicit in this story is the Maori emphasis on tattoos as abstract art. From the Maori perspective some designs are considered more aesthetically pleasing than others, but all appear to be for purposes of viewing and critical review by the public. Thus, attempting to discover more specific cultural functions of tattooing for the Maori has proved difficult.

Tattooing has also been practiced in traditional Japanese society. Japanese men, especially in the past, had elaborate designs (primarily faces and flowers) embedded onto their backs. Some historians have suggested that tattooing originated in Japan as a spiritual means for fisherman to scare off sharks. Other historians suggest that Japanese tattoos were originally used to brand individuals as criminals. Whatever the origins, today some traditional Japanese men have large, detailed tattoos on their backs and legs. In some cases tattoos may cover as much as 80 percent of the body.

Some Native American groups practiced tattooing. Among the Haida of the Queen Charlotte Islands of British Columbia's northwest coast, tattoos were used to depict a family crest. Many of these tattoos, typically designs of animal figures, were placed on men's chests. Among the Yurok of northwestern California, women received tattoos in the form of short radiating lines extending from the lower lip to the chin. At the age of five, girls received the first of these tattoos in the form of a single line. Every five years another line was added so that a Yurok woman's age could be determined in public.

Tattoos offer anthropologists an opportunity to interpret visual art for the purpose of discovering underlying cultural ideas. In some cases the use of tattoos in non-Western societies conveys highly specific ideas (such as marking clan membership, adult status, and so forth). In other cases, however, the cultural ideas conveyed through tattooing are unclear. In Western industrial societies (such as the United States, Britain, and many European countries) the use of tattoos is becoming widespread. The more traditional purposes for tattoo use do not necessarily apply to their use in Western societies. Many social scientists have described the use of tattoos in Western societies as multifunctional—serving numerous purposes. In many cases their use has been attributed to countercultural subgroups (subcultures such as punks, bikers, rock musicians, and surfers, among others). Since the

1980s, however, the frequent use of tattoos has been extended to more mainstream segments of Western society.

See also ADORNMENT.

Blackman, Margaret B. (1990) "Haida: Traditional Culture." In *Handbook of North American Indians*, vol. 7, *Northwest Coast*, edited by Wayne Suttles, 240–260.

Heizer, R. F., and M. A. Whipple. (1971) *The California Indians: A Source Book*.

McGuire, Edna. (1968) *The Maoris of New Zealand*.

Nanda, Serena. (1994) *Cultural Anthropology*.

Sutton, Douglas G. (1994) *The Origins of the First New Zealanders*.

Some human traits, both physical and cultural, are present in all human societies. These traits are said to be universal. In most cases universal traits are biological. Basic human anatomy, with some degree of variation, is biologically uniform across all human populations. Moreover, involuntary behavior traits such as crying, screaming in pain, and laughing appear to be manifestations of biological functions. Some universal traits, however, are cultural (acquired or learned) and do not appear to be biological in nature. The incest taboo rule (a person must marry outside of the family or group) is most likely a human "cultural" universal. Many anthropologists, after examining numerous cross-cultural studies, have concluded that cultural universal traits exist because they serve some basic purpose common to all human societies. The incest taboo, for example, prevents the breakup of the family unit by placing a strong sanction against family members having sexual intercourse with one another. This keeps marital units intact and forces siblings to establish social and economic ties outside of the immediate family or clan. Moreover, the rule makes it possible to keep families economically viable by bringing new economic resources (goods and labor) into a family unit through marrying out.

Defining what human traits are universal, in contrast to those that are "generalized" (present in many but not all societies) or "particular" (traits present in specific societies), is extremely important for cross-cultural studies of language and communication. Many nonverbal communicative cues appear to be universal. Facial gestures such as smiling, blinking when nervous, and yawning in the face of threats may occur in all human societies. However, many nonverbal cues appear to be specific to certain cultural traditions. Head nodding up and down for *yes* and laterally for *no* are not cultural universals; they are generalized for most parts of the world. In many parts of the Middle East nodding one's head up and down means *no*, and shaking the head laterally means *yes*.

Linguists such as Noam Chomsky have pointed out that some features of language grammar are universal. Question words tend to appear earlier in sentences; noun and verb phrases tend to be structured in the same way across all of the languages that Chomsky sampled. Some linguists have challenged Chomsky's basic contention that many aspects of grammar are universal. Admitting that some grammatical structures do appear to be universal, these linguists point out that many grammatical features are not (they are language specific). These linguists also point out that Chomsky's sample of languages is not representative of the total range of language variability found throughout the world. Finally, critics of Chomsky have suggested that those grammatical structures that seem to be universal may recur because certain utterances could not logically make sense unless they were organized in a particular grammatical order. Chomsky is not in total disagreement with this last position.

See also ANIMAL COMMUNICATION; GRAMMAR; SIGNS.

_____

Chomsky, Noam. (1965) *Aspects of the Theory of Syntax.*
Greenberg, Joseph H., ed. (1978) *Universals of Human Language.*
Premack D., and A. J. Premack. (1974) *Apes, Men, and Language.*

Typically associated with stage comedy, ventriloquists are found in most modern European and North American societies. Edgar Bergen and his famous dummy, Charlie McCarthy, are perhaps the best-known ventriloquist act of Western stage and film.

VENTRILOQUISM The art of making one's voice appear to emanate from somewhere other than one's mouth—"throwing" one's voice—is called ventriloquism. Ventriloquism is often performed with a dummy, a spirit object, or through implying the existence of an imaginary, secondary voice source (suggesting the existence of a hidden spirit, dead ancestor, or a character used for the purpose of entertainment). The ventriloquist must have the ability to produce a full range of vowel and consonant sounds (consistent with a parent language) without showing signs of speaking such as moving the lips and lower jaw. Ventriloquism also involves projecting the voice in the direction of the illusory second source. Ventriloquism therefore is usually performed by specialists of one type or another.

In societies where ventriloquism is practiced, its most common function is entertainment. Ventriloquists are found in modern European and North American societies and are typically associated with stage comedy. Edgar Bergen and his famous dummy, Charlie McCarthy, are perhaps the best-known ventriloquist act of Western stage and film. Ventriloquism is also practiced in some small-scale non-Western societies. In some traditional societies ventriloquism is sometimes used by shamans (traditional healers) as a means of enhancing their role as mystics. On occasion shamans might create the voices of spirits, dead ancestors, or invisible enemy shamans. For example, the traditional Inuit (Eskimo) shamans of the Arctic made extensive use of ventriloquism in their curing ceremonies. Inuit shamans sometimes produced the voices and sounds of animal and ancestor spirits as they called into an ice well (a deep cut in the ice). In the Inuit culture shamans were capable of slight of hand (similar to parlor magic) and trancing (going into an altered state of mind). Ventriloquism was essentially an extension of those shamanic practices. Slight of hand (using magic) generally created a sense of mystical awe in an audience and helped shamans establish reputations as effective curers. Trancing also contributed to their perceived role as spiritual healers. By creating the illusion of the existence of spirit voices, Inuit shamans further reinforced their positions as traditional healers and as masters of the spirit world. Moreover, through a single performance involving ventriloquism they could reinforce and perpetuate the traditional Inuit belief in nature spirits.

_____

Maxwell, James A., ed. (1991) *America's Fascinating Indian Heritage*.

VERBAL DUELING

See PLAY LANGUAGE; SONG DUELING.

and whisper to the young women they have chosen to court. The whispering is done out of respect for the mothers of the younger women and does not represent a form of covert communication between the young men and the young women they wish to date. The mothers are aware of the talk and actively consult with their daughters to make sure that the right dating partner is selected.

Clemmer, Richard O. (1978) *Continuities of Hopi Culture Change.*

WHISPERING The act of speaking in a soft, quiet voice is whispering. In most Western societies whispering is done to communicate covert (hidden) messages. In some non-Western societies whispering indicates respect for higher-status individuals, particularly elders. Among the Hopi, a Native American group in Arizona, young men often whisper in the presence of elder women. This cultural pattern is most evident when young men go to the outside of the Hopi buildings where young women and their mothers grind corn. A small rectangular hole in the wall of the building, placed approximately one foot off the ground, provides an audioduct (a hole to talk through) for young males wishing to talk to young women. This is the first step in the Hopi dating/courtship process. When the young men talk through the audioduct they must kneel down close to the ground

WHISTLING Although it is rare, some cultures have developed forms of communication based on whistling. In all cases whistle speech, as it is sometimes called, is made up of modified elements of the parent spoken languages. Some whistle languages are extremely basic. In such cases, only simple messages can be communicated. In other cases, however, whistle speech can be quite complex and can be used to carry out complicated communicative transactions. In many instances whistle languages are used to communicate over long distances (at least farther than a person can shout). Whistle languages have been observed in the Canary Islands, Myanmar (formerly Burma), West Africa, and Mexico.

The Mazateco Indians of the Oaxaca Valley of southern Mexico employ a whistle language. The parent Mazateco spoken language is tonal. Tonal languages employ changes in pitch and tone at the ends of words to signal changes in meaning. The Mazateco whistle language follows the contours of four recurring tones (high, low, and two intermediate tones) of the Mazateco spoken language and attaches these tones to whistle elements that imitate the syllables of actual spoken Mazateco words. The whistle language is thus an approximation of Mazateco spoken language. In 1948 the linguist George Cowan recorded a business transaction conducted through whistle speech between two Mazateco men (only men use the whistle language). The transaction involved describing corns leaves, their relative worth, and the establishment of a finally agreed-upon price for the leaves. The entire transaction was carried out in whistle speech. Although Mazateco whistle language follows the contours of the spoken language, it is not an exact representation. In fact, the Mazateco whistle language is limited to the correspondence of tones with syllables. Therefore the equivalent of homonyms often arises (whistle words that are identical to others in sound form but carry completely different meanings).

In the Canary Islands the Spanish-speaking inhabitants of the town of La Gomera use a form of whistle speech (*silbo*, which means whistle) to communicate over long distances (sometimes as much as 3 miles), particularly across wide valleys. In contrast to the Mazateco whistle language, the whistle language used in La Gomera more closely approximates the spoken language, which is Spanish. Since Spanish is not a tonal language the problem of recurring homonyms is significantly less than in the Mazateco case.

Whistle speech has also been observed among the Mexican Kickapoo (a group that split off from the Kickapoo of the Great Lakes area). Among the Mexican Kickapoo both men and women use whistling to communicate. This form of whistling is more like "fluting." The hands are cupped together with the knuckles of the thumbs pressed against the lips. Air is pushed through the narrow space between the thumbs. The fingers are used to regulate differences in pitch and tone. This form of whistling (fluting) is traditionally used only in conjunction with courtship.

See also DRUMMING.

Classe, Andre. (1957) "The Whistle Language of La Gomera." *Scientific American* 196 (April): 111–112, 114–118, 120.

Cowan, George. (1948) "Mazateco Whistle Speech." *Language* 24: 280–286.

Ritzenthaler, Robert E., and Frederick A. Peterson. (1954) *Courtship Whistling of the Mexican Kickapoo Indians.*

Salzmann, Zdenek. (1993) *Language, Culture, and Society: An Introduction to Linguistic Anthropology.*

Taylor, Allan R. (1996) "Nonspeech Communication Systems." In *Handbook of North American Indians*, vol. 17, *Languages*, edited by Ives Goddard, 275–289.

Voorhis, Paul H. (1971) "Notes on Kickapoo Whistle Speech." *International Journal of American Linguistics* 37(4): 238–243.

WRITING The process of using marks or graphic notation (symbols placed on surfaces) to represent spoken language is called writing. The origins of writing occurred independently in several parts of the world. In the Middle East the Sumerians may have developed writing as early as 5,000 or 6,000 years ago. This particular writing system, called cuneiform, was produced by cutting small markings into soft clay tablets. It is also possible that writing was developed around the same time in Egypt. Writing also subsequently emerged in Asia (China and India) and in the Maya area of the New World.

Although writing systems vary somewhat across time and cultures, the evolution of writing systems has tended to progress along similar paths. There is, for example, a tendency through time for writing systems to increase in complexity and abstractness. The earliest systems tended to be bulky (some employing thousands of symbols); they were also limited to the expression of relatively tangible (less abstract) ideas. It is generally believed that the earliest forms of writing were notation series used as mnemonic devices (graphic systems of notation used to enhance memory). Moreover, it is generally believed that picture language (using pictures to represent words) played a significant role in the emergence of subsequent writing systems. In theory, many notation and picture writing forms were eventually transformed into complete or comprehensive and detailed writing systems when additional elements where added to allow for more precise representations of spoken language.

Basic notation and picture writing are extremely limited in that the symbols used only refer to fundamental things, actions (generally nouns and verbs), or numerations. They lack the capacity for

The ancient Sumerian writing system, called cuneiform, was produced by making small incised markings into soft clay tablets. This particular tablet contains the world's oldest known medical handbook. A translation of a portion of the right column reads: "White pear tree, the flower of the 'moon' plant, grind into a powder, dissolve in beer, let the man drink."

representing other parts of speech such as adverbs, adjectives, and prepositions (although some marks such as arrows and circles have been used to suggest spatial relationships among nouns and verbs [such as prepositions for *in, on,* and *beyond*]). Notation and picture systems are also extremely limited by the inability to indicate highly abstract ideas. The picture of a house in picture language refers literally to a house. The central idea in Abraham Lincoln's famous maxim "A house divided against itself cannot stand" thus cannot be conveyed through the strict use of a picture language. "House" in Lincoln's statement refers to the abstract idea of a nation-state (the United States), not to an actual house.

Notation systems are equally limited. Notations for numbers only represent those numbers indicated by the number of marks made in a visible series. They cannot be used directly for conveying information about abstract ideas such as metaphors, analogies, or other literary devices. For these "proto-writing" (prewriting) systems to evolve into full writing, these various limitations had to be overcome.

The first breakthrough in writing came when people discovered how to make use of the *rebus* principle. Rebus constructions are made when pictures are used to represent spoken words that are homonyms with the objects represented by the picture-graphs. The anthropologist Michael Coe demonstrates the rebus principle clearly with an example from English. Pictures of an eye, a saw, an ant, and a rose, placed in a linear order, stand for the sentence "I saw aunt Rose." The pictures do not literally refer to an eye, a saw, an ant (the insect), and a rose (the flower). The pictures are used as symbolic representations of other words (homonyms of the picture words). Once this breakthrough occurred, writing systems could produce a large number of symbols that more precisely reflected actual spoken language.

Historical linguists interested in describing and comparing writing traditions have organized writing systems into three basic categories. First, *logographic writing* is composed of characters that contain both pictures and phonetic references. Second, *alphabetical systems* use a small number of symbols to represent the range of separate or contrasting sounds of spoken languages. Third, *syllabary writing* uses compact symbols that correspond to the syllables of spoken words.

Logographic characters, or *ideograms*, are essentially based on the rebus principle. The most well known examples of logographic writing are the Chinese character system, Egyptian hieroglyphics, and the glyphic system of the ancient Maya. The advantage of logographic systems of writing lies in their capacity to transcend differences in spoken languages. In China, for example, there are a significant number of languages that are not mutually understandable. Even many related Chinese languages (such as Mandarin, Cantonese, and so forth) are not mutually intelligible. Chinese logographic writing, which relies on symbols universally recognized across most of China, allow people in Shanghai, Beijing, and Hong Kong to pick up the same daily newspaper and read it, despite the fact that these individuals most likely speak different Chinese languages. The primary disadvantage of logographic systems is that they are bulky; in order to become reasonably literate, a person must memorize thousands of symbols (characters). A separate, conventional character for each word in any given vocabulary must be learned in order for Chinese literacy to persist. Thus logographic systems of writing are cumbersome and difficult to learn.

In the second type of writing system, the alphabetic system, specific signs or symbols are used to represent the sounds of a language. The first phonetic alphabet was most likely developed in Syria as early as 1700 B.C. The symbols (letters) are combined and recombined to create representations of spoken words. Writing systems of this type are sometimes called *phonetic systems*. The number of symbols used in phonetic systems varies according to the number of sounds incorporated into a spoken language and the need to represent significant features or qualities of particular sounds. For example, the Laotian Hmong of Southeast Asia were taught to use a romanized alphabet for their spoken language. Missionaries working in Laos during the early 1950s developed the system for representing the complex set of sounds contained in the Hmong language (some 80 to 85 contrasting sounds [phonemes]). Instead of inventing new symbols, the missionaries made use of the standard romanized symbols used in the graphic construction of most European languages. For example, a standard *p* sound is indicated with a *p*. An aspirated *p*, in which a puff of air is expelled during the production of the sound, is written *ph*. In Hmong it is important to differentiate between unaspirated and aspirated *p* sounds because they alter the meaning of words. Various combinations of the 26 Roman letters allow for the description of all Hmong sounds. Moreover, the use of *b, j, v, s, m, g,* and sometimes *d* at the end of words signals the different Hmong tones (significant changes in pitch and sound quality) that directly alter the meaning of words.

Most contemporary writing systems are based on phonetic alphabets (the Chinese systems are a notable exception). The advantage of phonetic writing can be found in the small number of symbols used to convey language. Phonetic systems are economical or streamlined. In order to become literate in English, for example, a person must learn only 26 symbols. However, a few variant uses of the symbols (such as long and short vowel alterations represented by the same symbol, or the sounds indicated by certain combinations of letters such as *th* or *sh*) must be learned to have a full command of the English phonetic system.

Phonetic alphabets do have some limitations. Perhaps the most serious problem has to do with historical inconsistencies in spelling. For instance, throughout the course of the history of English, several competing orthographic (writing and spelling) systems have been employed at various times. In England and subsequently in other parts of the English-speaking world these various writing schemes have caused some confusion with regard to matching spoken sounds with symbolic representations. During the eleventh century in England, after the Norman (French) invasion, French spellings for both French and English terms became common. In some cases English spellings for French words were used; in other cases French spellings remained for French terms that had become incorporated into the English vocabulary. Until the eighteenth century there were no standardized rules for spelling in English. As a result, standardizing English, while maintaining spellings for indicating the various linguistic origins of particular words (such as words from Greek, Latin, German, French, Chinese, and African languages), has been an almost impossible task. Why, for example is *phonics* spelled with a *ph* instead of an *f* (as in *fonics*)? The reason, at least in part, is that the word derives from the French word *phonique*, which most likely came originally from the Greek *phone*. The spelling suggests derivations and the history of the word itself, yet the spelling is inconsistent with most phonetic rules for spelling in English. The same problem can be found in the word *pneumonia*. In English we pronounce the first sound as an *n*. The silent *p* at the beginning is consistent with the Greek spelling, from which the word derives.

Consistent and accurate (standardized) phonetic alphabets have been developed and used by linguists for the purpose of describing languages. However, these systems of phonetic writing have not been employed by the general public (in most societies). The writing systems generally employed by nonlinguists (the general public) in most of the world's languages do not exactly correspond to spoken language the way that formal phonetic transcription does. In the English lexicon (vocabulary), for example, there are many words that have, throughout the history of English, been borrowed from other languages (particularly languages such as Greek, German, Italian, Latin/French, Spanish, Polynesian, Malaysian, and so forth). In many cases these words have brought with them unconventional spellings (that is, unconventional with regard to typical English spelling). The /p/ in *pneumonia*, to illustrate, is not pronounced in English although the /p/ is present in the English written forms. Some writers of dictionaries have suggested that these nontypical spellings

should be maintained because they indicate the historical derivation of the word. The word *pneumonia*, along with its spelling, derive from Greek. Although most phonetic writing systems do not correspond in all cases to their associated spoken language, the primary advantage of phonetic systems, in contrast to logographic or character systems, still rests with the fact that phonetic systems have fewer symbols to learn.

The third type of writing system, the syllabary system, is based on symbols for representing syllables. In most spoken languages many words contain more than one syllable; languages that have numerous words with more than one syllable are called *polysyllabic*. In spoken language, syllables are always composed of various combinations or clusters of vowel and consonant sounds. Moreover, syllables correspond to singular rhythmic beats. The English word *adjustable* has four syllables: *ad, jus, ta, ble*. Indicating syllables can be done using the letters *V* and *C* for vowels and consonants, respectively. The syllables for the word *adjustable* are thus described as follows: *ad* (VC), *jus* (CVC), *ta* (CV), and [*a*]*bl* (VC) (the *a* vowel extends into the last syllable).

The best-known example of a syllabary alphabet is perhaps Sequoya's Cherokee alphabet. Developed in 1821 by the half-Cherokee scholar Sequoya, this syllabary alphabet was composed of 86 symbols, with each symbol corresponding to a syllable that recurred in Cherokee spoken language. Syllables could be combined and recombined to produce literally any Cherokee word or phrase. Sequoya's syllabary closely matches Cherokee spoken language, and this particular syllabary proved to be quite useful as a writing system. Initially Sequoya felt that the only way to resist Euro-American expansion was for the Cherokee to become literate in their own language. By creating a Cherokee system of writing, he felt, Cherokee culture could be preserved through creating documents describing Cherokee history and culture. Furthermore, more efficient communication among Cherokee speakers might be carried out over long distances if communications were written down and sent by couriers. The test of Sequoya's syllabary alphabet is marked by its continued use among the contemporary Cherokee. Many Cherokee children in Oklahoma and elsewhere use primer readers that are written in Cherokee. Also, many Cherokee adults still read newspapers and other publications written and published in the Cherokee syllabary system.

Writing systems in general have greatly facilitated mass communication on a global basis. However, writing has been more beneficial to people living in large-scale societies. Complex histories, legal and economic documents, and other sources of information have provided a kind of collective memory for most people living in contemporary societies. Libraries and other repositories could not exist without writing. Referencing information relies extensively on these external sources of information (encoded in writing).

Small-scale traditional societies, in contrast, have tended to rely more on oral communication. Traditional knowledge is normally passed down through face-to-face interactions across generations. In these traditional oral societies the ability to memorize lengthy narrative texts was essential. In our modern reliance on writing as an external source of information we have, to some degree, compromised our capacity for real mental memory. On the other hand, without the benefit of writing, many of the world's oral traditions might have been lost forever (many oral traditions have become extinct). If the stories, narratives, and proverbs expressed in traditional oral societies are not maintained by the members of these rapidly disappearing societies, then the task of preservation will fall to outsiders. For this reason the task of most cross-cultural anthropological research has been to use writing to record, translate, and interpret the many histories and forms of cultural expression found in oral societies.

See also PICTURE WRITING.

Coe, Michael D. (1993) *Breaking the Maya Code.*

Hock, Hans Henrich, and Brian D. Joseph. (1996) *Language History, Language Change, and Language Relationship: An Introduction to Historical and Comparative Linguistics.*

Jaisser, Annie. (1995) *Hmong for Beginners.*

Salzmann, Zdenek. (1993) *Language, Culture, and Society: An Introduction to Linguistic Anthropology.*

Senner, Wayne M., ed. (1989) *The Origins of Writing.*

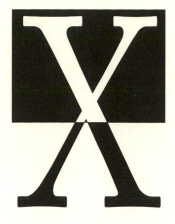

observed xenoglossia among the Haida of British Columbia's (Canada) Queen Charlotte Islands. During some emotionally charged religious ceremonies, Haida shamans (traditional healers) sometimes switched from the Haida language to Tlingit (a language spoken by a neighboring tribe). The switch produced a sense of mystical awe in the shaman's Haida-speaking audience and had the general effect of enhancing the shaman's role as a religious functionary.

See also ARGOT.

Swanton, John R. (1905) *The Haida*.

XENOGLOSSIA Xenoglossia refers to the switching of one language to another by individuals operating in situations dominated by religious emotion. The anthropologist John R. Swanton

cific animals. However, with added elements taken from the images of secondary animals and from human beings, most Maya zoomorphs appear as abstract otherworldly creatures. The description of zoomorphs across cultures is important because the images contained in them often represent characters or elements that derive from important myths. Myths, in turn, are important as a primary means in all human societies for conveying essential cultural ideas, values, and information. The zoomorphs of the ancient Maya appear to represent supernatural characters that featured prominently in Maya cosmology (worldview). According to Schele and Miller, Maya zoomorphs "manifest the power and animate force of objects, locations, and substances in the Middleworld" (the one in which we live). Zoomorphs, in this case, are symbolic emblems that stand for the Maya belief in real and supernatural realms.

ZOOMORPH The unnaturalistic depiction of images that seem to appear to have both human and animal characteristics is what epigraphers (people who study inscriptions) call zoomorphs. Mayanists Linda Schele and Mary Ellen Miller have observed that ancient Maya zoomorphs, typically depicted in stone carvings, seem to derive from spe-

Schele, Linda, and Mary Ellen Miller. (1986) *The Blood of Kings: Dynasty and Ritual in Maya Art.*

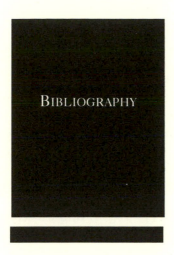

BIBLIOGRAPHY

Abrahams, Roger D. (1977) "Black Talking on the Streets." In *Explorations in the Ethnography of Speaking*, edited by Richard Bauman and Joel Sherzer, 240–262.

Alford, Richard D. (1988) *Naming and Identity: A Cross-Cultural Study of Personal Naming Practices.*

Armstrong, David F., William C. Stokoe, and Sherman E. Wilcox. (1995) *Gesture and the Nature of Language.*

Barnard, Alan. (1992) *Hunters and Herders of Southern Africa: A Comparative Ethnography of Khoisan Peoples.*

Basso, Keith H. (1979) *Portraits of "The Whiteman": Linguistic Play and Cultural Symbols among the Western Apache.*

Bergman, Robert. (1993) "A School for Medicine Men." In *Magic, Witchcraft, and Religion: An Anthropological Study of the Supernatural*, edited by Arthur C. Lehmann and James Myers, 153–157.

Berlin, Brent, and Paul Kay. (1969) *Basic Color Terms: Their Universality and Evolution.*

Bickerton, Derek. (1981) *Roots of Language.*

———. (1984) "The Language Bioprogram Hypothesis." *Behavior and Brain Sciences* 7: 173–221.

Birdwhistell, Ray. (1970) *Kinesics and Context: Essays on Body Motion Communication.*

Blackburn, Thomas C. (1975) *December's Child: A Book of Chumash Oral Narratives.*

Blackman, Margaret B. (1990) "Haida: Traditional Culture." In *Handbook of North American Indians*, vol. 7, *Northwest Coast*, edited by Wayne Suttles, 240–260.

Bliatout, Bruce, Bruce T. Downing, Judy Lewis, and Dao Yang. (1988) *Handbook for Teaching Hmong-Speaking Students.*

Boas, Franz. (1966) *Kwakiutl Ethnography.*

Bogoras, Waldemar. (1922) *Chukchee.*

Bolinger, Dwight. (1968) *Aspects of Language.*

Bonvillain, Nancy. (1993) *Language, Culture, and Communication: The Meaning of Messages.*

Bradley, David G. (1963) *A Guide to the World's Religions.*

Brown, Gillian, and George Yule. (1983) *Discourse Analysis.*

Brown, Penelope, and Stephen Levinson. (1987) *Politeness: Some Universals in Language Usage.*

Burling, Robbins. (1964) "Cognition and Componential Analysis: God's Truth or Hocus Pocus?" *American Anthropologist* 66: 20–28.

———. (1966) "The Metrics of Children's Verse: A Cross-Cultural Study." *American Anthropologist* 68: 1418–1441.

———. (1973) *English in Black and White.*

Burrus, Thomas L., and Herbert J. Spriegel. (1976) *Earth in Crisis: An Introduction to the Earth Sciences.*

Campbell, George L. (1995) *Concise Compendium of the World's Languages.*

Campbell, Joseph. (1969) *The Masks of God: Primitive Mythology.*

Carroll, John B., and Joseph B. Casagrande. (1958) "The Function of Language Classifications in Behavior." In *Readings in Social Psychology,* edited by Eleanor E. Maccoby, Theodore M. Newcomb, and Eugene L. Hartley, 18–31.

Cathcart, Robert S., and Larry Samovar, eds. (1984) *Small Group Communication: A Reader.*

Chagnon, Napoleon A. (1992) *The Yanomamo,* 4th ed.

Chambers, J. K., and Peter Trudgill. (1980) *Dialectology.*

———. (1991) *Dialects of English: Studies in Grammatical Variation.*

Chan, Sucheng. (1994) *Hmong Means Free: Life in Laos and America.*

Chance, Norman A. (1966) *The Eskimo of North Alaska.*

Cheney, Dorothy, and Robert Seyfarth. (1991) *How Monkeys See the World.*

Chomsky, Noam. (1957) *Syntactic Structures.*

———. (1965) *Aspects of the Theory of Syntax.*

———. (1968) *Language and the Mind.*

Classe, Andre. (1957) "The Whistle Language of La Gomera." *Scientific American* 196 (April): 111–112, 114–118, 120.

Clemmer, Richard O. (1978) *Continuities of Hopi Culture Change.*

Clyne, M. (1981) "Cultural Discourse Structure." *Journal of Pragmatics* 5: 61–66.

Coe, Michael D. (1993) *Breaking the Maya Code.*

Cohen, A., and M. Swain. (1976) "Bilingual Education: Immersion Model in the North American Context." *TESOL Quarterly* 10: 45–53.

Conklin, Harold. (1959) "Linguistic Play in Its Context." *Language* 35: 631–636.

Coulthard, Malcolm. (1985) *An Introduction to Discourse Analysis.*

Cowan, George. (1948) "Mazateco Whistle Speech." *Language* 24: 280–286.

Crawford, James. (1993) *Bilingual Education: History, Politics, Theory, and Practice.*

Croker, William, and Jean Croker. (1994) *The Canela: Bonding through Kinship, Ritual, and Sex.*

Crystal, David. (1987) *The Cambridge Encyclopedia of Language.*

———. (1997) *Languages: When the Last Speakers Go, They Take Their History and Culture.*

Cutler, Charles L. (1992) *O Brave New Words: Native American Loanwords in Current English.*

Degh, Linda. (1994) *American Folklore and the Mass Media.*

Devereux, Eve. (1994) *Flags.*

Dorson, Richard. (1983) *Handbook of American Folklore.*

Eastman, Carol M. (1975) *Aspects of Language and Culture.*

———. (1978) *Linguistic Theory and Language Description.*

Eckert, Penelope. (1996) "The Whole Woman: Sex and Gender Differences in Variation." In *The Matrix of Language: Contemporary Linguistic Anthropology,* edited by Donald Brenneis and Ronald K. S. Macaulay, 116–138.

Emerson, Gloria. (1983) "Navajo Education." In *Handbook of North American Indians*, vol. 10, edited by Alfonso Ortiz, 659–671.

Erickson, Frederick, and Gerald Mohatt. (1988) "Cultural Organization of Participation Structures in Two Classrooms of Indian Students." In *Doing the Ethnography of Schooling: Educational Anthropology in Action*, edited by George Spindler, 133–174.

Evans-Pritchard, E. E. (1948) *Nuer Modes of Address*.

———. (1968) *The Nuer*.

Fang, Hanquan, and J. H. Heng. (1983) "Social Changes and Changing Address Norms in China." *Language in Society* 12: 495–507.

Farb, Peter. (1978) *Word Play: What Happens When People Talk*.

Ferguson, Charles A. (1959) "Diglossia." *Word* 15: 325–340.

Findlay, Michael Shaw. (1989) *Paul Bunyan and the North American Ethos*. (unpubl.)

———. (1992) "American Hmong High School Students: An Ethnographic Study of Communication and Cultural Adaptation." Ph.D. dissertation, University of Oregon.

———. (1994) "Structure and Process in Speech Subcommunities of Hmong Students at a Northern California High School." *Language and Education* (6)3: 245–260.

———. (1995) "Who Has the Right Answer? Differential Cultural Emphasis in Question/Answer Structures and the Case of Hmong Students at a Northern California High School." *Issues in Applied Linguistics* (6)1: 23–38.

Firth, Raymond. (1997) "An Anthropologist's Reflections on Symbolic Usage." In *Magic, Witchcraft, and Religion: An Anthropological Study of the Supernatural*, edited by Arthur C. Lehmann and James E. Myers, 53–56.

Fiske, Shirley. (1978) "Rules of Address: Navajo Women in Los Angeles." *Journal of Anthropological Research* 34(1): 72–91.

Fox, Robin. (1967) *Kinship and Marriage: An Anthropological Perspective*.

Frake, Charles. (1964) "How to Ask for a Drink in Subanun." *American Anthropologist* 66(6, part 2): 127–132.

Freeman-Larsen, Diane. (1980) *Discourse Analysis in Second Language Research*.

French, David H., and Kathrine S. French. (1996) "Personal Names." In *Handbook of North American Indians*, vol. 17, *Languages*, edited by Ives Goddard, 200–221.

Frickeberg, Walter, et al. (1968) *Pre-Columbian American Religions*.

Frigout, Arlette. (1979) "Hopi Ceremonial Organization." In *Handbook of North American Indians*, vol. 9, *Southwest*, edited by Alfonso Ortiz, 564–576.

Gardner, Beatrix, and Alan Gardner. (1969) *Teaching Sign Language to a Chimpanzee*.

Gearing, Fred O. (1973) "Where We Are and Where We Might Go: Steps toward a General Theory of Cultural-Transmission." *Council on Anthropology and Education Quarterly* 4(1): 1–10.

Georges, Robert A. (1969) "Toward an Understanding of Story Telling Events." *Journal of American Folklore* 82: 313–328.

Giglioli, Paolo, ed. (1973) *Language and Social Context*.

Gleason, Harold. (1961) *An Introduction to Descriptive Linguistics.*

Goffman, Erving. (1959) *The Presentation of Self in Everyday Life.*

———. (1967) *Interaction Ritual.*

Good, Kenneth. (1991) *Into the Heart: One Man's Pursuit of Love and Knowledge among the Yanomami.*

Goodenough, Ward H. (1956) "Componential Analysis and the Study of Meaning." *Language* 32: 195–216.

Goodman, Felicitas D. (1969) *The Acquisition of Glossolalia Behavior.*

Greenberg, Joseph H. (1963) *The Languages of Africa.*

———. (1987) *Language in the Americas.*

———, ed. (1978) *Universals of Human Language.*

Gregor, Thomas A. (1969) *Social Relations in a Small Society: A Study of the Mehinacu Indians of Central Brazil.*

Grice, H. P. (1975) "Logic and Conversation." In *Syntax and Semantics,* edited by P. Cole and J. L. Morgan, 41–58.

Griffin, Em. (1991) *Communication: A First Look at Communication Theory.*

Gumperz, John. (1964) "Linguistic and Social Interaction in Two Communities." *American Anthropologist* 66(6, part 2): 137–153.

———. (1982) *Discourse Strategies.*

Gumperz, John, and Dell Hymes, eds. (1972) *Directions in Sociolinguistics: The Ethnography of Communication.*

Haarmann, Harald. (1986) *Language in Ethnicity: A View of Basic Ecological Relations.*

Haas, Mary. (1944) "Men's and Women's Speech in Koasati." *Language* 20: 142–149.

Hakuta, Kenji. (1990) "Language and Cognition in Bilingual Children." In *Bilingual Education: Issues and Strate-gies,* edited by A. M. Padilla, H. H. Fairchild, and C. M. Valadez, 47–59.

Hall, Edward T. (1959) *The Silent Language.*

———. (1963) *A System of Notation of Proxemic Behavior.*

———. (1966) *The Hidden Dimension.*

———. (1968) *Proxemics.*

———. (1981) *Beyond Culture.*

Hall, Edward T., and Mildred Reed Hall. (1994) "The Sounds of Silence." In *Conformity and Conflict: Readings in Cultural Anthropology,* edited by James Spradley and David McCurdy, 61–72.

Hand, Wayland D. (1989) "Folk Medical Magic and Symbolism in the West." In *Magic, Witchcraft, and Religion: An Anthropological Study of the Supernatural,* edited by Arthur C. Lehmann and James E. Myers, 192–202.

Hanks, William. (1996) *Language and Communicative Practices.*

Harris, Marvin. (1985) *Good to Eat: Riddles of Food and Culture.*

———. (1989) *Our Kind.*

Hatch, Evelyn. (1978) "Discourse Analysis and Second Language Acquisition." In *Second Language Acquisition,* edited by Evelyn Hatch, 401–435.

Haugen, Einer. (1950) *The Analysis of Linguistic Borrowing.*

Hayes, Alden C., and Thomas C. Windes. (1975) *An Anasazi Shrine in Chaco Canyon.*

Heath, Shirley Brice. (1993) *Ways with Words: Language, Life, and Work in Communities and Classrooms.*

Heimbach, Ernest E. (1979) *White Hmong-English Dictionary.*

Heizer, R. F., and M. A. Whipple. (1971) *The California Indians: A Source Book.*

Herzog, George. (1945) *Drum-Signaling in a West African Tribe*.

Hewes, Gordon. (1973) "Primate Communication and the Gestural Origin of Language." *Current Anthropology* 14: 5–24.

Hickerson, Nancy Parrott. (1980) *Linguistic Anthropology*.

Hock, Hans Henrich, and Brian D. Joseph. (1996) *Language History, Language Change, and Language Relationship: An Introduction to Historical and Comparative Linguistics*.

Hockett, Charles F. (1960) "The Origins of Speech." *Scientific American* 203(3): 88–96.

Hodge, Robert, and Gunther Kress. (1988) *Social Semiotics*.

Hoebel, E. Adamson. (1960) *The Cheyennes: Indians of the Great Plains*.

———. (1974) *The Law of Primitive Man*.

Hoijer, Harry. (1951) "Cultural Implications of Some Navajo Linguistic Categories." *Language* 27: 111–120.

Holloway, Ralph. (1985) "The Poor Brain of Homo sapiens neanderthalensis: See What You Please." In *Ancestors: The Hard Evidence*, edited by E. Delson, 319–324.

Holm, John. (1989) *Pidgins and Creoles*.

Hong, Beverly. (1985) "Politeness in Chinese: Impersonal Pronouns and Personal Greeting." *Anthropological Linguistics* 27: 204–213.

Hymes, Dell. (1962) *The Ethnography of Speaking*.

———. (1967) *Models of Interaction of Language and Social Setting*.

———. (1971) "Competence and Performance in Linguistic Theory." In *Language Acquisition: Models and Methods*, edited by R. Huxley and E. Ingram, 3–28.

———. (1971) "On Communicative Competence." In *Sociolinguistics*, edited by J. B. Pride and Janet Holmes, 269–293.

———. (1972) "Models of Interaction of Language and Social Setting." In *Directions in Sociolinguistics: Ethnography of Communication*, edited by John Gumperz and Dell Hymes, 35–71.

Irvine, Judith. (1977) "Strategies of Status Manipulation in the Wolof Greeting." In *Explorations in the Ethnography of Speaking*, edited by Richard Bauman and Joel Sherzer, 167–191.

Jackson, Michael. (1977) *The Kuranko*.

Jaisser, Annie. (1995) *Hmong for Beginners*.

Johnson, Charles, and Se Yang. (1992) *Myths, Legends, and Folk Tales from the Hmong of Laos*, 2d ed.

Johnson, Thomas Wayne. (1997) "Japanese Mnemonic Devices." From the Folklore Archives at California State University, Chico.

Jones, A. H. M. (1964) *The Later Roman Empire*.

Jones, Sir William. (1786) *The Third Anniversary Discourse on the Hindus*.

Kehoe, Alice B. (1992) *North American Indians: A Comprehensive Account*, 2d ed.

Khubchandani, Lachman. (1983) *Plural Languages, Plural Cultures: Communication, Identity, and Sociopolitical Change in Contemporary India*.

Kinkade, Dale M., and Anthony Mattina. (1996) "Discourse." In *Handbook of North American Indians*, vol. 17, *Languages*, edited by Ives Goddard, 244–274.

Kochman, T. (1970) "Toward an Ethnography of Black American Speech Behavior." In *Afro-American Anthropology: Contemporary Perspectives*, edited by

Norman E. Whitten and John F. Szwed, 145–162.

Kramsch, Claire. (1981) *Discourse Analysis and Second Language Teaching.*

Krashen, Stephen D., and Tracy D. Terrell. (1983) *The Natural Approach: Language Acquisition in the Classroom.*

Kroeber, Alfred L. (1925) *Handbook of the Indians of California.*

———. (1932) *The Patwin and Their Neighbors.*

Kroeber, Theodora. (1961) *Ishi in Two Worlds.*

Labov, William. (1963) "The Social Motivation of a Sound Change." *Word* 19: 273–309.

———. (1970) *The Logic of Nonstandard English.*

———. (1970) "The Study of Language in Its Social Context." *Studium Generale* 23: 30–87.

———. (1972) "On the Mechanics of Linguistic Change." In *Directions in Sociolinguistics: The Ethnography of Communication,* edited by John Gumperz and Dell Hymes, 512–538.

———. (1982) "Objectivity and Commitment in Linguistic Sciences: The Case of the Black English Trial in Ann Arbor." *Language in Society* 11: 165–201.

Lakoff, George, and Mark Johnson. (1980) *Metaphors We Live By.*

Lakoff, Robin. (1975) *Language and Woman's Place.*

———. (1990) *Talking Power: The Politics of Language.*

Lee, Richard Borshay. (1969) "A Naturalist at Large: Eating Christmas in the Kalahari." *Natural History* 78: 10.

———. (1993) *The Dobe Ju/'hoansi.*

Lehiste, Ilse. (1988) *Lectures on Language Contact.*

Lewis, David. (1972) "General Semantics." In *Semantics of Natural Language,* edited by Donald Davidson and Gilbert Harman, 169–218.

Lewis, Elaine, and Paul Lewis. (1984) *People of the Golden Triangle.*

Lieberman, Philip. (1971) *On the Speech of Neanderthal.*

———. (1984) *The Biology and Evolution of Language.*

Loeb, Edwin Meyer. (1932) *The Western Kuksu Cult.*

Malandro, Loretta A., and Larry Barker. (1983) *Nonverbal Communication.*

Malefijt, Annemarie de Waal. (1968) *Religion and Culture: An Introduction to Anthropology of Religion.*

Maltz, Daniel N., and Ruth A. Borker. (1996) "A Cultural Approach to Male-Female Miscommunication." In *The Matrix of Language: Contemporary Linguistic Anthropology,* edited by Donald Brenneis and Ronald K. S. Macaulay, 81–98.

Matisoff, James A. (1990) "On Megalocomparison." *Language* 66: 106–120.

Matsumoto, Yoshiko. (1989) *Politeness and Conversational Universals: Observations from Japanese.*

Maxwell, James A., ed. (1991) *America's Fascinating Indian Heritage.*

McClure, Erica. (1977) "Aspects of Code-Switching in the Discourse of Mexican-American Children." In *Linguistics and Anthropology,* edited by Muriel Saville-Troike, 93–116.

McGuire, Edna. (1968) *The Maoris of New Zealand.*

McLuhan, Marshall. (1964) *Impact of Electronic Media.*

Meggitt, Mervyn. (1977) *Blood Is Their Argument: Warfare among the Mae Enga Tribesmen of the New Guinea Highlands.*

Merton, Robert K. (1967) *Manifest and Latent Functions*. In *Theoretical Sociology*, 79–91.

Miller, Wick R. (1983) "Uto-Aztecan Languages." In *Handbook of North American Indians*, vol. 10, *Southwest*, edited by Alfonso Ortiz, 113–124.

———. (1996) "The Ethnography of Speaking." In *Handbook of North American Indians*, vol. 17, *Languages*, edited by Ives Goddard, 222–243.

Momaday, Scott. (1976) *The Names*.

Moss, Peter. (1985) "Rhetoric of Defense in the United States: Language, Myth, and Ideology." In *Language and the Nuclear Debate: Nukespeak Today*, edited by P. Chilton, 45–63.

Myerhoff, Barbara G. (1974) *The Peyote Hunt: The Sacred Journey of the Huichol Indians*.

Nanda, Serena. (1994) *Cultural Anthropology*.

Newman, Stanley S. (1955) "Vocabulary Levels: Zuni Sacred and Slang Usage." *Southwestern Journal of Anthropology* 11: 345–354.

Obeidelman, T. O. (1971) *The Kaguru: A Matrilineal People of East Africa*.

Ochs, Elinor. (1976) "The Universality of Conversational Postulates." *Language in Society* 5: 67–80.

———. (1996) "Norm-Makers, Norm-Breakers: Uses of Speech by Men and Women in a Malagasy Community." In *The Matrix of Language: Contemporary Linguistic Anthropology*, edited by Donald Brenneis and Ronald K. S. Macaulay, 99–115.

Ochs, Elinor, and Bambi B. Schieffelin. (1982) *Language Acquisition and Socialization: Three Developmental Stories and Their Implications*.

O'Grady, William D., and Michael Dobrovolsky, eds. (1993) *Contemporary Linguistics: An Introduction*, 2d ed.

Parker, Sue T., and Kathleen R. Gibson. (1990) *Language and Intelligence in Monkeys and Apes: Comparative Developmental Perspectives*.

Philips, Susan Urmston. (1988) "The Language Socialization of Lawyers: Acquiring the 'Cant.'" In *Doing the Ethnography of Schooling: Educational Anthropology in Action*, edited by George Spindler, 133–175.

———. (1993) *The Invisible Culture: Communication in Classroom and Community on the Warm Springs Indian Reservation*.

Pike, Kenneth. (1954) *Language in Relation to a Unified Theory of the Structure of Human Behavior*.

Pinker, Steven. (1994) *The Language Instinct: How the Mind Creates Language*.

Powers, William K. (1992) "Translating the Untranslatable: The Place of Vocable in Lakota Song." In *On the Translation of Native American Literatures*, edited by Brian Swann, 293–310.

Premack D., and A. J. Premack. (1974) *Apes, Men, and Language*.

Reisman, Karl. (1970) "Cultural and Linguistic Ambiguity in a West Indian Village." In *Afro-American Anthropology: Contemporary Perspectives*, edited by Norman E. Whitten and John F. Szwed, 129–144.

Ritzenthaler, Robert E., and Frederick A. Peterson. (1954) *Courtship Whistling of the Mexican Kickapoo Indians*.

Sahlins, Marshall. (1963) "Poor Man, Rich Man, Big Man, Chief: Political Types in Melanesia and Polynesia." *Comparative Studies in Society and History* 5: 285–303.

Salmond, Anne. (1977) "Ritual Encounter among the Maori: Sociolinguistic

Study of a Scene." In *Explorations in the Ethnography of Speaking*, edited by Richard Bauman and Joel Sherzer, 192–212.

Salzmann, Zdenek. (1993) *Language, Culture, and Society: An Introduction to Linguistic Anthropology.*

Samovar, Larry A., and Richard E. Porter, eds. (1991) *Intercultural Communication: A Reader*, 6th ed.

Sandy, J. E. (1921) *A History of Classical Scholarship.*

Sapir, Edward. (1915) *The Na-Dene Languages: A Preliminary Report.*

———. (1921) *Language.*

———. (1929) "Male and Female Forms of Speech in Yana." In *Selected Writings of Edward Sapir*, edited by D. Mandelbaum, 206–212.

———. (1931) *Conceptual Categories in Primitive Languages.*

———. (1933) "The Psychological Reality of Phonemes." In *Selected Writings of Edward Sapir*, edited by David G. Mandelbaum, 46–60.

Saussure, Ferdinand de. (1966) *Course in General Linguistics.*

Savage-Rumbaugh, Sue. (1991) "Language Learning in the Bonobo: How and Why They Learn." In *Biological and Behavioral Determinants of Language Development*, edited by N. A. Krasnegor, D. M. Rumbaugh, R. L. Schiefelbusch, and M. Studdert-Kennedy.

Saville-Troike, Muriel. (1989) *The Ethnography of Communication: An Introduction*, 2d ed.

Schele, Linda, and Mary Ellen Miller. (1986) *The Blood of Kings: Dynasty and Ritual in Maya Art.*

Searle, John. (1969) *Speech Acts: An Essay in the Philosophy of Language.*

Sebba, Mark. (1986) "London Jamaican and Black London English." In *Language and the Black Experience*, edited by D. Sutcliffe and A. Wong, 123–135.

Senner, Wayne M., ed. (1989) *The Origins of Writing.*

Seymore, Dorothy Z. (1975) "Black English." In *Introductory Readings on Language*, edited by Wallace L. Anderson and Norman C. Stageberg, 239–245.

Shaw, Daniel R. (1996) *From Longhouse to Village: Samo Social Change.*

Sherzer, Joel. (1976) "Play Language: Implications for Sociolinguistics." In *Speech Play: Research and Resources for Studying Linguistic Creativity*, edited by Barbara Kirshenblatt-Gimblett, 19–36.

Shibamoto, Janet. (1987) "The Womanly Woman: Manipulation of Stereotypical and Nonstereotypical Features of Japanese Women's Speech." In *Language, Gender, and Sex in Comparative Perspective*, edited by Susan U. Philips et al., 26–49.

Shuter, Robert. (1991) "The Hmong of Laos: Orality, Communication, and Acculturation." In *Intercultural Communication: A Reader*, 6th ed., edited by Larry A. Samovar and Richard E. Porter, 270–276.

Speck, Frank. (1945) *The Iroquois: A Study in Cultural Evolution.*

Spradley, James. (1979) *The Ethnographic Interview.*

Stewart, William A. (1975) "A History of American Negro Dialects." In *Introductory Readings on Language*, edited by Wallace L. Anderson and Norman C. Stageberg, 246–255.

Sutton, Douglas G. (1994) *The Origins of the First New Zealanders.*

Swadish, Morris. (1955) "Towards Greater Accuracy in Lexicostatistical Dating." *International Journal of American Linguistics* 21: 121–137.

Swain, M., and S. Lapkin. (1982) *Evaluating Bilingual Education: A Canadian Case Study.*

Swanton, John R. (1905) *The Haida.*

———. (1905) *Haida Texts and Myths.*

Tannen, Deborah. (1984) *Conversational Style: Analyzing Talk among Friends.*

———. (1986) *That's Not What I Meant!: How Conversational Style Makes or Breaks Your Relations with Others.*

———. (1990) *You Just Don't Understand: Women and Men in Conversation.*

Taylor, Allan R. (1996) "Nonspeech Communication Systems." In *Handbook of North American Indians*, vol. 17, *Languages*, edited by Ives Goddard, 275–289.

Tedlock, Dennis. (1972) *Finding the Center: Narrative Poetry of the Zuni Indians.*

———. (1985) *Popol Vuh: The Definitive Edition of the Mayan Book of the Dawn of Life and the Glories of Gods and Kings.*

Tenhula, John. (1991) *Voices from Southeast Asia: The Refugee Experience in the United States.*

Terrace, Herbert. (1979) *Nim.*

Thompson, Lawrence C., and Dale M. Kinkade. (1990) "Languages." In *Handbook of North American Indians*, vol. 7, *Northwest Coast*, edited by Wayne Suttles, 30–51.

Trask, Robert. (1994) *Language Change.*

Trechter, Sara. (1995) "Categorical Gender Myths in Native America: Gender Deictics in Lakhota." *Issues in Applied Linguistics* (6)1: 5–22.

Trudgill, Peter. (1984) *Applied Sociolinguistics.*

———. (1990) *The Dialects of England.*

Turner, Terence S. (1969) "Tchikrin: A Central Brazilian Tribe and Its Language of Bodily Adornment." *Natural History* 78: 8.

Turner, Victor. (1967) *The Forest of Symbols: Aspects of Ndembu Ritual.*

Tyler, Stephen. (1978) *The Said and the Unsaid: Mind, Meaning, and Culture.*

Valdes-Fallis, Guadalupe. (1978) "Code-Switching among Bilingual Mexican-American Women: Toward an Understanding of Sex-Related Language Alternation." *International Journal of the Sociology of Language* 17: 65–72.

Van Zandt, Howard F. (1970) "How to Negotiate in Japan." *Harvard Business Review* 48(6): 45–56.

Voegelin, C. F., and F. M. Voegelin. (1977) *Classification and Index of the World's Languages.*

Voorhis, Paul H. (1971) "Notes on Kickapoo Whistle Speech." *International Journal of American Linguistics* 37(4): 238–243.

Wallace, Anthony F. C. (1970) *Culture and Personality.*

Welty, Paul Thomas. (1971) *Pageant of World Cultures.*

Whorf, Benjamin L. (1952) *Collected Papers on Metalinguistics.*

Wong, Ansel. (1989) "Creole as a Language of Power and Solidarity." In *Language and the Black Experience*, edited by D. Sutcliffe and A. Wong, 109–122.

Woodburn, James. (1968) "An Introduction to Hadza Ecology." In *Man the Hunter*, edited by Richard B. Lee and I. Devore, 49–55.

Young, Robert W. (1983) "Apachean Languages." In *Handbook of North American Indians*, vol. 10, *Southwest*, edited by Alfonso Ortiz, 393–400.

Zuengler, Jane. (1985) *English, Swahili, or Other Languages? The Relationship of Educational Development Goals to Languages of Instruction in Kenya and Tanzania.*

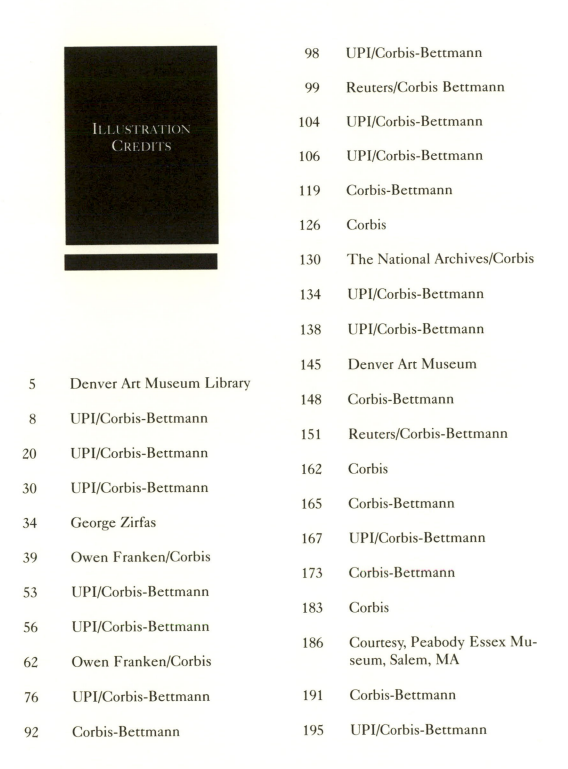

ILLUSTRATION
CREDITS

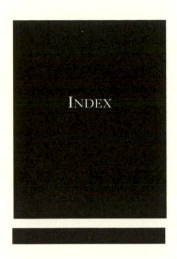

INDEX